japanese
farm food

Nancy Singleton Hachisu

Foreword by Patricia Wells
Photographs by Kenji Miura

**Andrews McMeel
Publishing, LLC**
Kansas City · Sydney · London

Andrews McMeel Publishing, LLC
an Andrews McMeel Universal company
1130 Walnut Street, Kansas City, Missouri 64106
www.andrewsmcmeel.com

15 16 17 18 19 TEN 11 10 9 8 7 6

ISBN: 978-1-4494-1829-8

Library of Congress Control Number:
2011944586

www.nancysingletonhachisu.com

Design: Julie Barnes and Diane Marsh

Photography: Kenji Miura

Additional photography:
Kelly Ishikawa: pages iii, 183, 200, 216, 322, 323; Junichi Takahashi: pages 164, 240, 241; Toshiji Tomori: pages 83, 84, 85.

Japanese editorial content and consulting: Kim Schuefftan

ATTENTION: SCHOOLS AND BUSINESSES
Andrews McMeel books are available at quantity discounts with bulk purchase for educational, business, or sales promotional use. For information, please e-mail the Andrews McMeel Publishing Special Sales Department: specialsales@amuniversal.com

THIS BOOK IS DEDICATED TO MY HOUSE,
MY FAMILY,
AND THE MAD COUNTRY WHERE I LIVE.

Remembering Baachan

On November 14, 2011, my eighty-three-year-old mother-in-law, affectionately known as Baachan ("Granny"), climbed into the bath and peacefully slipped away from us. She appears often in this book because we had lived together since the fall of 2000 and because she embodied all of those farmwife traits I emulate but can never quite live up to. We often sat together at our round breakfast room table and chatted about her life as a young bride in a farmer's house. She came from a wealthy farming family and was not accustomed to the work or the life of an underling. She spent her younger years saying *hai*, *hai* ("yes, yes"), so as she got older she just spoke her mind. She drove us all a bit crazy, but there is not any minute of any day that we do not miss her in our lives.

CONTENTS

FOREWORD

Nancy Hachisu is a treasure in a land that already acknowledges humans for their unique specialness. She's intrepid. Outrageously creative. Intensely passionate. Committed. True and real.

This California native who fell madly in love with a Japanese organic egg farmer and became, in her own words, "a stubbornly independent foreign bride," now calls herself an impostor farmer. But she is hardly an impostor anything. Just the real deal.

A part of Nancy's world lives with me everywhere I go in my French life. Well-crafted wooden boxes, ceramic serving bowls, hand-painted lacquered soup bowls with lids, and delicate baskets that serve a myriad of purposes connect me to Nancy, all of them gifts offered over time. The fat blue Japanese noodle bowl becomes a salad bowl in my kitchen in Provence. One of her son's handmade pottery cups is used each morning for a steaming espresso. A hand-crafted Japanese knife from husband Tadaaki is the go-to knife in my Paris kitchen.

And this book captures Nancy in all her guises: wife, mother, farmer, home cook, yes. But she is also a brilliant, careful writer who knows how to communicate pleasure as well as disappointment (in herself and others) and her words teach us as much about life as about food and cooking.

We join her planting rice in her bare feet, spending hours plucking feathers from a wild duck, making her own tofu "from scratch." We watch as husband Tadaaki makes illegal home-brewed sake; we join in the pleasures of hand-made country sushi rolls and read in amazement as she creates homemade udon noodles from her own homegrown flour.

She teaches us to "listen to the vegetables," touching them while they are still alive. She teaches us to trust our instincts in the kitchen and describes her food as "bold, clear, and direct," just the way she is.

As you read on, you fall in love with her rough-hewn life, and want to venture out with her into the soybean fields to harvest fresh edamame; you crave a tour of the local flea market to unearth pottery, wicker, and enameled treasures. You applaud her valiant efforts to (sometimes) be the good farmwife even though she's a complete foreigner. And you admire her strict code of ethics for growing, pickling, curing all that the family grows on the farm. Hers is a made-up life, but one that Nancy, Tadaaki, and sons Christopher, Andrew, and Matthew made up to suit themselves.

I urge you to cook from this book with abandon, but first read it like a memoir, chapter by chapter, and you will share in the story of a modern-day family, a totally unique and extraordinary one.

—Patricia Wells

Trusting Your Instincts

I came to Japan for the food, but stayed for love. Organic farmer boy Tadaaki Hachisu captured my heart with his, "Would you like to be a Japanese farmer's wife?" So I said yes (though not right away). Japanese clothes didn't quite fit Tadaaki, who was strikingly handsome, with a lean six-foot body, but he looked great in jeans.

Besides his good looks and solid country values, one more thing drew me to this guy. He loved food as much as I did and went to great lengths to grow it or find it. And like me, he knew a lot about it. But as a California girl, I never really knew about seasons. Until I moved to Japan.

I couldn't understand why Tadaaki would bring me so many of one kind of vegetable when he came to visit. Later, I found out why. When you have a lot of something, you eat it at every meal. You don't choose the vegetables, they choose you. My education was a slow process, and I was typically stubborn. It took me many years to wean myself off of planning a meal around recipes. Or even from planning meals ahead.

As my sons got older and my husband got busier, I started picking the vegetables. Walking among the rows, I would stroke them and feel their energy. Touching vegetables while they are living is something every cook should do. You have to accept them, not force your will on them. A huge turning point in my cooking came the day I really began to listen to the vegetables.

Cooking farm-to-table food from another country is easy if you source your ingredients thoughtfully and take care to understand the heart of the food. Japanese farm food is both logical and simple to execute. There is a small array of preparation techniques for plain fish or vegetables, and vegetables are flavored with a handful of interchangeable "dressings." Fish can be salt-broiled, miso-broiled, sake-steamed, or deep-fried after being dredged in flour or dipped in tempura batter. Vegetables are most often boiled, then plunged in running water to cool, squeezed, and dressed with dashi, soy sauce, sesame-miso, or a miso and sesame tofu dressing. Alternatively, they are stir-fried with aromatics such as ginger and hot pepper before being seasoned with salt, soy sauce, *shottsuru* (Japanese fish sauce), or miso thinned with sake. Raw vegetables can be salt-massaged; served with soy, citrus, sesame, or miso-flavored vinaigrettes; or just thrown in batter and deep-fried as tempura. Armed with some basic high-quality, preferably organic, Japanese pantry staples (I recommend visiting online macrobiotic sites for these items; see Resources), a trip to the farmers' market or local fish market is all you need to start cooking Japanese farm food. Learning to trust your instincts in cooking is the only way to get beyond the recipe, and the more you touch farm vegetables, or the more you observe the seasonal fish available, the more you will be able to do this.

ABOUT OUR FARMHOUSE

Our eighty-year-old family farmhouse is a destination.

Foreigners and Japanese friends travel two hours on the local train from Tokyo to get to our house in rural Saitama prefecture. The kids at my English immersion school pester me with pleas of "I wanna go to Nancy's house" (inexplicably not organic farmer husband Tadaaki's house).

Friends come for the relaxed feeling in our wide-open farmhouse, my husband's family home. Comfortably cluttered with stacks of books and pottery bowls, our house is the heart and soul of our lives. It is the *honke*, the main house of an extended family and the place where the house gods reside. Shinto, the native Japanese belief system, shares similarities with the Native American spiritual belief in animism—that every stone, river, and tree is imbued with divinity. There are gods around the house as well, and they are housed in stone shrines placed in hidden corners of the garden.

In the past, family members gathered to celebrate Japanese holidays at the *honke*. Today, we still follow that custom, but have added a few Western holidays such as Thanksgiving and Christmas and have revived some long-lost Japanese lunar ceremonies. In September at the full moon, we leave steamed *manju* buns on the inner passageway that opens up to the garden, inviting neighborhood children and friends to creep in and grab a couple without our seeing. And then we say how lucky we are because "the moon ate our *manju*."

After the rice harvest, in the late autumn we make "straw guns" called *wara deppo* for Tokanya, a farming rite to send off the rice field god to the mountains. Our friends come over to help us pound *mochi*. We eat in the garden at torchlight then head to the narrow street in front of our house, where we whack the long straw cylinders on the pavement, yelling, *"Tokanya, waradeppo yomochi kutte, buttatake!"* (Tokanya, straw gun, eat *mochi* in the nighttime, shoot!) The crack of the "straw gun" hitting the pavement wakes up the sleeping winter

bugs and kills them (metaphorically). We also invite a handful of my preschool students and their families to participate in these ancient practices, since my husband believes it important to pass these customs on to the younger generations.

At our house, we don't stand on ceremony. Everyone is family and everyone can be put to work at any time. Surrounded by antique American dining tables intermixed with old Japanese *tansu* chests and cushy sofas, Japanese find themselves able to let go and enjoy themselves in this cross-cultural environment. We usually draw an eclectic, unconventional crowd, and lively conversation spills out as we mill about the kitchen and breakfast room, sampling hors d'oeuvres before moving to the tables.

Ten years ago we renovated the farmhouse that my husband's grandfather rebuilt in 1930 using recycled beams and posts from the original 200-year-old structure. We ripped out false ceilings to expose blackened beams and restored many of the papered shoji doors that my father-in-law had removed and replaced with modern wooden sliding doors. The old doors still have their original antique glass, made from patterns that are no longer produced. My mother-in-law and I hauled out heaps of futons from a back storage room where mice had taken up residence. The mouse room, scoured, floors planked and walls resurfaced, is now our laundry room. We live amidst my collection of antique Japanese chests, bowls, and baskets culled from local flea markets. Our life is at once traditional Japanese (intergenerational living) and modern American (central heating, Viking Range), an anomaly in contemporary Japan.

These days the younger generations of farming families have little desire to carry on the agricultural traditions and even less desire to live in a dusty old (inconvenient) farmhouse that is piled full of decades of stuff accumulated by the grandparents or parents. Tadaaki and I chose to preserve the intrinsic beauty of the house but make it more livable for our version of farm life.

Unlike his parents' generation, we use the 100-year-old baskets and bowls in our everyday life that were stored away after the war—too impractical, not modern enough. Postwar Japan was an extremely frugal time (by necessity), when plastic and stainless steel became favored over ceramic bowls, bamboo baskets, and iron pots. When a recent visitor from Berkeley walked into our house, he looked around and said, "Your life is ten times more than any picture I could have created in my mind." It's because people just don't live like we do. Perhaps because we are creating our own world and do not feel constrained to follow rules. We make our own.

Our house is almost like a living creature. It breathes. Instead of interior walls, we have movable wood and paper doors that are always open, creating a feeling of spaciousness. The air flows throughout the house and from the outside gardens. The smell of the house changes with the seasons but is always a mixture of earth and green: inside from whitewashed earthen walls and woven rush tatami matting, outside from the dirt and plants. And there is also that inviting mingling of fresh vegetables and lingering last meal aromas, the smell of a well-used farm kitchen, the same anywhere in the world.

Japanese Farm Food is a collection of recipes from my husband's family farm and from twenty-three years of our collaboration in the kitchen. My hope is that the recipes and photos of our farm and our food will entice you to step into our kitchen to feel, smell, and taste with us. And through experiencing our meals, I hope you will feel nurtured and comforted from having shared this simple, warm, and welcoming life on our Japanese farm.

ABOUT FARM FOOD

Our life centers on the farm and the field. We eat what we grow. Additional ingredients are sourced carefully: meat from the butcher and fish from the fish market. You will find the recipes to be both simple and approachable because that is how we like to eat and that is how we like to live.

Tadaaki and his two brothers grew up cooking with their grandmother, a formidable matriarch who raised silkworms and spun thread for her loom. A gifted and curious cook, Tadaaki has updated family recipes and created his own. And over the years I have put my own touch on the family fare. The traditional sesame dressing used in *kyuri momi* (salt-massaged cucumbers with sesame-miso) becomes a pecan dressing on *koshi abura* when Tadaaki pairs a local mountain vegetable with our homegrown pecans and organic miso. The classic stir-fried *gobo no kinpira* (burdock root with soy sauce) is reborn as a bright celery *kinpira* in my hands. Tadaaki replaces the usual beef in shabu-shabu with sashimi fish, giving this typical *nabe* (one-pot dish) a lighter, clearer taste. And the quintessential summer soul food of the Japanese farmer, *abura miso* (stir-fried eggplant slices with red pepper and miso) gets an extra flavor kick from the slivered ginger and shiso leaves that I throw into my rendition.

Our food is bold, clear, and direct. Age-old cooking methods complement and enhance the natural flavors of vegetables, fish, and meat. Unlike most modern Japanese fare, farm food was unsweetened. Authentic Japanese farm food is uncomplicated and intuitive, with a limited number of easily learned methods. Armed with the basics, even a novice cook can re-create this food in a home kitchen anywhere in the world. One doesn't need to build a complete Japanese meal. A Japanese vegetable makes a perfect side for a simple grilled piece of fish or meat.

ABOUT MY LIFE IN JAPAN

"Just call me Rodrigo," said my lanky, handsome English conversation student in 1988. He had a smile as well. Half a year later he asked, "How would you like to be Japanese farmer's wife?" The next year we were married.

Tadaaki was a farm boy who had grown up without hot water in the kitchen. I was an urban American girl who couldn't live without a clothes dryer. But we found common ground in food. Before Tadaaki had even met me, he was growing basil. Why? Because he wanted to see how it tasted. When I carried Williams-Sonoma wine vinegar back from California, his response was, "Why don't you make your own?" And now I do.

Today, some two decades later, Tadaaki and I have two teenage boys and another away at college, all three homeschooled until September 2009; and I run a small fifty-student English immersion school called Sunny-Side Up! currently in its twenty-second year. Originally called Nancy's English Club, the school is in the site of our first family home, a ski cabin—style cedar house we built when we first married. Now a dedicated school, Sunny-Side Up! has three programs: an English immersion preschool/kindergarten (ages one to six), an all-day Saturday program (ages two to thirteen) and an after-school club (ages five to twelve). Our family is composed of husband Tadaaki, his mother Obaachan (Granny), Christopher Kiroku, Andrew Takeshi, Matthew Saburo, myself, Kitty, a bouncy-jouncy black Lab puppy named Hana, and the House. And each and every day, I am thankful for the food we grow and the life we lead.

Tadaaki had spent a year in Brazil as a cowboy, hence the "Rodrigo" handle (that didn't stick). He had also traveled to the USSR on the Peace Boat and had been part of an early farming mission to North Korea and Mao Tse-tung's China. He was, and still is, an odd mix of traditional Japanese with a global viewpoint that this town girl from Atherton, California, could not resist.

—August 2011

ABOUT RATIOS

Having spent the better part of two decades converting recipes created in imperial measurement back to metric, I can tell you with great conviction that the classic recipes in this world were most likely originally developed using the metric system. Through seeing these recipes written as how I believe they were intended (using metric measurements), the logical relationship of the ingredients is unequivocal. It just makes sense to understand these elemental ratios when cooking.

A few years ago, I met Michael Ruhlman, the author of many smart (thoughtful and well-thought-out) books. In *Ratio*, Michael talks about the fact that basic doughs and sauces can be broken down into an easy-to-comprehend set of ratios. That Michael was astute enough to write a book about this subject reveals his ability to perceive universal truths in cooking (and serve them up to the public in a simple and clear fashion).

Over the years, I moved away from converting other people's recipes and began writing more of my own—mainly for the staff at my English immersion school, where we serve lunch six days a week, but also for the occasional cooking students and my college-aged son. I found myself creating recipes that made sense logically in their proportions, especially vis-à-vis ratios. I wanted the recipes to be easy to multiply and easy to reproduce for a busy staff member, mother, or student, Recipes in which the ingredients have a logical relationship make the person cooking feel comfortable. Arbitrary, odd, or random ingredients undermine the integrity of recipes.

As I set to paper our Japanese farm food family recipes or developed my own new ones, it became clear that creating recipes taking ratios into account was eminently applicable to Japanese cooking. I found that often a recipe was better explained in ratios (e.g., 1 cup vegetables to 1½ teaspoons oil to 1½ teaspoons soy sauce)—thus allowing people to make the amount that worked for them. And wherever possible, I have included those ratios.

When you pick vegetables or buy at a farmers' market, you choose what looks good. And CSA boxes are like Christmas packages—always a delightful surprise. Some days you end up with an abundance of one kind of vegetable and small amounts of other kinds. It is this element of serendipity that makes cooking from the farm so creatively stimulating. Understanding the ratio of ingredients allows you to adapt to the amount of vegetables you have without fussing about recalculating the recipe.

1

the japanese
farmhouse kitchen

Where Is Home?

Japanese farmhouses are built with posts and beams, though one main post (the *daikoku bashira*) is the center of the structure. The post that runs through the living room up to our bedroom is made of Japanese cypress. When Tadaaki was a boy, he remembers his grandmother rubbing the post with sesame oil to enhance the grain of this treasured pillar that holds up the house. While the rest of the beams and posts are typically made from rougher cuts or recycled wood, the Japanese carpenter selects a particularly beautiful piece of wood with a distinct personality for the main bearing post of a house.

I often feel like that post is the backbone of our family, and the house is the frame that keeps us together. So when I go out from the house, in some way I am without my center. That does not mean I experience some wrenching sensation when I finally heave myself onto the bus bound for Narita airport, bags stowed and airplane sandwiches on ice. Strangely, I leave easily. It is the coming back that is hard. Funny, the words used to describe this process: I am a "registered alien" and have a "reentry permit" to come back into Japan. In many, many senses of the word, "reentry" does prove to be a jarring transition.

The house almost seems to have spurned me. Somehow life has gone on without me; there are changes that Tadaaki has effected in my absence—some not so subtle. The clutter has grown, and the same things that were on the counter when I left don't appear to have shifted position. In one sense, life has stood still, but in another sense it has taken another direction and my space has closed up, leaving me almost an outsider.

One fall had been particularly busy with trips abroad. I spent a couple of weeks "interning" in the kitchen at Chez Panisse in September, ten days in Italy for Slow Food in October, and then two weeks in California to visit family and attend a Japanese food event at the CIA in Napa. When I got back from Italy, I found a dog in my kitchen. Tadaaki had decided to give himself

a dog for his birthday. Never mind that I had strongly vetoed the idea when Matthew began lobbying for a dog a few years previously.

When the boys were small, the need to get out of Japan mounted like a pressure cooker. The longest time between trips was an unbearable eighteen months. In those days, the stress of running a small business, demands of farm life, bringing up bicultural children, and living as a foreigner in Japan were sometimes too much to endure. These days, I'm older, hopefully wiser, but certainly more prosaic. I don't "need" to get out of Japan anymore, but I am pulled by the feeling of being connected to a larger world food community, and those bonds draw me to Berkeley, California, or Portland, Oregon, and sometimes to the countryside of France or Italy. In those places I am quasi-normal and don't stand out (much).

Several years ago Christopher told me he was done going to Italy or France because we only "moved house," so to speak. We had the same daily life in Italy or France that we had in Japan: hang around the house, read, watch videos, and eat good food. The big difference he overlooked was that although this was his daily life in Japan, mine was not one of leisure, so for me this routine was heaven. I'm not a fan of sightseeing; I go abroad for the chance to eat

a favorite cook's food and a chance to use a foreign language (other than Japanese). And I go for the guilt-free ability to hang around and be lazy (though these days, I often write all day and I don't feel at all guilty about being "lazy").

Now that my originally-homeschooled sons are all in school, I miss that they don't come with me, though I carry the memories I had with them. That fall trip to Italy was the first without any of the boys, but I retraced our steps, staying in our favorite room in the castle and eating at our favorite restaurant, La Libera. In my transits between Pollenzo and Alba, I often found myself taking a wrong turn. But with those wrong turns came an accompanying feeling of warmth from that familiar feeling of getting lost in the same spot, that feeling of "I've been here before" accompanied by a strange impression of being home.

I thought about that sensation over the course of the following weeks and realized that despite my visceral connection to the old Japanese farmhouse in which I live, I also had a few other spots in the world that conjured up in me a different sense of home. And all of those places are where I spent time with my boys, away from Japan and away from them being predominantly Japanese. I will always be the odd one here in Japan, and maybe I will always be the odd one in other countries, but somehow in

California, Italy, or France, I introduced another world to my boys, and we shared that world in a different way than we can ever share Japan. Because in Japan, their father is the conduit to how they enter society, but in foreign countries I am. And I liked that feeling of being in charge and that feeling of being completely comfortable outside in the outside world. My outside world.

But once again I am home—installed in the house. Writing at my laptop, I've taken back possession. Sick of the dog dishes sloshing water on the floor, I moved them out of the way, but when no one is looking I give that incorrigible black Lab of Tadaaki's a surreptitious pat. Her name is Hana, but for now I call her Dog.

PANTRY

Perhaps the most intimidating aspect of cooking food from another culture is the daunting number of unfamiliar ingredients needed to make many dishes. Not so with Japanese farm food—with only miso or soy sauce in your kitchen, you can make stir-fries from farmers' market vegetables. Many Japanese ingredients have incomprehensible labels full of kanji characters. Off-putting, to say the least. But I have found the best-quality versions of most of the items essential for a Japanese pantry are available through macrobiotic Internet mail-order sites, such as Gold Mine Natural Food Company (see Resources). Any other ingredients can be found at a Japanese (or Asian) grocery store.

I visited several Japanese grocery stores in the San Francisco Bay Area and Portland, Oregon, for the purpose of researching this book. My advice to you when standing in front of a shelf of nori, or konbu, or whatever: Pick the one that has the coolest packaging or looks most esthetically (beautifully) Japanese. I would steer clear of messy, gaudy labels or food that lists more than a small number of ingredients. Also I would avoid anything labeled with アミノ (amino); that indicates the presence of MSG. I have organized the Pantry section by order of importance, more as a reference than as a must-have list for your kitchen. The basic Japanese ingredients you will need for the recipes in this book are miso, soy sauce, *katsuobushi*, konbu, rice vinegar, sake, *hon mirin*, and of course, japonica rice. Your food will only be as good as the ingredients you choose, so choose wisely. Organic, small-producer miso and soy sauce may cost double the industrially produced ones. But consider the quantity of these condiments that you put into any given dish—merely tablespoons—which translates into but a few pennies. Beyond that, you will need top-quality sea salt; a very good, bright, clear oil, such as rapeseed; good-tasting flour (preferably unbleached and organic); and organic sugar. After that, get thee to the famers' market, butcher, or fish market and buy what's in season and looks good. Simple.

SALT FLAVORS

SOY SAUCE: You will find a myriad of soy sauces out there on the supermarket shelf, but why complicate things? We use only one kind of soy sauce in our house, made locally by Yamaki Jozo, but readily available in the U.S. packaged under the Ohsawa brand. If the Ohsawa soy sauce is too pricey, my college-student son buys Kikkoman organic and reports it is "not bad." Producing soy sauce naturally is a process that should not be hurried. Large companies have a large output, so most must boost production through various means, such as starting from acid-hydrolyzed soy protein instead of soybeans and wheat. I prefer naturally fermented soy sauce (for obvious reasons).

MISO: Selecting miso can be bewildering. I would stick with one semimild, pleasant-flavored miso before you start experimenting with others. After all, unless you are preparing Japanese food on a daily basis, it may take you a while to make it through one container of miso. Here again, we buy miso from our local producer, Yamaki, who ferments the soybeans and grain with a natural mold (*koji*) for more than a year. And again the Yamaki miso is available in the U.S. under the Ohsawa label. I use brown rice miso, but barley miso is an excellent (though a bit darker-flavored) alternative. I have also noticed local miso in the Portland, Oregon, area, but have not tried it. Steer clear of miso with unusual flavors, such as dandelion-leek (at least for Japanese food).

SEA SALT: To be completely true to the integrity of your food, I would choose Japanese sea salt. I use finer sea salt (sold in 1-kg bags) for large pickling jobs or cooking and a shiny, slightly crystallized sea salt (sold in 200-g bags) for dipping tempura or salting simple vegetable stir-fries. This salt, an unforgettable Japanese fleur de sel produced by a fisherman in Wajima, is the best salt I have ever tasted. Product information in English for Wajima no Kaien is available through Good Food Japan (see Resources).

SHOTTSURU: Also known as *ishiru* and *ishiri*, *shottsuru* is a native Japanese fish sauce typically fermented from *hata hata* (sandfish) or squid. Splash on a raw cucumber salad, garnished with slivered ginger or use in place of salt in a stir-fry. Experiment. *Shottsuru* generally is given a longer fermentation than most Southeast Asian fish sauces and is not at all fishy. My hands-down favorite *shottsuru* is produced by Moroi Jozojo in Akita prefecture. They have a 10-year-old one that is like elixir. Pure heaven. (If you can say that about fish sauce!) Once I mentioned I wanted 6 bottles to bring to chef friends, and they sent them double-packed in bubble wrap along with nifty gift bags and assorted extras. Who would not love these people?

SEAWEED

KONBU: Kyoto chefs are particular about the konbu they use, for the good reason that they are producing a famous, highly stylized, precisely flavored cuisine called *kaiseki ryori*. For Japanese farm food (or any home cooking), buy good-looking, thick, folded sheets of this dried kelp—it will usually come in long packages and most likely will be the *ma-konbu* variety, which is gathered in southern Hokkaido. Break into manageable pieces and store in a well-sealed plastic bag.

WAKAME: If you can find fresh wakame, grab it and put it in miso soup or vegetable salads. Wakame is a seaweed that is invasive to the point of being a pest but is much favored in Japan. It is usually sold dried in the U.S., but sometimes can be found salted in the refrigerator section. Either way, you will need to soak the wakame at least a half hour in cold water to desalinate or to reconstitute before using.

NORI: Anyone who has ever eaten sushi is familiar with these sheets of red algae that have been air-dried in a process not unlike papermaking. There are many grades of nori; though perhaps the highest grade (read most expensive) will yield the best results. Sometimes called "laver" in English, nori is typically sold toasted, ready to use. Nowadays nori packages have small zips to keep the nori from getting floppy, but I recommend putting the bag in one more resealable plastic bag to double seal it. Nori can be recrisped by waving it (carefully) over a stove burner flame. Avoid the seasoned/ flavored sheets or small packs of nori cut into eighths (designed for scooping up rice) unless you are fond of MSG.

KATSUOBUSHI

WHOLE: Dried, smoked skipjack tuna (usually called bonito) that is shaved on a razor-sharp planing blade set into a wooden shaving box (*katsuobushi kezuriki*). The curled flakes are used to make stock or to flavor vegetables.

ARAI-KEZURI: Thickly shaved (slightly leathery), rust-colored pieces good for making stock. Once opened, store in the fridge.

HANAKATSUO: Pinky-tan, fine flat shavings for topping vegetables or making stock. Once opened, store in the fridge.

CHILES

TOGARASHI: Chile japones, a small, hot chile used extensively in Japanese farm food. Found easily, but you can also substitute with chile de árbol. Usually used dried.

SHICHIMI TOGARASHI: 7-spice powder that contains red pepper, *sansho,* tangerine peel, white and black sesame seeds, hemp seeds, ginger, and *aonori.* Used for shaking on *nabe* (one-pot dishes) or hearty soups. Readily available at Asian markets. Buy one that is roughly ground and has visible colors (not pulverized into a homogeneous powder). Store in the fridge and replace every few months.

KOCHUJANG: Korean red pepper paste made from chiles, glutinous rice, fermented soybeans, and salt. Good with *yakiniku* (page 276).

RAYU: Chile-infused sesame oil used when eating *gyoza* and ramen. Also good on soy sauce–dressed salads. Easy to make (page 315).

YUZU KOSHO: A recently popular condiment made from pounded yuzu peel and green chiles (page 316); traditionally made in a few local areas of Japan, but now available everywhere. Good dabbed on salt-flavored ramen or country soup (page 87).

SOYBEANS

TOFU: There is no comparing freshly made tofu to the spongy long-shelf-life blocks of bean curd often found in U.S. supermarkets. If not locally available, with a little forethought and patience, it is not difficult to make your own (page 104).

USUAGE: Tofu blocks are sliced horizontally into thin (about ¼-inch/6-mm) slabs, weighted to press out liquid, and deep-fried to puff up. *Usuage* ("thin fried") is also known as *abura age* ("oil fried"). Look for bright-colored pieces that do not appear saturated in inferior oil. Alternatively, degrease by pouring hot water over the *usuage* before using. If eating as a snack, recrisp briefly in a hot frying pan with a small amount of oil. Good as is for stir-fries or soups, or simmered in dashi and stuffed with sushi rice (page 148).

ATSUAGE: Deep-fried tofu blocks that have first been weighted to express water. Good in hearty soups or stir-fries.

GANMODOKI: Mashed and squeezed tofu is mixed with hand-grated *yama imo* (mountain yam) as a binder and seasoned with diced carrot, mushroom, and konbu. This tofu-vegetable mixture is formed into patties and deep-fried (page 110). Traditionally

ganmodoki were used to add depth of flavor to *nimono* (dashi and soy sauce–flavored simmered root vegetables) or *nabemono* (one-pot dishes).

NATTO: Fermented soybeans inoculated with *Bacillus natto,* a "good" bacteria. In the U.S., most natto is sold frozen, in small foam packs with minute little packages of hot mustard and dashi-infused soy sauce included. However, local, organic natto is being produced in Sebastopol, California, and is available through Japan Traditional Foods via the Internet (see Resources). You will need to whip up the natto with chopsticks to create a creamy mass of beans full of sticky threads. Natto keeps for several weeks in the fridge.

OKARA: Soybean pulp—a by-product of making soy milk. Usually given away free by tofu shops and good stir-fried with vegetables (page 111).

YUBA: Soy milk skin skimmed off the surface of scalding soy milk during the tofu-making process and rolled into delicate cigar-shaped cylinders. Highly perishable, so must be eaten within a day or so of making.

OILS

RAPESEED: More commonly known as canola oil, rapeseed oil is extracted from rape blossoms (similar to rapini) and is the oil used by generations of Japanese farm families. My first taste of organic small-scale–produced rapeseed oil was eye opening. The oil had a clarity and brightness that I had heretofore not tasted in other so-called flavorless oils. I buy two varieties in 16.5-kg drums (big). One oil is made from organic Australian rapeseed, the other from Japanese. Both are excellent, but the Japanese oil is lighter, more elegant, and cleaner for deep-frying (but about 50 percent more expensive). I strongly urge you to discover your own "eye-opening" oil; be sure to pour out a little in a spoon and taste. The oil should be pleasant and fresh tasting, not flat, heavy, or flavorless.

COLD-PRESSED SESAME: Otherwise known as light sesame oil, a good alternative to the heavier dark sesame oil if you like a fresher taste. Organic cold-pressed sesame oil is easily found at health food stores.

DARK SESAME: I don't use dark sesame oil much anymore because I often find the roasted sesame flavor too insistent. Nonetheless, we stock dark sesame oil in our pantry, since my husband and sons continue to love it. The oil is available in most Asian grocery stores and mainstream American supermarkets as well, though you may have better luck finding a high-quality organic sesame oil on the Internet.

LIQUORS

MIRIN: Seek out *hon mirin* (true mirin) since you will use only a little at a time—the flavor profile should have some depth and character. Mirin (a brewed condiment) is available in varying degrees of alcohol content (from 1 percent to 14 percent), with *hon mirin* having the highest level, thus giving a needed nuance to the food. Organic mirin is also available (and recommended). Avoid *aji mirin*, because the prefix *aji* typically refers to added "flavor" (MSG).

SAKE: As with wine, the better the sake, the better the end taste when cooking. But as with wine, the better the sake, the higher the price, so perhaps a middle ground needs to be considered. You can probably find a good-quality sake in the ten-dollar range for a 720-ml bottle. I have always found Harushika to be readily available in the States and an excellent mid-range choice.

SHOCHU: Low-grade *shochu* is often sold as "white liquor" in Japan and is used to make fruit-flavored cordials from summer fruits or tonics from medicinal mountain roots. *Shochu* is commonly distilled from sweet potatoes, barley, or rice, but can be made from other substances as well. *Shochu* is a popular liquor used in Japanese cocktails, while high-grade *shochu* is savored on the rocks by connoisseurs.

RICE

JAPANESE SHORT-GRAIN (JAPONICA) RICE: Often misnamed "sticky rice," Japanese rice is part of the same family of rice as Arborio, one of the rice varieties used to make Italian risotto. While the Japanese cooking method does produce a fairly homogeneous rice that tends to clump together, if cooked well, the grains should break away from each other in your mouth. The rice should not be mushy. To remove any bran, Japanese rice needs to be scrubbed and rinsed until the wash water runs clear.

BROWN RICE: Brown rice is merely hulled, unpolished rice. Because the bran is intact, brown rice is healthier than white rice. Bran provides needed roughage to the body. Brown rice is cooked with a 1.5:1 water-to-rice ratio, rather than the usual 1:1 for white rice. Massa Organics in California sells top-quality organic brown rice grown on a family farm along the Sacramento River (see Resources).

GLUTINOUS RICE: For some reason glutinous rice (otherwise known as "sticky rice") is often sold under the misnomer "sweet rice" and can contain cornstarch, iron, niacin, thiamine, and folic acid. Which begs the question . . . why? Be careful to check the label before buying. Glutinous rice contains no gluten; however, the grains exude a glutinous texture that results in a pleasantly tacky rice good for sweets (page 352) or a savory steamed with azuki beans (page 158). Cooked glutinous rice keeps well for a couple of days at room temperature.

SEEDS, NUTS, BEANS, AND FLOUR

GOMA (SESAME): Avoid the roasted sesame seeds (*iri-goma*) sold in Japanese grocery stores. The sesame flavor will not be as pleasant as fresh-ground. Arrowhead Mills has unroasted, unhulled organic sesame seeds in 12-ounce (340-g) packages. You can also find them in the bulk section of some natural food stores.

ONIGURUMI (BLACK WALNUTS): Japanese native black walnuts are almost impossible to crack without a hammer (or wrecking ball), thus the name: "devil walnuts." These walnuts grow in the hills near us and are sold in early winter at the local farm stands, but most urban-dwelling Japanese have never seen or tasted these rich, intensely flavored nuts. They are particularly favored for grinding up and adding to soba dipping sauce (page 138). Local conventional walnuts substitute nicely.

AZUKI (RED BEANS): Small, shiny red beans used for making *anko* (Sweet Red Bean Paste, page 354) and *sekihan* (Red Bean Rice, page 158). Organic azuki beans are available in 16-ounce (453-g) bags from Arrowhead Mills (sold as adzuki beans). You can also find them in the bulk section of some natural food stores or at Japanese grocery stores.

KUROMAME (BLACK BEANS): Round black soybeans that are simmered, left whole, and seasoned with sugar and soy sauce when soft. Available at Japanese grocery stores.

KINAKO (ROASTED SOYBEAN POWDER): Commonly used in Japanese sweet making for dusting. I prefer the black soybean powder (*kuromame kinako*) because it has more flavor (and is readily available in the U.S. at Japanese grocery stores).

JOSHINKO (RICE FLOUR): Made from plain (as opposed to glutinous) rice and used by farmers to make *dango*—no steaming is necessary, thus rendering the whole process much easier than when using *mochiko*.

MOCHIKO (MOCHI FLOUR): Fine-ground glutinous rice that substitutes as a shortcut for making *mochi* (steamed and pounded glutinous rice)—typically for *kusa mochi* ("herb" *mochi* pounded with mugwort). The *mochiko* is mixed with water to form a dough that is steamed before pounding and shaping.

UNBLEACHED ALL-PURPOSE OR CAKE FLOUR: Periodically, I refer to "good-tasting flour," which may perplex some people. Most of us grew up only knowing industrialized flour and never realized flours from different locales had their own taste. I used to buy 20-kg sacks of flour from a miller and thought I was doing well to avoid supermarket shelf generic flour. Around that time, my husband began growing wheat. At first there were problems with the low gluten content in the wheat, then in overheating in the drying process, thus giving baked goods a slightly gummy consistency. But the flour tasted good. This was a kind of a life-changing revelation. It took Tadaaki about three more years to get the wheat right and the drying process worked out, but he did. Good-tasting flour will blow your socks off. Really. King Arthur Flour and Guisto's are two excellent sources for flour that are available online (see Resources).

PANKO (DRIED BREAD CRUMBS): Made from dough cooked by electric currant rather than heat. I prefer to make my own from traditionally baked bread. Grate French or Italian-style white bread with the grating disc of a food processor, or in a blender. Preheat the oven to 300°F (150°C). Spread the grated bread out on a cookie sheet, no deeper than ½ inch (12 mm). Place in the middle of the oven and stir a couple of times while baking to evenly distribute the drier cooked edges with the middle soft area. Bake for 12 minutes or until dry to the touch but not browned (it may take an additional 2 to 4 minutes). When cool, store in a plastic container or sealed plastic bag in the refrigerator (or dry pantry with good air circulation). Keeps for several weeks or more.

SWEETENERS

ORGANIC GRANULATED SUGAR: I specify organic granulated sugar because the taste difference is remarkable and because I see no reason to use a tasteless agent that only adds sweetness and no other complexities. I strongly recommend finding good-quality organic granulated sugar (taste to evaluate), but ultimately the choice is yours.

KUROZATO (OKINAWAN BROWN SUGAR): This dense, fine-grained (flavorful) native sugar is available at Japanese grocery stores. Do not substitute American "brown" sugar because it is not at all the same.

KUROMITSU (BROWN SUGAR SYRUP): There is no need to purchase this separately, since *kuromitsu* is easily made by simmering *kurozato* with water (page 319). The flavor of dark molasses or blackstrap molasses is similar.

HOSHIGAKI (DRIED PERSIMMON): Dried in the early winter from tannic oval-shaped persimmons. Used to naturally sweeten dressings such as *shira-ae* (page 299). Substitute unsulfured dried apricots.

THICKENERS

KATAKURIKO (POTATO STARCH): The most common thickener or binder used in Japanese cooking. Also good for coating marinated chicken pieces before deep-frying (page 267).

KUZU (KUDZU): A starch made from the root of *kuzu* vines, used as a sauce thickener and in sweets. Real *kuzu* powder (*hon kuzu*) is difficult to find and expensive (even in Japan).

KANTEN (AGAR-AGAR): A natural jelling agent produced from red algae. Favored for making gelatin-based sweets or savory custards such as *gomadofu*. Historically, *kanten* was sold in various forms, from stick to strings, but today the powdered variety is most common. Available at Japanese grocery stores. Agar jelly is more delicate than gelatin and starts to set at room temperature.

MISCELLANEOUS

DRIED SHIITAKE: Often added to simmered foods (*nimono*) for a deep, earthy component.

ITO KONNYAKU OR *SHIRATAKI* (DEVIL'S TONGUE NOODLES): No-calorie slippery noodles made from *konnyaku* (page 364) that hold up well in soupy dishes such as *Gyudon* (page 272), Sukiyaki (page 278), or *Nikujaga* (page 281).

KANPYO (DRIED GOURD STRIPS): Used in country sushi rolls (page 146) and as a tie for simmered foods.

KURAGE (JELLYFISH): Salted jellyfish used in country sushi rolls after soaking and flavoring.

SURUME (AIR-DRIED SQUID): Used in *matsumae zuke* (page 71) or as a healthy snack. Look for whole, flat squid and avoid shredded *surume* as it contains MSG.

NIGARI (MAGNESIUM CHLORIDE): Extracted from seawater, sold in liquid or crystal form. Essential in tofu-making and available from Gold Mine Natural Food Company (see Resources).

NUKA (RICE BRAN): The highly perishable outer layer of the white rice kernel after the rice has been hulled. Commonly available at Japanese grocery stores or health food stores. Used to make many kinds of Japanese pickles, including *nukazuke* (page 77).

KOJI (*ASPERGILLUS* MOLD): Used to make miso and sake or as a pickling agent for fish and vegetables. Available in Japanese grocery stores or online through Natural Import Company (see Resources).

SAKE KASU (SAKE LEES): Used to pickle fish or vegetables, available in Japanese grocery stores or from sake breweries.

AMAZAKE (SWEET "SAKE"): A nonalcoholic cultured rice product sold as *amazake* concentrate. Used in *sakamanju* (page 356), but can also be heated with water 1:1 for a warm pick-me-up on a blustery afternoon. Available online through Natural Import Company (see Resources).

OUR LOCAL FLEA MARKET

Twenty years ago some fellow foreign wife friends coerced me into helping raise money by selling odds and ends at a flea market in Omiya, a sprawling suburb of Tokyo. The sixty-meter high banner spanning the blocked-off shopping street splashed "Free Market" in red letters. It should have been a free market for all the junk that people were selling that day.

Ten years later, we embarked on a house renovation project with the intention of converting the house we had built into a dedicated school and moving into Tadaaki's parents' (then) seventy-year-old farmhouse. And so began a year of designing, scrubbing, and scavenging for old *tansu* (chests) and shoji doors. When Tadaaki started coming home from our local flea market with very cool, unusual pieces, I found myself haunting that market, too. Winding my way through the rows of dealers on that dusty ground, I have become pals with some of them, and no matter what I say, they still think I'm a dealer as well, maybe because I buy wisely and in volume. It's hard to pass up an intricately woven basket for ¥1,000 ($8) that probably took a skilled craftsman several painstaking days to produce fifty or more years ago. Heartbreaking, really, when you think how undervalued that basket has become. But then I tend to buy big things: baskets, mixing bowls, and wooden buckets, often affordable because Japanese today have little storage space and houses are no longer designed for large pieces. Farmhouses have cavernous closets with few shelves, so oversized nesting baskets and wooden boxes were used to store clothes and papers. Sometimes the traditional storage style in our farmhouse is inconvenient, but at least we have space for my finds.

It's mostly the wealthy Tokyoites or other antique dealers who see the value in much of what is being sold at our local flea market. Even in our old neighborhood, the typical modern couple will tear down their parents' (or grandparents') farmhouse and replace it with a super-sized prefab house slapped together in a few months. While many Japanese may see the intrinsic beauty in old things, those objects have become far removed from their lives. Old is cool, just not in their house. Old is dirty.

But I don't mind a little dirt, and for me, old has flavor ("*aji*"). In Japan, the dealers buy up the contents of entire storage houses from farming or merchant families, sight unseen. The older generation (as well as the younger), see no inherent value in the "junk" stored from the past and are happy to unload the stuff and have someone haul it away. So, when I haggle, I have that in mind. Also, I look for unusual or well-crafted wooden boxes, ceramic serving bowls (often cracked), hand-painted, lacquer soup bowls with lids (sometimes with shell inlay), and baskets—glorious, glorious baskets. And I buy *tansu*—though less now that one of our ex-chicken coops is storing about twenty or more *tansu* scavenged from abandoned farmhouses due to be demolished.

In the end, though, the dealers at our flea/antique market are not getting rich, so there is a limit on how much I try to get the price down. And it's all about the relationships we form. I trust their pricing, and they know I value the things I buy because I have an eye for humble artistry.

I've got my favorite guys at the flea market, though they're not always there. Some have given up, while others hang in there despite age or shaky health. My favorite vendor wears a jaunty fishing cap and speaks with a charmingly shy hesitation. But he always puts together an irresistible package for me, so of course I come away with way more than I intended. The prices he offers me are too good to pass up. One time I bought an alligator purse for $25 and an antique round wall clock for $45. I still haven't figured out where I'll put the clock or where I'll carry the purse. But they were great buys. The flea market in our little town of 15,000 has grown from once a month to a weekly affair and now sometimes spreads out to an adjacent parking lot. I'm not sure why our little area has become a magnet for old things and borderline junk, but the hard-packed dusty ground is mobbed on the first and last Sundays of the month (the main markets), and new vendors seem to pop up each time I go.

I often encounter friend Kim Schuefftan at the market. He lives in a dilapidated farmhouse in a hamlet of ten houses about forty minutes west of us and is addicted to cool folk junk and patched and mended things. Our flea market is very different from the trendy Sunday antique markets in Tokyo because here you can find just about anything and everything, from farm machinery to saws and chisels to modern paintings to goldfish to ammonites . . . to . . . to . . . a mad hodgepodge that ranges from pure junk to rare finds. I think what attracts Kim, Tadaaki, and me to the market is the messy jumble of life that is put on display each Sunday. For us, this reflects the real Japan, not the manicured gardens at Buddhist temples or Shinto shrines that most people abroad associate with this country. For us, Japan has a rough-hewn underside well worth experiencing, which is only found in rural Japan. And that is why we live there.

TOOLS AND KNIVES

The Japanese farm kitchen is a low-tech affair. Traditionally, the farmwife made due with a grinding bowl, ginger grater, thick dowel used as a rolling pin, and sharp knife. Those days have come and gone; nonetheless, our Japanese kitchen remains fairly simple. Also, a Western substitute can be found for most common Japanese kitchen tools. The list I have compiled is meant to give you a sense of what implements were typically used in the Japanese farm kitchen (and may no longer be used in the urban one). I have organized the tools section by usage sequence (e.g., grinding, noodle making, charcoal barbecuing, sushi making, etc.). However, besides a grinding bowl, the only other absolutely necessary tool would be a sharp all-purpose knife (preferably Japanese) and a good sharpener. We use a *banno bocho* for vegetables and meat, and a *sashimi bocho* for slicing fish, but the *banno bocho* cuts fish nicely (provided it is razor sharp). Ultimately, sharpening your knife on a whetstone is the only way to create an edge, though a diamond-surfaced sharpening tool is useful for daily maintenance (or at least weekly, if you are busy). Any other all-purpose knife (*bunka bocho*), such as a *funayuki bocho* or *santoku bocho* perform the same multiple duties as our *banno bocho*. Hida Tool, an authentic Japanese neighborhood hardware store in Berkeley, California, sells various tools online (see Resources). One excellent knife is worth more than three mediocre ones. But keep the blade sharp!

TOOLS

SURIBACHI: A ceramic bowl with grooves combed into the surface used for grinding seeds or nuts. This is the one tool essential for making Japanese farmhouse food with ease. You can substitute a mortar, but the results will not be quite the same, and the process will be more arduous. Do not be tempted to save money and buy a small *suribachi* because seeds will jump out and you will regret your choice. Get the biggest one you can find (if possible, with at least the capacity of a medium-sized mixing bowl). You can find these at Japanese grocery stores, Korin (see Resources), or Amazon.

SURIKOGI: The grinding pestle that is used with the *suribachi*. While difficult to find these days, the best *surikogi* are made from the thick trunk of a *sansho* (prickly ash) bush. The knobby surface makes getting a purchase on the pestle easier than slick wood. Also the *sansho* adds some hint of flavor to what you are grinding (*sansho* is a relative of Sichuan pepper). Don't bother with thin, feeble *surikogi*; go for the thickest one.

TAKE BURASHI: A small, rectangular bamboo "brush," sometimes sold with *suribachi* sets. Useful for removing ground seeds that stubbornly remain in the grooves of your *suribachi*. Also works for getting the last grated ginger off of the *oroshigane* grating plate.

OROSHIGANE: The best tool for fine-grating ginger and daikon. Plastic grating plates are most common, though perhaps the least useful since they are brittle and do not stand up to big grating jobs. We use a circular ceramic grating plate (*oroshiki*) with a trough surrounding the raised and textured grating area (think flat volcano with a moat); the finely grated daikon slides down and is held in the trough as you grate. For ginger, a rectangular metal plate with sharp, raised teeth is best, though a wide-bladed Microplane with fine teeth pinch-hits admirably.

WASABI OROSHI: Wasabi is typically grated on a flat wood-handled board covered in sharkskin. The sharkskin tends to warp over time and eventually will separate from the board. A metal-toothed grinder also works well (sometimes better).

OTOSHI BUTA: A wooden or stainless steel drop-lid used when simmering vegetables in soy sauce–sweetened dashi. Parchment paper makes a fine substitute.

URAGOSHI: A straight-sided wooden sieve with metal mesh used to sift flour or separate chaff (or debris). Comes in many grades of mesh from coarse to fine. A Western sieve works almost the same, though the handled variety does not provide as stable a sifting action as one with graspable sides.

MENBO: A wooden dowel about 3 feet (90 cm) long and about 1¼ inches (3 cm) in diameter for rolling out Japanese noodles. An approximate tool can be purchased at any hardware store. French rolling pins are similar, though they have a wider diameter (and are expensive).

SEIMENKI: A standing Japanese noodle rolling machine made from cast iron and brass, with a rectangular wooden base. Since noodles were eaten nightly, every farm family in our area had a noodle roller to make quick work of the meal. We use ours often for rolling out both Western and Japanese noodles. These noodle rollers are costly even in Japan but extremely useful if you can find one. An Italian pasta roller will also work.

SUINO: A long-handled woven bamboo noodle scooper. New ones are pretty—old ones, patinaed by the wood-burning fire, are gorgeous (page 252).

ZARU: A round flat bamboo basket used to serve noodles that allows any excess water to drain off naturally. Available at Japanese cookware stores.

MUSHIKI: A tiered bamboo steaming basket easily available in Chinese or Japanese cookware stores or online at Korin (see Resources). Square wooden or metal steamers are known as *seiro.*

HIOKOSHI: A small, wood-handled, cast-iron charcoal starter. Available online at Korin (see Resources).

SHICHIRIN: An inexpensive round tabletop barbecue used for grilling *yakiniku, yakitori,* or fish in the garden. *Shichirin* (and *konro*) are often made from diatomaceous earth (*keisodo*), a naturally insulating material. Available online through Korin (see Resources).

KONRO: A rectangular "hibachi"-style tabletop barbecue. Note that *konro* are used for cooking. Available through Korin, but expensive. (The traditional hibachi are not cookers but wooden or porcelain containers filled halfway with ash to hold smoldering charcoal embers and provide heat for the house. Of course such traditional hibachi are anachronisms, but are much-sought-after antiques.) The term *konro* is also used for a butane-fueled tabletop burner, useful (or perhaps essential) when making sukiyaki or *nabemono* (one-pot dishes). Easily available through cookware supply stores or Amazon.

SUIHANKI: Japanese-style rice cooker—commonly available in any cooking store.

DONABE: A lidded ceramic casserole-style vessel used for cooking *nabe* or rice over a flame. Meant to simulate the traditional method of cooking food in an iron pot on top of a low charcoal-fueled kitchen cooker (*kamado*). The earthenware conducts the heat evenly but also (like rice cooked in an iron pot set over a *kamado*) enables the rice to form a favored delicacy called *okoge,* the crispy brown crust that results from cooking rice over a fire. The rice produced in a *donabe* is certainly more delicious than that steamed in the rice cooker, but the *donabe* has one disadvantage: The rice does not stay warm. Black-glazed Iga *donabe* from Nagatani-en (the same *donabe* I use) are available in the U.S. from Toiro Kitchen (see Resources), though for a hefty price. If you buy one *donabe,* buy the one that can cook rice because, depending on the style, many *donabe* meant to cook *nabe* will never work for cooking rice (but the rice cooker *donabe* serves admirably when throwing together a *nabe* dinner).

SHAMOJI: A thick, flat cedar paddle for serving rice, now commonly made of textured plastic. The cedar paddles are much more aesthetically pleasing, but there is no denying the ease of serving with the plastic, since the textured surface allows the rice to fall off nicely rather than stick stubbornly to the wooden paddle. You decide. I prefer the wooden ones, but my husband and sons use the plastic.

HANDAI: A round, low-sided, wide wooden tub used for cooling and aerating sushi rice as you add in the sweetened vinegar. The back of a large wooden cutting board can be substituted very successfully.

MAKISU: The bamboo mat used for rolling country sushi or any other rolled sushi meant to be cut into thick rounds.

OHASHI: Chopsticks (usually made of wood, but also of bamboo, iron, or bone) are extremely useful when deep-frying and the perfect implement to fluff up your rice when done steaming. Cooking and serving chopsticks are longer than those used for eating. In most Japanese households, each person has his or her own personal pair of chopsticks, and they are used at every meal.

WARIBASHI: Disposable chopsticks commonly used all over Japan when serving guests or eating outside of the house, though some eco-minded people carry their own chopsticks. Over the years I have collected a large number of extra chopsticks and no longer stock *waribashi*. Nonetheless, sometimes using them is unavoidable; in this case, please do not scrape *waribashi* against each other after breaking. This is considered bad manners because it signals to the host that he or she has provided cheap chopsticks that easily splinter. Making a person feel badly or ashamed goes deeply against the Japanese grain and should be avoided.

TAWASHI: An extremely stiff brush made of hemp palm that is the perfect vegetable brush. The bristles are rough enough to create the necessary friction to rub off the dirt and hard part of vegetable skins without having to peel them (and remove flavor). You can use a green "scrubby," but it won't do quite the same job. I use the "Turtle" *tawashi* made in Japan (see Resources).

TOFU TSUKURIKI (WOOD TOFU PRESS): Made from Japanese cypress. Along with other tofu-making supplies, it is available online (See Resources).

TOISHI (WHETSTONE): There is no substitute for this to sharpen kitchen knives (and any blade tools), though diamond-surfaced hand sharpeners are good stopgap tools to use for maintaining the edges of your knife blades. There is no need to feel intimidated by the stone or the hand sharpener. Like all things, learning how to sharpen knives well takes time, patience, and personal balance. But it is worth it in the long run! Without a sharp knife, it is impossible to cook.

KNIVES

BANNO BOCHO: This is the knife we use every day on just about everything (and we have a few of them). The blade is brittle, so it is not good for cutting hard surfaces such as crusty bread or kabocha. The *banno bocho* is made by our local knife maker and is meant to be a multipurpose knife that can be used on vegetables, fish, or meat. Similar styles of all-purpose knives (*bunka bocho*) are *santoku bocho* and *funayuki bocho*. If you buy one knife, choose a *bunka bocho*. To keep things simple, just look for a knife that has a curved blade to the end point and is described by the seller as all-purpose. There are many sources for Japanese knives, but I tend to trust a small, family-run business. I recommend talking to the guys at Hida Tool & Hardware in Berkeley, California—what you will gain in knowledge and expertise is worth the cost of a phone call (see Resources). Alternatively, skip the phone call (and the lesson) and just order directly from their online site.

DEBA BOCHO: A wide-bladed knife of varying sizes, heavy enough to cut through fish bones (sometimes called a *sakana bocho*—"fish knife"). A medium-sized *deba bocho* would be the second most useful knife to add to your kitchen. The *deba bocho* does a good job of cutting meat and, depending on the heft (and size) of the blade, can cut through poultry bones as well (using the corner nearest the handle).

SASHIMI BOCHO: A long, thin knife that comes in handy when slicing sashimi. We have several styles of *sashimi bocho*, but Tadaaki favors the squared-off rectangular type (*takobiki*) over the pointed tip style (*yanagiba*). Either works well. This is a specialty knife, only to be purchased when you are ready to step up your knife skills and start slicing your own sashimi.

HASAMI: Butterfly-shaped iron scissors whose design dates back to the Roman Empire. Japanese scissors are one of my most favorite Japanese tools because of their intrinsic beauty and superb workmanship. I get pleasure from holding them in my hand and love using them in the field to cut our gorgeous vegetables.

SHAGUJI

My husband fell into the family well when he was five and almost drowned—no surprise when you see his little brown monkey face grinning impishly out from the family albums—definitely a kid who got into scrapes. As the story goes, his parents hauled him out of the well, and, assuming him dead, began to perform a ritual cleansing by washing his body. Tadaaki regained consciousness during the cleansing—much to the surprise of all present. But this is not the whole story. While he was unconscious, Tadaaki saw three wise men with white beards and flowing robes. He asked them if he was going to die, and they told him that of course he would die someday. But not that day.

Today, Tadaaki, with vestiges of that impish little get-into-trouble boy still remaining, nonetheless lives his life closely connected to some undefined, yet no less real spiritual world. One night a few years ago, Tadaaki had a dream. In this dream a voice said, "Go to the local shrine. There will be a round stone in that area and you must bring it home. You should take care of the stone and pray before it. The name of the god in the stone is Shaguji."

Being a busy farmer, Tadaaki did not take the dream seriously until six months later, when he suddenly decided to visit the shrine and satisfy his curiosity. And there he found a round stone where the shrine borders the road, guarding the entrance. Finding this stone stunned Tadaaki, and consequently he felt compelled to ask the priestess to allow him to take it home. After listening to his unusual story, she agreed. To honor the stone, he bought a mammoth garden rock from a stonemason and constructed a shrine upon which he rested Shaguji. Around the shrine, he planted flowers.

Tadaaki later researched the name Shaguji and discovered that, in fact, a god named Shaguji did exist. Shaguji is but one of numerous variations of the name, for the god is of great antiquity, thought to date back even before the advent of Shinto, Japan's native religion. Shaguji is from Japan's Neolithic Jomon period, which lasted some 10,000 years until about 300 B.C.—an era to which Tadaaki has always felt a great affinity.

Where a natural object is known to be imbued with divinity—tree, rock, whatever—a straw rope (*shimenawa*) is tied around it, and this is draped with sacred zigzag (lightning-shaped) folded papers (*shige*). Tadaaki has honored Shaguji in our garden in this way, as he has the god of the kitchen, with a row of *shige* strung on the hood above our stove. I cannot pretend to understand all of these customs; nonetheless they are an essential part of what my husband believes and how he lives his life and so are part of my daily life as well.

CUTTING AND COOKING TECHNIQUES

Probably the biggest hurdle for Western cooks preparing Japanese food is the difference in fish and meat cuts. After that, the vegetable cutting style is slightly elusive, since skilled Japanese home cooks typically keep much sharper knives in their kitchen than most homes in the West do. In general, Japanese cuts are much finer (and thinner) than most Western vegetable cutting styles. To this end, you will need a sharp knife. Also there are a few miscellaneous, easily learned techniques such as vegetable squeezing or tofu grinding clearly illustrated by photos. If you study the photos included in this section, you will have a visual reference to help you better understand the techniques or cutting style you want to achieve for any given dish. There really is no mystery. Japanese techniques may be different from Western techniques, but they are no more difficult.

COOKING TECHNIQUES

Roasting sesame

Squeezing pressed tofu

Grinding tofu

Scooping greens
from pot

Refreshing greens

Scrubbing daikon
with brush

Grating wasabi

Parboiled *konnyaku*
pieces

Massaging salt into
cucumbers

COOKING TECHNIQUES (CONTINUED)

Adding oil to egg
for mayonnaise

Deep-frying (tempura)

Deep-frying (*kara age*)

Swirling egg onto
katsudon

Searing bonito
over straw

Cooking yakitori
on a *shichirin*

COOKING VEGETABLES

Finely chopped green
onion (*mijingiri*)

Julienned vegetables
(*sengiri*): carrot and *negi*

Finely sliced vegetables
(*usugiri*): cucumber

Eggplant cut for frying:
shigiyaki

Shiso chiffonade

Boiled vegetables
to be dressed

CLEANING AND SLICING FISH

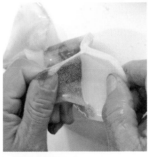
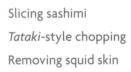

Slicing sashimi

Tataki-style chopping

Removing squid skin

Lining fish with konbu

Filleting jack mackerel

Filleting sardines

MEAT CUTS

Sukiyaki

Gyudon

Katsudon

This chapter was designed as a sort of exhaustive overall look at Japanese ingredients, implements, and typical kitchen skills. You need not have even a fraction of these ingredients or implements in your pantry or kitchen. And you need not master a good portion of the kitchen skills because the majority of young Japanese today have not. Focus on getting a few quality tools and kitchen staples; and start small, making one dish at a time from the freshest ingredients you can find. Look to what you do have, not what you don't.

2

small bites with drinks

TSUMAMI

TSUMAMI: SMALL BITES

Most Japanese dishes are suitable for *tsumami*, small bites before dinner. My husband's method of cooking involves standing at the stove turning out one dish at a time, tossing it on the table, and yelling, *"Tsumami desu!"* (something akin to "Munchies are done!"). I sit down and have a few searing hot bites (because that's how I like them, hot from the stove). Unlike me, Tadaaki isn't too concerned with timing all the dishes to arrive on the table at the same time, so when he cooks, I often just start sampling one of them as an hors d'oeuvre, then call the boys and my mother-in-law to the table when the rest of the meal is ready.

Any of the dishes in this section will work well as finger food before dinner or even as a side dish with a meal. I prefer not to serve meat before meals, so with the exception of Salmon Roe (page 26) and Deep-Fried Little Fishes (page 57), they are all vegetarian. I include Japanese-Style Potato Salad (page 54) because it is the quintessential farmer's dish in early summer, when potatoes are freshly dug and full of flavor. Potato salad can be used as a dipper for green peppers, rolled in lettuce leaves, or even served on plain rice crackers. The dishes are arranged from light, oil-free vegetarian bites to more substantial egg, rice, and stir-fries.

Umeshu, also known under the misnomer "plum wine," is the traditional cordial made in every farm household from native sour plums (which are really members of the apricot family). In addition to *umeshu*, my husband's parents made a number of unsweetened (or minimally sweetened) medicinal cordials by steeping various wild sour berries, quince, or ginseng in a clear, inexpensive spirit (*shochu*). These cordials are used to perk you up when feeling droopy or as a homeopathic remedy for colds. *Umeshu*, however, is served on the rocks in a little roly-poly tumbler—and was even given to children in my husband's childhood. While *umeshu* is the best-known cordial made from fruit in Japan, I also like to make cordials from apricots, blueberries, and raspberries, all readily obtainable in the West. The basic technique is the same no matter what the fruit or berry.

Ikura is well known by sushi aficionados and is often served in the U.S. with a small quail yolk perched on top to mitigate the saltiness. *Ikura* quickly gets tacky when not fresh, so salt (or soy sauce) is added to preserve and flavor the eggs. Home-cured salmon roe does not require as much salting agent because the eggs will be consumed within a few hours. It takes a little time and patience to coax the luminescent eggs from their thready sac. Keep your hands gentle and know that you will end up with beautifully fresh *ikura* like you have not tasted elsewhere (except perhaps at a top, top sushi shop). In the cold months, when salmon are spawning, we occasionally buy salmon roe sacs from the local fish market. The roe sacs are not cheap, but conversely a side of salmon is, and can be had for about $10 (dirt cheap). The roe sacs should be readily available from any reputable fishmonger outside of Japan during this same season.

salmon roe SERVES 6
IKURA

1 sac salmon or salmon trout roe (about 7 ounces/200 g)

1 teaspoon sea salt

1 teaspoon sake

Grated zest of ½ yuzu or Meyer lemon

Set a medium-sized bowl in the kitchen sink and fill with tepid water. Submerge the egg sac in the water and gently pry the roe from the outer membrane by scraping your fingertip along the membrane. Remove the membrane tendrils from among the eggs. Drain the eggs as you go in a wire mesh strainer set over a bowl.

Season with salt, sake, and grated yuzu (or Meyer lemon) zest. Taste and add more salt if necessary. The eggs should remain naturally sweet with a slight background taste of salt. They should not be too salty.

Serve as an appetizer in a small colorful bowl with soy sauce dishes and chopsticks alongside.

VARIATION: Use 1 teaspoon soy sauce in place of the salt.

My favorite miso is made in Kamiizumi-mura, a mountain town bordering ours. Yamaki Jozo is family owned and part of our Slow Food community. The brown rice miso has enough depth of flavor to hold up to the wild scallion, with no distraction from the underlying wheat grains that you get with barley miso. I couldn't have told you that a month ago, but recently I've been yanking off stalks of wheat to taste wheat kernels in the field with my preschool kids, and they share similar characteristics with barley. I use wild scallions that grow by a riverbank. They are almost a cross between garlic and green onion, but have very thin green stalks and small curved pinky white bottoms. This simple dish makes a fresh before-dinner appetizer and is especially good with mixed drinks such as mojitos or gin and tonics . . . or beer.

young scallions and miso
NOBIRU TO NAMA MISO

Very thin, young scallions

Organic brown rice miso

Clean the scallions. Cut off the root bottoms and any brown or tapering tops. Peel off the tough or discolored outside layers.

Spoon out a dollop of miso onto a medium-sized plate. Curl the scallions attractively on the plate with the miso. To eat, dip the scallion in the miso, scooping up about the same volume of miso to scallion.

VARIATIONS: Fantastic with Japanese cucumber sticks (cut in half across the middle, then quarters lengthwise), green pepper wedges, whole mild chiles, radishes (washed and tailed, but leave the greens on if fresh picked) or heavenly with very young garlic cloves or green garlic.

Once, on the way back home to Japan from California, my friend Sam White and artist girlfriend Jessica Niello were on the same plane. We had planned on rendezvousing in the Tokyo Narita Airport before heading out to our area by limousine bus, but by a lucky stroke, their flight was canceled, so Sam and Jessica were rerouted on my plane. When we finally arrived at our farmhouse (about fifteen hours later), Tadaaki had laid the table with a feast. I can't remember all he prepared that night, but the one dish that stood out was the *koshi abura*, a hauntingly bitter, yet earthy mountain vegetable gathered in the Japanese spring, which he served with homegrown pecans ground up with miso and *sansho* leaves from our shrub. The pecans stunned me. *Treviso* would make a good substitute for the *koshi abura*, since it is slightly bitter and has a touch of juicy crunch. *Sansho* leaves (page 366), from a similar bush to the one that produces Sichuan pepper, leave a peppery-tingling sensation that cannot be duplicated, though shiso leaves can be used instead.

treviso with pecan miso
and sansho leaves SERVES 6
TOREVISO TO PEKAN-MISO

4 small *sansho* sprigs
  (about 2 inches/5 cm)

¾ cup fresh pecans
  (3.5 ounces/100 g)

4 tablespoons organic brown rice
  or barley miso

12 treviso leaves

Pluck the leaves from the *sansho* sprigs and finely chop. Smash the pecans and chopped leaves in a *suribachi* or mortar. Grind by hand until smooth, then mash in the miso with a *surikogi* or pestle. Mound the pecan miso onto a medium-sized plate. Stack the treviso leaves attractively in a fan formation on the same plate. Pick up a leaf, scoop up some of the pecan miso, and eat.

VARIATIONS: Substitute garden chives, young celery, or just about any other juicy vegetables that go well with miso. Also fantastic rolled in a fresh shiso leaf.

PECANS: FROM NUT TO TREE

A couple of years ago, my husband dropped a ratty plastic bag bulging with something brown in the middle of my writing projects stacked all over the dining table. "A present," he said laconically, while lifting an eyebrow, telegraphing that I should be duly grateful for this mysterious manna. I dragged myself off the chair where I was writing. As I peered into the bag, my memory flooded back to a similar gift the previous year: one small precious bag of pecans.

Pecans? Yes, simple, incredible, perfect pecans.

These are homegrown pecans—so startlingly fresh. Mmm, my mouth is remembering that first bite last year, the surprise, the tingling feeling of "Oh, my god, this is one of the best things I have ever tasted."

I dug my hand into the bag of dusky nuts and felt their naturally powdered shells. I took a few out and admired them on my malachite counter. The pecans had teensy brown speckles on their buff shells with irregular dark brown streaks tapering down to the point.

They were almost too perfect to crack, but I did it anyway. I cracked open four. I'm not very good at this, so the nutmeat got a little smashed. I dug out all the meat, collecting my spoils on a small plate normally meant for soy sauce, and poured myself a glass of sauvignon blanc before sitting down for a quiet moment. I popped a small piece of pecan into my mouth and slowly bit down, savoring the slightly oily flesh. As I chewed, the pecan-ness flooded into my mouth. It was nothing like the organic pecans I usually bought. The pecan reached deep inside of me so I could taste the heart of the tree.

And my husband grew the trees from nut. Can any of us imagine this? I never understood when Tadaaki told me it would take twenty or thirty years to grow a tree. Why would you do that? Why not just buy something big enough to produce in, say, five years? That's pretty long to wait as it is. But now I get it. These pecans were worth the wait.

Oh, and these days, it's my husband who buys trees. He gave me a Japanese maple for my birthday. I wanted a goat but was properly thankful.

EDAMAME

"Don't eat the pod," Toshi-san warned as he set down a small saucer of what looked like pea pods with a slight peach fuzz.

That was my first taste of edamame. It was 1987, and I was in Palo Alto, California.

Those edamame were quite tasty . . . at the time. Slightly salty to the tongue, it was fun to run the pods through my teeth to pop out the green soybeans. I liked the idea of something green to go with my cold beer.

But those first edamame had certainly been frozen, and who knows where they were grown. I hadn't yet made it to Japan, so I didn't know how edamame should really taste.

Edamame season starts in early summer here in Japan and extends into fall. But really, edamame is all about cold beer and the hot, sultry summer. It's just like fresh corn. You yank the whole soybean plant from the earth, strip the pods right there on the field, then run quickly to the pot of boiling water you have prepared in your kitchen. And just like fresh corn, the frozen or canned variety is not at all the same. The frozen pods aren't so bad, though they don't have much taste—just texture—and I suppose protein.

The good news is that small farmers in the U.S. do grow soybeans and are selling edamame. Look around at the farmers' markets and encourage your local farmers to grow them for you. And tell your farmers to "please, please pick them in the morning before coming to market." Tell them you don't mind the bare roots or plucking them off the branch. Tell them it's just like shucking the corn at the farmers' market. It's part of the fun. Then run, run, run to the boiling water you have left in the kitchen (attended by your faithful mate or children . . . or whoever) and boil them for 3 or 4 minutes before you toss them with sea salt and serve with beer.

Edamame should be an almost luminous apple green and not dull, dark, or flat-colored. The inside beans should be straining against the pods. Feel them to know more—the pods should telegraph you their freshness. Unfortunately, most soybeans in the U.S. are grown on a gigantic scale and are from genetically modified strains that mandate the use of specific chemical fertilizers and pesticides for that particular seed. Finding a local farmer is the ticket. Here again, the type of bean is important. Heirloom Japanese varieties will probably taste best. Some soybeans are meant to be grown in the early summer, some in midsummer, and yet others in late summer. Our grower friend Suka-san grows a pleasantly nutty variety that I love called *chamame* ("brown beans"). Tadaaki's black edamame are similar, but we harvest them in August.

Our friend Matsuda-san lives up in the hills near here. He's another city transplant who has made a new life in our local area. We do a Slow Food edamame-picking event at Matsuda-san's place in early October every year because his area traditionally grows the late variety of soybeans. We all pile into small trucks and bounce across the land to his edamame field not too far away. We pull a big section of plants and then strip them right there so the stems can mulch back into the land. Matsuda-san leaves the rest to be harvested as soybeans, which he dries and uses throughout the winter. Kids love to help, and it's great fun working in the warm fall sun on the side of a green hill overlooking the valley. Back at Matsuda-san's little mayonnaise factory and organic café, we boil the beans in batches over a wood fire and make pizza in Matsuda-san's home-built brick pizza oven. Sometimes we roast chickens. And microbrewery beer on tap is always a must.

I don't think it's possible to get tired of fresh-picked, freshly boiled edamame, but I did fall in love with another method I read about on Hiroko Shimbo's blog. Hiroko is the author of *The Japanese Kitchen*, what I would call the "bible" of Japanese food (next to Shizuo Tsuji's *Japanese Cooking: A Simple Art*). Hiroko shared the roasting method in a dry wok that I describe in the variation. She credits her friend Jiro Iida, the chef at Aburiya Kinnosuke in New York City. You can only roast a small amount at a time, so the method is not good for crowds. Also it does take longer than the boiling method. But for just yourself or a couple of people, pan roasting yields remarkable pods that are smoky, intensely flavored, and crystallized with salt. Frozen pods are not too bad if you've never tried fresh edamame right off the branch (*eda*). But once you eat the real thing, you will be unable to go back to frozen pods. Guaranteed.

edamame and sea salt SERVES 4

1⅓ pounds (600 g) edamame
   (young soybeans)

1½ teaspoons best-quality sea salt

Fill a large stockpot with water and bring to a boil over high heat. Boil the edamame about 3 to 4 minutes, depending on the size of the beans. Scoop out with a strainer into a medium-sized crockery bowl and toss with sea salt. Serve immediately. The edamame should be so hot you can barely touch them.

Grab a handful and eat quickly because they cool quickly (and are particularly good burning hot). Don't forget to prepare the cold beer (if you like) and a bowl for the empty pods. Boil in batches for a big crowd so you can keep serving them hot.

If you have any left over, save the pods in a resealable plastic bag, then pop the beans out the next day and fold into a vegetable salad, potato salad, or any curry or stewlike dish.

VARIATION: Heat an iron wok over high heat and throw in a couple of handfuls of raw edamame pods. You want to make sure that each pod is in direct contact with the surface of the pan. Toss with two flat-edged wooden spoons to ensure even heat distribution. Cook until the skins are blistered and a little juice runs out. Taste to check for doneness. Sprinkle with sea salt, toss once or twice, and serve hot.

When developing the recipe list for this book, I originally intended to make this with sesame oil. In the meantime, I steadily began to dislike the overpowering heaviness of dark sesame oil, especially when compared to the beautifully elegant Japanese rapeseed oil I had recently begun using. To compensate for the lack of sesame flavor, I used toasted sesame seeds. As a result the dish became instantly less oily and also more pleasing to the eye—a win-win decision.

zucchini coins
with roasted sesame SERVES 6
ZUKKINI NO KARUPACCHO

1 tablespoon unhulled sesame seeds

2 medium yellow zucchini
  (about 1 pound/450 g)

½ teaspoon salt

1½ teaspoons organic rapeseed oil

Measure the sesame seeds into a small frying pan and roast over medium-high heat while lifting and shaking the pan to avoid burning the seeds (be careful—they burn easily!). When the seeds start to pop, remove from the heat, dump into a Japanese grinding bowl (*suribachi*) or mortar, and grind roughly.

Slice the zucchini into very thin (but not paper-thin) rounds with a razor-sharp knife. Starting with the coins of the largest diameter, fan the zucchini around the perimeter of a nice-looking large dinner plate (or small serving platter). Working down in size, make concentric, overlapping circles of zucchini coins. You may need to squish up the zucchini in places to fit all the coins in. You want to make sure that at least some of the surface of each coin is peeking out. You don't want to completely cover any of the zucchini as you are laying out the coins.

Sprinkle with the salt, and with gentle fingertips try to distribute the salt evenly over the surface of the zucchini. Drizzle with the oil, sprinkle with the ground sesame, and serve immediately but carefully. Invariably, the zucchini pieces will be unevenly seasoned, so be sure to give each person all of the layers from any given spot on the serving plate (and they should eat accordingly to get the full effect: less seasoned pieces layered with more seasoned pieces).

VARIATIONS: Substitute green zucchini, or mix the colors.

KATSUOBUSHI

A whole piece of *katsuobushi* looks like a dried-up old bone. But waft it under your nose and you'll get hints of the ocean and smoke. *Katsuobushi* is dried, smoked skipjack tuna (usually called bonito), which, along with konbu (dried kelp), is the essential element in making dashi, the ubiquitous stock that is the backbone of Japanese cooking.

Katsuobushi is pleasantly chalky to the touch. You grasp the dried bonito and scrape it over a razor-sharp planing blade in one quick motion. The blade is set into a *katsuobushi kezuriki,* the traditional wooden holding box, and the angle of the blade is adjusted precisely. It looks easy, but I have never quite mastered this trick. My husband shaves off beautifully curled large flakes—mine are gritty crumbles, but they still taste good.

Most Japanese have given up shaving their *katsuobushi* by hand, so many grades of shaved *katsuobushi* are readily available, ranging from thick shavings good for making stock to cheapo small packets that even my cat won't eat. Sadly, the small packets are quite popular, chosen more for convenience than flavor. In our house, we use the thick leatherlike strips (*arai-kezuri*) for stock and the airy fine shavings (*hanakatsuo*) for topping vegetables when we are feeling too lazy to shave our own (and sometimes for stock).

I almost can't squeeze enough vegetables into a meal, and am particularly addicted to raw ones. Okra has that slime thing going, so many people don't care for it, but I've found that some people who can't eat cooked okra can eat it raw. And slicing the okra into very fine rounds makes it all that more palatable, since it hinders telltale okra "threads" from forming. This is, hands down, my favorite way to eat okra.

thinly sliced okra with dried bonito shavings SERVES 6
OKURA NO OHITASHI

30 small or 15 medium okra (about 7 ounces/200 g)

2 tablespoons freshly shaved *katsuobushi,* or 3 tablespoons wide flakes (*hanakatsuo*)

2 tablespoons organic soy sauce

Cut off the tops of the okra and slice into fine rounds. Heap into a small serving bowl. Pinch up a small handful of *katsuobushi* and drop on top of the okra. Drizzle with soy sauce right before serving.

VARIATION: Substitute finely sliced tender asparagus spears for the okra.

There always comes a point during the summer when I start feeling like I don't want to cook another eggplant, Western style or Japanese. But I never get tired of eating eggplant raw, fatigued in salt—so very refreshing, and of course unusually low in calories, since most other eggplant recipes require oil (and eggplants soak up oil like sponges).

salt-massaged raw eggplant with ginger and shiso SERVES 4
NASU NO SHIOMOMI

2 (4½-ounce/125-g) Japanese eggplants

2½ tablespoons sea salt

1 teaspoon slivered ginger

½ tablespoon shiso leaves, cut in chiffonade

Slice the eggplants into very thin rounds with a razor-sharp knife or mandoline. Toss in a medium-sized bowl with salt and a handful of ice cubes. Let sit 15 minutes. Squeeze out the water, discard the salty water, and return the squeezed eggplant to the (wiped) bowl. Drop in the ginger slivers and shiso chiffonade and distribute gently with chopsticks. Mound in a small bowl and serve.

VARIATION: Replace the shiso and ginger with a small red pepper, cut into fine rounds.

Tadaaki loves to make huge bags of these eggs for workers' snacks or when he goes on the occasional road trip. There is something about the gently salty soy sauce enveloping the creamy egg that is irresistible.

eggs pickled in soy sauce SERVES 6 OR MORE
TAMAGO NO SHOYUZUKE

8 farm-fresh eggs, at room temperature

¾ cup (175 cc) soy sauce

Fill a medium-sized saucepan three-quarters full with water and bring to a boil. Place the eggs in a small strainer and lower into the boiling water. Boil for 8 to 9 minutes, depending on size. Set a large bowl in the kitchen sink and fill with cold water. Scoop the eggs from the boiling water with the strainer and immediately plunge into the water. Run more cold water if the water temperature feels warm. When the eggs are cool, gently crack by rapping and rolling on a cutting board. Put the eggs back in cold water for a few more minutes, then peel. Try to get to the inner membrane and peel by running your thumb under the membrane to free the shiny white egg.

Lay the peeled eggs on a dry dish towel. Pat dry, then place the eggs in a freezer-style gallon resealable plastic bag. Pour in the soy sauce, tip the bag to distribute, press out all the air, and roll up any unused portion of bag to create a tight cylinder. Refrigerate overnight. Serve before dinner with drinks or as a side dish for a barbecue or picnic. Best the first day.

I like to serve our guests what we produce, so with a free-range egg farmer husband, eggs are always high on the list. Whacking the eggs in half and scooping them out of the shells is a great chore to palm off on guests eager to help. These eggs are wonderful served nestled in a small pile of tender lettuce leaves filmed with soy sauce dressing, finished with a dollop of homemade mayonnaise and a sprinkling of chopped chives. Half-boiled eggs also add a creamy note to a bowl of homemade ramen. Use eggs of any shell color but white.

half-boiled eggs SERVES 6
HANJUKU TAMAGO

6 medium-sized farm-fresh eggs, at room temperature

Best-quality white sea salt

Fill a medium-sized saucepan three-quarters full with water and bring to a boil. Place the eggs in a small strainer and lower into the boiling water. Boil for 7 to 8 minutes, depending on size. Set a large bowl in the kitchen sink and fill with cold water. Use a strainer to scoop the eggs from the boiling water and immediately plunge the hot eggs into the cold water. Run more cold water until the water temperature remains cool.

When the eggs are completely cool, remove from the water and set on a kitchen towel to air dry (or hand dry individually).

Within an hour or so of serving, slice the boiled eggs in half vertically with a razor-sharp knife. Carefully scoop the eggs out from the shells with a soupspoon. Place the eggs on a pretty dinner plate and make a small mound of sea salt alongside for dipping. Serve as an hors d'oeuvre before dinner.

VARIATIONS: Serve with Japanese Mayonnaise (page 312), or substitute a small saucer of soy sauce for the salt.

It is worth tracking down good-quality *usuage* for this simple and immensely satisfying little before-dinner snack. Or you might try making the pouches yourself if you have access to local tofu. Slice the cotton tofu (*momendofu*) horizontally into ½- to ¾-inch (12- to 18-mm) thin slabs; lay out on a bamboo sushi rolling mat placed on a chopping block. Place another rolling mat on top of the tofu slices and another chopping board on top as a weight. Angle the boards into the sink (prop up one end with another board or plate). Let sit for 30 minutes, then deep-fry one by one until light brown on each side. Drain on paper towels set on top of a folded-up newspaper.

grilled tofu pouches with ginger and scallions SERVES 6
YAKI USUAGE NO SHOGA-ZOE

2 (4-ounce/112-g) packages *usuage* (deep-fried tofu pouches)

1 tablespoon rapeseed oil (if frying instead of grilling)

1 tablespoon grated ginger

1 tablespoon finely chopped scallions or chives

2 tablespoons wide bonito shavings (optional)

2 tablespoons organic soy sauce

Cut the *usuage* in half horizontally, then again diagonally into triangles. Cook over low embers on a charcoal grill, turning frequently, until gently sizzling but not tough. Alternatively, heat the oil in a wide frying pan over high heat and cook quickly by tossing and flipping the skins frequently.

Fan out the crisped tofu pouches in a circular fashion on an attractive dinner plate. Dab with ginger, strew with chopped scallions and bonito shavings, if using, and drizzle with soy sauce.

VARIATIONS: Do the same with thicker deep-fried tofu pieces such as *atsuage* or *ganmodoki* but heat slowly over a low flame or coals, covered. Again, getting top-quality fried tofu products is essential.

Konnyaku is pure fiber and contains virtually no calories. But *konnyaku* loves oil, so it makes a great stir-fry to eat with beer or drinks before dinner. Some people may be put off by the rubbery consistency of *konnyaku*, but I find the texture of the *konnyaku* works well against the scratchy *katsuobushi*. And soy sauce gives this dish a deep flavor that tends to be addicting. *Konnyaku* keeps for weeks in the refrigerator, so it's easy to have on hand at any time. And once the *konnyaku* is parboiled, this stir-fry is ready in a flash, making it convenient as well as tasty.

stir-fried konnyaku with shaved bonito SERVES 6 TO 8

KAMINARI KONNYAKU

2 blocks *konnyaku*
(1 pound/500 g each)

2 tablespoons rapeseed oil

3 small dried red peppers,
broken in half

3 tablespoons soy sauce

A couple of handfuls of large
katsuobushi flakes (*hanakatsuo*)

Tear the *konnyaku* into bite-sized pieces. Boil in salted water for 15 minutes to firm up and dispel any packaging taste. Drain in a strainer.

Heat the oil in a wide skillet or wok over a medium-high flame. Drop in the red peppers and fry for a few seconds until bright red and well roasted. Slide the drained *konnyaku* pieces into the hot oil and toss for several minutes until heated through. Splash in the soy sauce, stirring once. Throw in the handfuls of *katsuobushi*, toss one more time, and serve hot.

KONNYAKU

When I cut through the back roads of our town and head up toward the hills, I pass by densely green fields of *konnyaku*. *Konnyaku* is planted in the spring and harvested in November and December. A mottled brown stem juts out vertically from the root and umbrella-like leaves sprout from the top of the stiff stems, producing a canopy effect. Eventually the root will grow into a dark globular mass weighing several kilos.

One day during a photo shoot with Miura-san, we saw some *konnyaku* farmers cropping, so we stopped to chat and snap a few shots. The *obaachan* had one of those deeply lined farm faces that tell a story of a lifetime out in the fields working the land. She also had a smile that reached inside of her, and welcomed the chance to sit her heavy body down on a crate and exchange a few words.

I showed interest in making *konnyaku* at home, and she kindly walked me through the process (not without a little amusement at the crazy foreigner). A few days later, a *konnyaku* worker showed up at our door with one of those monstrous corms. It sat in my front hall through the Christmas holidays and eventually disappeared. No time to make *konnyaku*—it's a major undertaking. No wonder almost all the *konnyaku* found today is made industrially. The small town of Shimonita, about an hour's drive west of us, is said to be where 70 percent of Japan's *konnyaku* is processed.

The traditional process was explained to me as follows: Peel the *konnyaku* and grate the firm flesh on a large wooden spike grater. Boil the goop in water for several hours, then add calcium carbonate (lime) to coagulate the *konnyaku*. Ladle the mass into rectangular forms stored in cold water to set.

Hmm . . . don't think I'll be making that anytime soon.

Nowadays, the *konnyaku* processors slice, then gas-dry the roots to make chips that can be stored indefinitely and ground into a powder as needed. The powder is then boiled and coagulated with calcium carbonate. Not as interesting, but certainly more practical.

Goya Champuru is one of my favorite Japanese dishes. *Goya* is the Okinawan word for "bitter melon" and *champuru* is Okinawan for "stir-fry." *Goya* looks more like a cucumber than a melon and has the texture of a hard zucchini. This *champuru* combines four tastes into an explosive finale: bitter (*goya*), sweet (egg), hot (red pepper), and salt. My husband often whips up *champuru* for a bite to eat with drinks before dinner in summer. We review the day while standing around the counter, pinching up bright green and yellow mounds of *champuru* with our chopsticks as soon as Tadaaki turns it into a waiting pottery bowl.

bitter melon stir-fried with egg and red pepper SERVES 6
GOYA CHAMPURU

3 small to medium bitter melons (*goya*), about 1 pound/500 g

2 small dried chile peppers (japones or árbol)

6 eggs, at room temperature

2 tablespoons rapeseed oil

¾ teaspooon sea salt

Slice the bitter melons in half lengthwise and scoop out the seeds with a spoon. Cut off the ends and slice crosswise into ⅛-inch (3-mm) half-rounds.

Tear the chile peppers in half or thirds and reserve in a small bowl.

Break the eggs into another bowl and whisk with a fork or chopsticks.

Heat the oil in a large frying pan or wok over medium-high heat and drop the chile peppers into the hot oil. Immediately decrease the flame to low and fry the peppers to infuse the oil. Throw in the bitter melon slices and toss over high heat until no longer raw (about 4 minutes or so). Add the salt as you are cooking the bitter melon.

Mix in the beaten egg and toss quickly as the egg curds form. Remove from the heat when the eggs are still not quite set. Stir until just set and turn into a medium-sized serving bowl. Eat hot.

Tadaaki loves this dish beyond reason, since eating it propels him back to his childhood. He makes it countless times over the course of the long, hot summer months. The backs of the eggplant halves are scored in crosshatch slits, and when fried resemble the feathers of a bird, hence the name. *Shigi* is the Japanese word for "sandpiper," one of the many water birds in a country surrounded by water and dotted with water-flooded rice fields.

fried eggplant halves with sweet miso SERVES 4

NASU NO SHIGIYAKI

About 1⅓ cups (150 cc)
  Sweet Miso Sauce (page 317)

1 pound (450 g) Japanese eggplants
  (4 or 5 small)

2 cups (500 cc) organic rapeseed
  or cold-pressed sesame oil

Make the sweet miso sauce, but reserve the finely sliced shiso leaves and ginger slivers separately until the eggplant has been cooked.

Slice the eggplants in half lengthwise and score the backs with a crosshatch pattern at ⅛-inch (3-mm) intervals and about the same depth.

Line a cookie sheet with several sheets of folded newspaper topped with paper towels and set next to the stove.

Heat the oil in a deep-frying pan (such as a wok) over medium- high heat until hot but not smoking. There should be enough oil so that the eggplant pieces are submerged; otherwise they will become overly brown. Slip the eggplant halves in, skin side down, and fry gently for several minutes, until the cut surface of the eggplant has a golden sheen. Turn the eggplants, cook a couple of minutes more, and remove to drain on the prepared paper-lined cookie sheet.

Stack attractively (cut side down) on a large dinner plate or small serving platter. Warm the sauce briefly, stir in the shiso threads, and pour over the fried eggplant. Sprinkle with the slivered ginger and serve immediately.

top: salt-massaged raw eggplant with ginger and shiso, page 40.

Potatoes aren't very sexy. Not like a slender stalk of spring asparagus or those first delicate snap peas. They don't have the natural beauty of a gorgeous leafy red speckled head of heirloom lettuce. But fresh-dug potatoes are beyond memorable. We crop potatoes in late June or early July, though sometimes Tadaaki is busy and we end up cropping them later. And some years, Tadaaki is able to get a second crop planted for late fall or early winter eating.

The big difference between Japanese and Western potato salad is that you mash the potatoes before adding vegetables and mayonnaise. It took some getting used to at first, but now I prefer the Japanese style. The only thing I object to is adding the mayonnaise when the potatoes are still warm. It's worth tracking down a clear-tasting neutral oil for the mayonnaise since oil is the main ingredient. I use rapeseed, but a good-quality peanut or safflower oil would also work.

japanese-style potato salad SERVES 6
POTETO SARADA

8 large yellow-skinned potatoes

2 medium carrots, peeled

3 small Japanese cucumbers, thinly sliced

1 teaspoon salt, plus more to taste

2 very small red onions (or 1 medium)

2½ to 3 cups (600 to 700 cc) Japanese Mayonnaise (page 312)

Rice vinegar to taste (1 to 2 tablespoons)

Peel the potatoes and cut into large (2½-inch/6-cm) chunks. Boil the potato pieces in salted water with the carrots. Cook the carrots halfway (around 7 minutes—they should not be soft) and remove to a cutting board. Continue cooking the potatoes until the centers have no resistance (about 15 minutes or more, depending on the heat of your flame and the variety of the potato).

Sprinkle the cucumber slices with 1 teaspoon salt, toss, and let sit for 5 to 10 minutes before squeezing out the excess cucumber water. Slice the cooled carrots into thin half-moons. Mash the hot potato pieces until fluffy, cool, then add the sliced cucumbers and carrots. Cut the ends off the onions and slice in half vertically. Peel, cut into thin half-rounds, and mix into the smashed potatoes with the other vegetables. Fold in the mayonnaise to taste; add salt and vinegar as needed.

VARIATIONS: In the summer, skip the carrots and use any combination of the following instead: cooked edamame beans, finely sliced raw okra, raw corn kernels shaved from the cob, or chopped peppers (green, red, or yellow). Substitute chopped scallions for the sliced onions.

There is something about fried food that is madly appealing, but it does create a bit of a mess in the kitchen. Nonetheless, for a casual before-dinner snack, little fried fishes are worth the effort of having to stand over a hot pot of boiling oil. The trick here is to pour yourself a small glass of crisp wine and prepare a little plate of fish for yourself to munch as you cook. These really need to be served hot as they come out of the oil and don't hold up too well. Also, using the best-quality oil you can find is essential, as is skimming off flour particles between batches. When frying with excellent organic oil, the oil remains crystal clear and almost sparkles. The difference is visually palpable, and the taste is incomparable.

deep-fried little fishes SERVES 6
MAMEAJI NO FURAI

Best-quality rapeseed or peanut oil

⅔ cup (100 g) low-gluten good-tasting flour (page 10)

1 teaspoon fine white sea salt, plus more for sprinkling

½ pound (225 g) small fish, such as anchovy, smelt, or whitebait

2 or 3 lemon wedges

If the fish are larger than a child's pinky, remove the guts by poking your finger into the tummy area and smooshing them out toward the head. Wash and dry the fish, making sure to remove any lingering sand, silt, or guts.

Line a cookie sheet with a thick piece of newspaper, then top with a layer of paper towels. Set next to the stove. Over low heat, heat 4 inches (10 cm) of oil in a medium-sized heavy saucepan.

Measure the flour into a small- to medium-sized bowl and whisk in 1 teaspoon salt. Have a pair of long cooking chopsticks or tongs ready.

Increase the heat on the oil to about medium-high. The oil should not be smoking. Test the oil with a drop of flour. It should sizzle and immediately form a small ball as it hits the oil but should not brown. Adjust the oil temperature as needed.

Working with 6 or 8 fish at a time, toss the fish in the flour. Pick them up in your palm, spread your fingers, shake off the excess flour with a couple of vigorous shakes, and drop into the hot oil. Turn gently as the fish become a light golden color. When both sides are cooked and the oil bubbles around the fish have quieted down a little (about 3 to 4 minutes, depending on the size of the fish), remove to the prepared cookie sheet. Serve immediately on a dinner plate lined with attractive blotting paper, sprinkled with fine white sea salt and a few squeezes of lemon.

Come early summer, every home center in our area brings out the fixings for making *umeshu*, the traditional cordial fashioned from rock-hard sour "plums." The sugar commonly used is a rock sugar called *korizato* ("ice sugar"), though I prefer organic sugar for the floral notes it adds to the cordial, especially since the *shochu* (sold here as "white liquor") is fairly generic. My friend Amy Dencler, a longtime downstairs cook at Chez Panisse, sometimes gives me a jar of her strawberry gin made from artisanal gin and organic strawberries ripened under the sun. In this case, she uses a tasteless (easy-to-dissolve) sugar. That makes sense because the organic sugar would muscle out the beautiful gin and strawberries. It's all about balancing your flavors. If you use organic sugar, it will take a bit longer to dissolve and you'll need to shake the jars a tad more often. Producing your own homemade cordial is simple, but I suspect this custom is no longer followed as much in urban areas because the majority of city people are fairly removed from the land and country customs. Also the jars are large and hard to store for apartment dwellers, and we live in an impatient world. Perhaps the minimum of three months it takes for *umeshu* to mature is too long to wait to taste the "fruits" of your labor. But do not be deterred. The wait is more than worth it.

apricot cordial
MAKES ABOUT 2 QUARTS/2 LITERS
ANZUSHU

2 pounds (1 kg) apricots

1 pound (500 g) organic sugar
  or white rock sugar

2 quarts (1.8 to 2 liters) white liquor
  (or plain vodka)

Wipe the apricots and place them in a large clean jar or sealable crock. Add the sugar and liquor, and cap securely. Shake to distribute and help dissolve the sugar.

Let the fruit and liquor macerate for at least 3 months in a cool, dark place. Shake occasionally. Taste after 3 months, and if the liquor is sufficiently infused with apricot, it is ready to serve. This cordial keeps practically indefinitely, though the taste will intensify over time.

Serve cold over ice as a before-dinner drink in the summer.

RATIO: fruit : sugar : liquor—2 : 1 : 2 quarts (1.8 liters—a large bottle of *shochu*)

VARIATIONS: Raspberries, blackberries, boysenberries, and blueberries make lovely cordials as well. When the liquor is fully infused, strain and discard the berries because they will discolor the cordial.

left to right: apricot, *ume*, and blueberry cordials

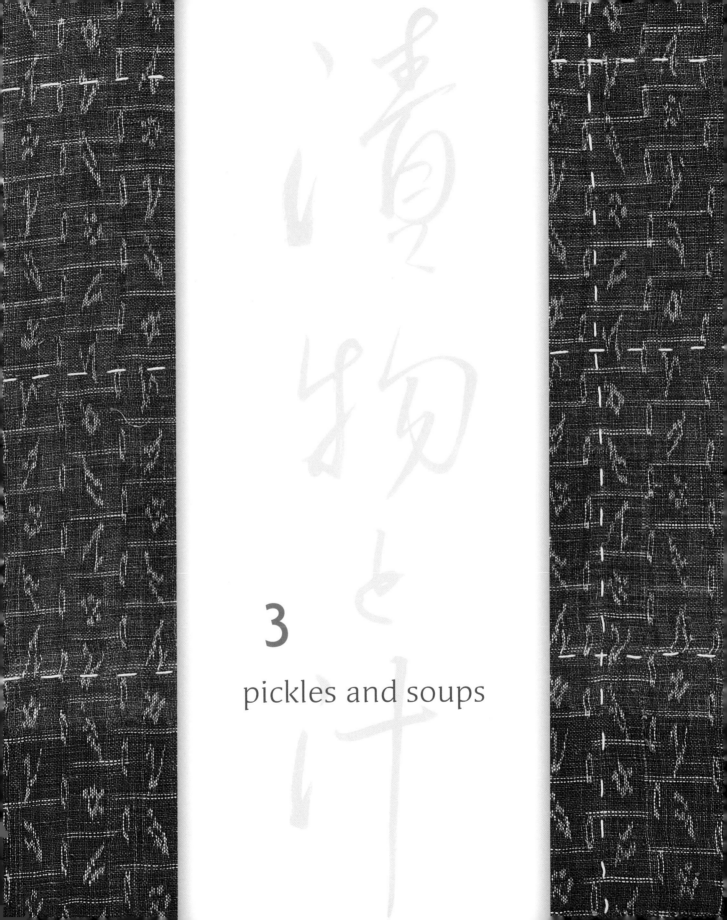

3

pickles and soups

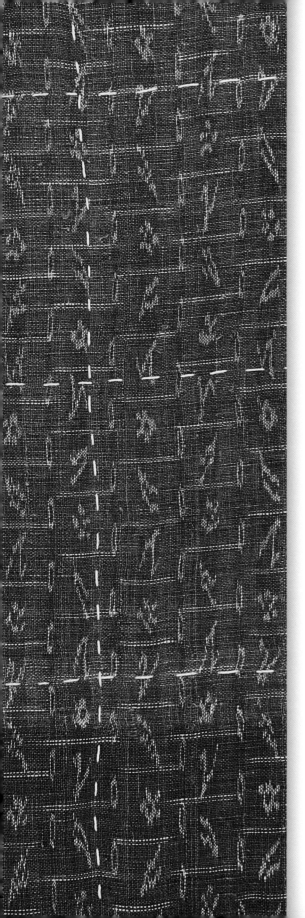

When vegetables are in season, we eat them madly and at every meal. But often we have more than we can possibly eat (or give away), so we make pickles, a time-honored tradition on farms all over the world. Farm vegetables are pickled not only for storage, but also for variation in flavor. We use salt, soy sauce, miso, vinegar, rice bran, or sake lees—alone or in combination—to preserve and enhance the vegetables. Pickles meant to be eaten quickly are treated raw, while pickles destined for long-term storage must first be salted and dried for several days (or longer). I could write a whole book dedicated to Japanese pickles, but in the meantime, I have chosen a sampling of fairly easy to execute but deliciously representative farmhouse pickles. The long-term pickles require patience more than hands-on preparation time, and the quick pickles are more like salted vegetables. All pickles are wonderful served alongside a bowl of rice. Accompanied by a bowl of miso soup, that's the quintessential Japanese meal and follows the *ichiju issai* formula—one soup, one dish—the basic Buddhist repast, which dates way back in time.

Japanese love a bowl of soup at each meal, be it miso soup with tiny clams, clear fish broth with delicate slivers of green onion floating on the surface (a personal favorite), or a *nabe* (one-pot dish) cooked over a tabletop burner on a cool evening. In fact, one of the first meals I shared with my husband was a *nabe* he prepared in the woods, with a bunch of us squatting under the trees, plunking vegetables into an earthenware pot. The girls had brought *onigiri* (rice balls) so perfectly shaped I was sure they had been fashioned in a mold. Those rice balls lacked soul, but the *nabe* did not. Tadaaki had brought the pot and vegetables from his farm. The water we fetched from a nearby stream. The drink we had bought at a roadside stand driving up the mountain, a cloudy-white unfiltered sake called *nigorizake*. The contrast between the restrained rice balls and the wild *nabe* was remarkable. And that was the day Tadaaki told me he had always thought that he was a throwback to Jomon man (from prehistoric Japan) and that he was more hunter than farmer. I think that was the day I really fell in love with him.

UMEBOSHI

One thing is patently clear—we can never do everything. We can never be that perfect mother, farmwife, or person. As such, I gladly let Baachan make the Japanese pickles. I had my hands full doing the Western ones. And as Baachan got older, Tadaaki often pitched in or made his own style of farm pickles (some successful, some not). It was a relief to be a team: Baachan, me, and Tadaaki. Each of us did what we could, and each of us took up the slack when the others could not.

But writing this book, I knew it was time for me to start assuming more of the traditional Japanese wife's (*oyome*) tasks, such as pickle making for the family, especially since pickles are one of my favorite foods. The *oyome* is the bride in her husband's household regardless of age, and her duties are set in stone. Being a bad American *oyome*, I took another path—one I knew I could follow one day at a time—thus making it possible to live out my whole life in this sometimes restrictive culture.

Furiously testing recipes and writing at every available opportunity made for an extremely busy summer recently. I had also been away in the States for a couple of weeks in early June, and a week after I got back we did rice planting. Rice planting (*taue*) is an all-day affair that involves me cooking lunch and dinner for about thirty-five helpers (plus lunch for the twenty-odd kids and staff at Sunny-Side Up! that day).

A few days before the rice planting, Tadaaki's youngest aunt, Katchan, drove into our courtyard and hauled out a couple of buckets of *ume* she had just picked. Her seventy-something freckled face was beaded with sweat, and she could barely catch her breath. But she was so proud of picking the last of the *ume* off the family tree—her family tree, since she had grown up in our house. My gratitude was intermixed with a sense of dismay. Yikes! Two more buckets of *ume* (hard sour "plums," actually of the apricot family) that needed to be dealt with.

I had already salted my local *ume* for *umeboshi* pickles and wasn't planning on making more. Also I was deep into the housecleaning and menu planning for rice planting, all the while trying to write my book. I wanted to cry, but instead smiled and thanked her. I knew she had put enormous effort into picking the *ume* from the low-hanging branches and had searched through the grasses under the tree to gather the fallen fruit. I could be nothing but thankful—truly. Katchan ran cold water in the buckets to soak the fruit and said something about Tadaaki dealing with them, so I turned back toward the house and my kitchen to continue with dinner preparations.

I found the *ume* a couple of days later, still soaking (one day is all you need; two days in the summer heat was pushing it). There were some frothy bubbles forming on the surface of the water: not a good sign. I dumped out the water and freshened up the *ume* with clear cold water before laying them out to dry on flat farm baskets I had perched on the hood of my car. Later that evening, after the sun went down, I passed the baskets through the sliding glass door onto the veranda-cum-hallway that faces the garden (still hoping that Tadaaki would deal with them).

The following day was rice planting, and the *ume* sat in their baskets in the hallway until 9 p.m. the following night. Most of the rice planting helpers had trickled off to their respective homes, while a few die-hard friends and over-night guests were still winding down the hard day of labor in the rice fields, sharing a last beer or glass of wine. I had finally finished putting the food away and washing the dishes, and I too wanted to sit and share a glass of wine and some relaxed conversation, but the *ume* still sat there, waiting, and they would not wait another day. I knew I could not turn my back on Katchan's effort. And after all they were our *ume*, from a family tree that has been loyally producing *ume* for generations of Hachisu.

Gathering up some last vestige of energy, I hefted the *ume* onto our breakfast room table, found a several-gallon pickling bucket outside the kitchen, and set about washing it (cursing a little). The *ume* and Katchan pushing me, I picked through the fruit, discarding bad ones but keeping ones that were slightly discolored or even slightly smashed (at Tadaaki's advice). "They're fine," he tossed off casually. Engrossed in conversation, he did not offer to help.

I lined the pickling bucket with a thick plastic bag specifically made for pickling operations and gently slid in the *ume*, to which I added sea salt at 8 percent of the *ume* weight. After squeezing out the air and cinching up the bag, I laid the drop lid on the *ume* and placed a pottery bowl (of the same weight as the *ume*) directly on top. The *ume* stayed like that for a few weeks, hap-pily sitting on my kitchen floor. I kept thinking I should check them, but it was a busy, busy sum-mer. After a few rainy days, the sun appeared, and as luck would have it, I caught the *ume* just before they went bad.

I learned a few things: Don't worry about how pretty the container is, make sure you use a

plastic pickling bag to keep the air out, and check your *ume* to see if the salt is melting and the brine is well distributed around the fruit—occasionally massage a little to distribute. And don't wait too long before you dry the *ume*.

The ones I had put in crockery containers did not fare as well as the Hachisu *ume* Katchan had picked and I had packed in the ugly (but practi-cal) plastic pickling bucket. I dried the *ume* for three days in bright sunlight, returning them to their naturally exuded pickling brine (*umesu*) at night. And now my *umeboshi* (dried *ume*) sit in the kitchen closet, stored in a celadon Korean pickling pot bought at the local flea market. This time I was the good farmwife.

My friend Sharon Jones still talks about when Tadaaki whipped up a simple little Japanese breakfast for her while I slept in. He made her a quick bowl of miso soup, and while the *katsuobushi-konbu* dashi was steeping, he sliced up some turnips he had grown, threw in the leaves as well, and tossed them with sea salt and aromatics. A bowl of rice with a raw egg rounded out the meal, and Sharon was hooked. Mother of a budding farmer and a chef, Sharon is also on the board of directors of Chez Panisse and tends goats in her spare time. But something about the food and the feeling of Japan captured her heart during the three months she spent in this country, and that feeling pulls her back here. This dish epitomizes everything I love about Japanese farm food: simple, pristine flavors of the field and quick to prepare.

turnips and turnip leaves pickled in salt SERVES 6
KABU NO SHIOZUKE

8 tender turnips with leaves
   (about 1½ pounds/675 kg)

Scant 2 tablespoons sea salt (27 g)

2 yuzu or 1 Meyer lemon

2 small fresh or dried red chile
   peppers

1 teaspoon slivered ginger (optional)

Slice the tops off the turnips and reserve. Pare away any discoloration on the turnips and cut them in half vertically, then crosswise into thin (⅛-inch/3-mm) half rounds. Pick through the leaves and slice a couple of small handfuls into 2 by 1¼-inch (5 by 3-cm) pieces. Toss the turnips and leaves together in a medium-sized bowl and sprinkle with salt. Gently but firmly massage the salt in to distribute well to encourage the turnips to exude a bit of their water.

With a very sharp knife or vegetable peeler, shave off the outer yellow zest of the yuzu or lemon, taking care to avoid the bitter white pith. Stack small slices of zest and slice into very thin strips. Slice the chiles into thin rounds. Slide the zest, chiles, and ginger slivers, if using, into the bowl with the turnips. Massage one more time and serve immediately or pack in a resealable plastic bag and chill for a couple of hours. These keep for a few days refrigerated; however, they will continue to leach out water so they will not retain their pleasing crispness.

RATIO: turnips : salt—10 : 4

VARIATIONS: Slice carrots into thin rounds or daikon into thin quarters (or halves, depending on the size of the daikon) in place of turnips; adjust the salt to taste. Be sure to slice carrots fairly thin, since they will not soften with salt as much as juicier roots such as turnips or daikon. Include the leaves if at all possible, because they not only add color to the dish but also give the sweet vegetables an added earthy, piquant pizzazz.

Napa cabbage (*hakusai*) and daikon are to Japanese winter as eggplant and cucumbers are to summer. If a farming family grows nothing else, at least they will be growing those two vegetables during their seasons. As my father-in-law approached his eighties, he grew fewer and fewer vegetables, but I can still picture him out in the field tying up his heads of napa cabbages to prevent them from spreading out loosely, as is their natural tendency. The Japanese value the white juicy stalks with pale crinkly leaves that form when tied; also the tight cylinder shape is necessary for making cabbage pickles, since the cabbages are sliced vertically and dried in quarter wedges. *Nappa* is the generic term for leafy greens in Japanese, so most likely the American name derives from that term. The Japanese word for napa cabbage, *hakusai*, means "white vegetable."

We don't tie all of our *hakusai* because we also like the leafy green part, not just the crisp white stems. While not as useful for pickles, the green leaves are more versatile for salads. When we did a soba dinner at Chez Panisse in 2010, the chef, our friend Kanji Nakatani (Kanchan), made a salt-massaged (*shiomomi*) dish with radicchio tardivo, sorrel, and chervil—it was stunning. So feel free to experiment, though if you are using strong greens such as sorrel, just a little goes a long way. This kind of salt-massaged treatment works beautifully as a fresh relish-type addition to a plate and makes a nice accompaniment to salt-grilled fish.

salt-massaged napa cabbage with yuzu slivers SERVES 6
HAKUSAI NO SHIOMOMI

½ napa cabbage, sliced vertically through the head (about 1½ pounds/600 g)

1½ tablespoons sea salt

Slivered zest from 2 small or 1 large yuzu, or Meyer lemon

½ small dried or fresh red pepper, sliced into fine rounds (optional)

Remove the core with a V cut and slice the cabbage crosswise into fine strands. Scrape into a large mixing bowl and toss with the salt, yuzu zest, and red pepper, if using. Massage the cabbage gently until its natural juices have run out but it is not completely fatigued.

Pack into a resealable plastic bag, squeeze out all the air, and roll tight. Chill in the fridge for about 15 minutes. Remove from the fridge, lift the cabbage from the accumulated liquid, and squeeze. Taste, add a touch more salt if needed, and serve.

This is the kind of uninhibited style of cooking Tadaaki loves. It is very manly and visceral as you get right in there with the smashing and breaking. We eat baskets and baskets of cucumbers during the summer and somehow never seem to tire of their crispness. Our teenage sons love this approach to pickling because it is one we only started using a couple years ago and the novelty has not faded.

smashed cucumber pickles with garlic SERVES 6

TATAKI KYURI

1¾ pounds (800 g) Japanese
  cucumbers (5 or 6 medium)

2 cloves garlic, roughly chopped

2 teaspoons fine sea salt

Lay the cucumbers on a large cutting board and bang them gently but firmly with a Japanese pestle (*surikogi*) or rolling pin to crack (and slightly smash) the surface of the cucumbers. Break into rough chunks with your hands and drop into a freezer-style gallon-sized resealable plastic bag. Mash the garlic with a pinch of the salt in a mortar with a pestle. Sprinkle the remaining salt over the cucumbers, scrape in the mashed garlic purée, and massage in lightly to distribute the salt and garlic. Roll up the bag and squeeze out the air, then refrigerate for about 10 minutes.

Remove from the fridge when ready to eat, and drain the cucumbers in a wire mesh strainer set over a bowl. Serve before dinner with drinks or as a side dish with any broiled fish, teriyaki-style meats, or steak.

VARIATIONS: Stack 8 shiso leaves, roll into a cigar shape, and slice into fine tendrils; toss gently but well with the cucumbers before serving. Finely slivered ginger (about ½ tablespoon) also adds a bright note—massage in with the garlic. Substitute Western cucumbers, but peel and seed first.

Tadaaki made these pickles while I was writing this book. I had more than enough recipes already, so tried to ignore his inpromptu pickle-making project, but they were so good I had to include the recipe. These full-flavored pickles have a hint of sweetness that I somehow like, and are quite addicting.

cucumbers pickled in soy sauce and mirin SERVES 6

KYURI NO AMAJOYU-ZUKE

1½ cup (375 cc) organic soy sauce

1 cup (250 cc) best-quality mirin

½ cup (125 cc) organic rice vinegar

2 pounds (1 kg) Japanese cucumbers (7 or 8 medium)

1 (1-inch/2.5-cm) knob of ginger, peeled

A small handful (about ½ cup/ 125 cc) of konbu threads (*ito konbu*)

4 *myoga*, quartered lengthwise (optional)

Measure the soy sauce, mirin, and rice vinegar into a large saucepan and bring to a boil. (Remove from the heat once the liquid has boiled, if you have not finished cutting the cucumbers.)

While the pickling liquid is coming to a boil, cut the cucumbers into ¼-inch (6-mm) rounds and the ginger into very fine slivers.

Drop the cucumber slices, ginger slivers, konbu threads, and optional *myoga* into the boiling pickling liquid and cook 1 minute over medium-high heat. Remove the pan from the heat and let cool for about 1 hour.

Strain out the liquid and reserve the cucumbers, ginger, konbu, and optional *myoga* in a medium-sized bowl. Bring the strained pickling liquid to a boil again, throw the cucumbers and all the other aromatics back into the boiling liquid, and cook for 1 minute over medium-high heat. Remove the pan from the heat and let cool for 1 hour.

Repeat this step once more for a total of three times. After you have heated the pickles three times, let them cool in their pickling solution, covered. They are now ready to eat and can be stored in the refrigerator for up to 1 week.

RATIO: soy sauce : mirin : rice vinegar—3 : 2 : 1

My brother-in-law, Noriaki, makes *matsumae zuke* at New Year, and these garlic-infused carrots, more a salad than a pickle, are one of the dishes I look forward to most during the holidays. The fresh, crunchy julienned carrots and konbu strips are subtly flavored with garlic, and the salty sea taste of the dried squid (and konbu) comes through in the background, tantalizing your tongue. *Matsumae zuke* is a relief from the characteristically sweet New Year foods (*osechi ryori*) such as dried fish simmered in sweetened soy sauce until dense and syrupy. In the past, as each New Year approached, the whole family (including the men) helped do a big cleaning, and the women cooked sweet-simmered foods that would keep well at room temperature for about a week. During the New Year holiday, shops and markets were closed, and this was the time women were "allowed" to take a break from preparing the daily meals. When we were first married, there was a steady stream of visitors during the days after New Year, now not so much. And today the shops remain open. For many families, the custom of doing the big New Year cleaning has slipped away, and many families just buy their *osechi ryori*. You can even buy a set at 7-Eleven. I know because my mother-in-law bought one a few years ago. (She tried to bring it out at the traditional family dinner on December 31. We gently but firmly vetoed that.)

carrots pickled with konbu and dried squid SERVES 6 TO 8
MATSUMAE ZUKE

1 (9 by 3-inch/22.5 by 7.5-cm) piece of konbu

2 tablespoons sake

1 pound (500 g) carrots

1 teaspoon salt

½ piece (MSG-free) dried squid (*surume*, page 11)

3 small cloves garlic, finely chopped

2½ tablespoons organic soy sauce

Break the konbu into 4 pieces, set on a small plate, and douse with the sake. Let soak while you cut the carrots into 1¾-inch (4-cm) julienned matchsticks, slide into a medium-sized bowl, and gently toss with salt. Let sit for 10 minutes, squeeze the carrots by handfuls to express out any accumulated liquid, and drop them into a clean medium-sized bowl as you go.

Remove the konbu from the sake, reserve the soaking liquid, and slice the soaked konbu into ⅛-inch by 2-inch (3-mm by 5-cm) strips. Add the konbu strips to the bowl of carrots.

Starting with the legs, snip the dried squid into ⅛-inch by 1-inch (3-mm x 2.5-cm) slivers with a pair of sturdy kitchen shears. Some legs will be too thick, so you will need to slice them up the center to thin; but be sure to cut the body portion laterally. Add the dried squid slivers to the bowl of carrots and konbu.

Season with the garlic, soy sauce, and 1 tablespoon of the sake reserved from soaking the konbu. Mix well and set aside for several hours to allow the flavors to intermingle and the squid and konbu to soften. This keeps well stored in the refrigerator for more than a week. It's good straight from the fridge or served at room temperature.

Often served at New Year, *namasu* is a bright and crunchy dish that acts as a refreshing digestive during the holidays when there are guests and we tend to overeat. The sugar-to-vinegar ratio is one of taste, but I prefer these a bit astringent, with not too much sugar, since daikon and carrots are especially sweet in the winter. *Namasu* keeps for about a week and is a pretty splash of color on the table with almost any meal. The carrots are a dominant color that can overwhelm the dish, so keep the balance of daikon to carrot at roughly 2:1 (or 70 percent daikon and 30 percent carrots). This dish is best made in winter from freshly picked daikon and carrots at their peak of flavor.

sweet-vinegared daikon and carrots SERVES 4 TO 6

NAMASU

1 cup (250 cc) organic rice vinegar

3 tablespoons organic granulated sugar

3 cups (700 cc) julienned daikon (1¾-inch/4-cm thin matchsticks)

1¼ cups (300 cc) julienned carrots (1¾-inch/4-cm thin matchsticks)

1½ teaspoons sea salt

Zest from 2 small yuzu or 1 large Meyer lemon, cut into fine slivers

Heat the vinegar and sugar together in a small saucepan over low heat to melt the sugar. Cool to room temperature before using.

Keep the daikon and carrots in two separate bowls. Sprinkle the daikon with 1 teaspoon salt and the carrots with the remaining ½ teaspoon salt. Massage the salt in gently and let sit for 10 minutes before squeezing out the excess water and dropping into a clean medium-sized mixing bowl. Toss the daikon and carrots with the slivered yuzu peel and cooled sweet vinegar. Chill for 1 day before serving cold.

Pickling is a way of life in Japan, though sadly the custom is waning. One element that comforts me is the logic in so many pickling methods. When you are in a hurry, you can just sprinkle juicy vegetables, such as turnips or cucumbers, with salt, massage, let sit a couple minutes and voilà—instant pickles. Using the liquid produced in making *umeboshi* (*umesu*) as the pickling agent accomplishes the same simple task. The air is heavy during our muggy Japanese summers, so the hot flash of ginger is quite nice at the end of the day. Tadaaki often stops by the field on his way home from egg deliveries and grabs some young summer ginger to eat raw, scooped into a mound of miso, as a before-dinner snack. Here, the young ginger is pickled in plum vinegar and good served with a bowl of rice and a fried egg for breakfast. Any way, young ginger gives you a hot zing.

young ginger pickled in plum vinegar SERVES 6
MESHOGA NO UMEZUKE

4 pale pink young ginger roots
(sold with green stems intact)

1 cup (250 cc) plum vinegar (*umesu*)

Separate the ginger into single stalks. Wash well and cut off the leaves and stalks about 3 inches (7.5 cm) above the root portion. Lay the roots in a plastic container along with the plum vinegar. Let marinate in the refrigerator for half a day before serving. Use fairly soon, maybe within a day or two, for the ginger will continue absorbing the salty/sour flavor of the plum vinegar.

DRIED EGGPLANT

A couple of years ago, I stepped outside and found my mother-in-law (Baachan) laying out thick rounds of eggplant on bamboo screens lined with rush mats. I had never seen her do this, so was intrigued. She was wearing a jaunty straw bonnet banded with a piece of blue-and-white-checkered gingham she had tied under her chin. She looked so happy to be out in the sunshine, doing something she used to do because she wanted to, not because she had to. And I know she felt a deep sense of pleasure in being useful—it had become harder and harder for her to get around with her bent back. Also her eyes are not really sharp enough to catch fine cracks in the eggs, so she is not able to help Tadaaki wipe and sort eggs anymore.

I stayed awhile to chat with Baachan and find out how she planned on using the dried egg-plant. She told me that they dried the eggplant for use in winter simmered dishes, and I under-stood immediately the dark flavor the eggplant would impart during those cold, barren winter days. It would be similar to dried shiitake, with

its deeply intense mushroom essence that in some way can replace meat or fish in a simmered vegetable dish. The eggplant is dried during the height of summer, when the sun is at its hottest and the glossy purple orbs are at their peak. The eggplant is cut into 1-inch (2.5-cm) thick rounds and laid out on bamboo racks for several days or until completely desiccated and hard to the touch. The balsa wood–like light pieces are then stored in a cool, dark place. During the winter, dried eggplant or shiitake that have been soaked for about 20 minutes give a simmered dish an in-tense flavor boost because their natural essence has been concentrated in the drying process.

I was surprised that I had not seen Baachan drying eggplant before, but comforted that even after more than twenty years in Japan, I was still learn-ing traditional ways. And I was enveloped by an incredible warmth from being part of this farming family that still carries out these thrifty country customs. No matter how tired I get, I love being part of that history and hope that I too will keep at it well into my eighties, just as Baachan has.

Years ago, when Tadaaki and I were first married, we made rice bran pickles (*nukazuke*). They immediately captivated me. The mildly sour rice bran imparts an unusual tang to the vegetables that is more subtle than the typical salt, soy sauce, or vinegar pickles. Also the rice pickling mash (*nukadoko*) creates wick-dry pickles with an indescribable flavor that is impossible to duplicate otherwise. *Nukazuke* often accompanies the bowl of rice served at the end of a casual-style Japanese meal. I've heard of people keeping their *nukadoko* fresh and alive for years. But we are not one of them—we would lose track of the days and forget to turn the *nukadoko* to keep it from getting sour. And eventually we had to toss the whole thing and start again, though often not until the next summer, at the height of eggplant and cucumber season—two vegetables that are transformed by *nukadoko* into cannot-stop-eating pickles. But now we have a rice polishing machine in the garage, so fresh rice bran is available when it is time to make our *nukadoko*. Because inevitably I still manage to forget to turn the mash, and inevitably the mash becomes sour. But that's okay. Life is a process, and so is pickle making. It's okay to make mistakes along the way. That's called being human.

zucchini pickled in rice bran SERVES 6
ZUKKINI NO NUKAZUKE

NUKADOKO

10 cups (1¾ pounds/800 g) rice bran (*nuka*, page 11)

11 tablespoons (about 6 ounces/165 g) salt

3 tablespoons brown rice miso

2 (4 by 2-inch/10 by 5-cm) pieces of konbu

5 dried red peppers

6 strips tangerine or sour orange peel, such as *daidai* or Seville (optional)

Mild vegetable cuttings or pieces: carrot, zucchini, squash, green beans, etc.

Parch the rice bran over a low flame in a large wok or frying pan until dry and powdery to the touch. (The bran should be warm but must not brown.) Remove from the heat and dump into a large mixing bowl.

Bring 4 cups (1 liter) water to a boil with the salt; stir to dissolve. Stir the brine into the parched rice bran to make a thick paste and fold in the miso. Mix well. Pack the bran mixture (*nukadoko*) into a large crockery pot with a lid or a plastic container. Poke in the konbu, dried red peppers, and citrus peel (making sure they are completely submerged).

Nukadoko is a living thing, so embrace the natural beauty of it and don't be afraid of it. The *nukadoko* needs about a week to ripen and grow "good bacteria." You will see no visible change each day, but you will be able to taste how the *nukadoko* progressively sours and develops a more complex flavor profile as each day passes.

continued on next page

zucchini pickled in rice bran

NUKAZUKE

4 small zucchini (or 1 large)

When starting your *nukadoko*, store the crock at room temperature, out of direct light. Each day, starting with Day One, put a few cuttings or pieces of vegetable into the mixture and let sit overnight. The following day, pick out the vegetables and discard. Turn the mixture over with your hands to aerate and promote its health. Taste the mixture each day to understand how it is changing and how it is alive. If you forget to turn the mixture one day, it may have formed a fine white bloom. Scrape it off. If you forget for two days in a row, you risk souring the *nukadoko*. Three days and it's gone—you might as well throw the whole thing out and start again.

After a week, the *nukadoko* should be nicely seasoned and ready to use. If tended, it will keep for years.

To make the *nukazuke*, roll the small zucchini in a little sea salt. If the zucchini is oversized, cut it in half crosswise, again lengthwise, and scoop out the center spongy part with seeds. Push the zucchini into the *nukadoko* until completely covered and leave for 4 to 6 hours. Remove the zucchini, wash off the bran mash, dry well, and slice into ½-inch (12-mm) rounds or half-moon shapes.

Whether you make pickles every day or not, you must turn the mixture every day, or it will go off—once a day in the winter, but twice a day in the summer. Most vegetables will be done in about a half day in the summertime but will take a few hours longer on cold winter days. Also the *nukadoko* should be saltier in the summer to hinder spoilage. As winter approaches, you can let the salt balance gradually soften.

Taste the *nukadoko* every day, and never forget that it is a living thing, so multiple variables come into play. It takes some trial and error, but don't be afraid to try and don't be afraid to fail. It's all a learning experience.

RATIO: rice bran : salt—10 : 2

VARIATIONS: Cucumbers, carrots, okra, green beans, thin-skinned mild green peppers, Japanese eggplants, radishes, *myoga*, turnips, squash, or daikon. Pink- or purple-skinned vegetables such as eggplant, radish, and *myoga* should be rolled in salt before putting them into the *nukadoko* to prevent discoloration. The softer vegetables will be done in about a half a day, but the daikon will take longer since it is thick and fibrous.

PLUCKING DUCK FEATHERS

Two and a half hours into the duck plucking, with all the feathers that hadn't already settled on some surface wafting gently in the kitchen, I began to regret forgoing the water dip. At least the ducks didn't smell.

My sons Andrew and Matthew couldn't be convinced to help, but Christopher (my eldest) wandered by and took pity on me. I passed him the duck I had given up on and he went to fetch pliers to remove the wing and tail feathers. Tadaaki breezed in, rolled his eyes at the mess I was making, grabbed a duck, and left. Christopher (more practical than I) followed him out not too long after. But before that, we got to talking about the yearly duck plucking. A bit like childbirth, it's an ordeal I always conveniently forget until Christmas overtakes us one more time and I'm back tugging at those impossibly recalcitrant feathers that don't seem to want to separate from their host. Someone told me recently that we should be plucking the ducks immediately upon killing. After all these years, why didn't I know that?

And why are the Muscovy ducks harder to pluck than the little wild mallard ducks? And why are the glossy green ones a bit easier than the plain white and black ones? And who cares anyway? But these are the things that went through my mind as I plucked the Christmas ducks with early Joan Baez cranked up high.

When we were having babies, we used to buy the ducks from a duck farm. The duck guy would kill to order (either Muscovy or mallard ducks, our choice), and then send them beautifully packed and separated by cut, down to individually wrapped livers, hearts, and gésiers. I often made confit in those days, so he also included extra duck fat, ready to render. I don't know how much the ducks cost, but those were glorious days. I reminisced with Christopher about those featherless Christmases, and he wondered if we wouldn't go back to ordering ducks from the duck man. The idea is seductively enticing, but I don't think we will. It's not about the money but about not giving up on how we choose to live our life and sticking to a code of ethics when it comes to creating our food. It's a lot easier to buy our rice or flour . . . or even vegetables for that matter. And it's a hell of a lot easier to buy our Christmas ducks, plucked and cleaned. But then we would lose that feeling—that feeling that tunnels into your core and spreads throughout your body when you take a bite of food that you have created from seed or have lovingly raised, respectfully killed, and then painstakingly cleaned. And that's a feeling for which there is no duplicate, and that feeling is addicting because it reaches in and grabs your soul.

I love wakame—slippery and tasting of the sea. And we are lucky to be able to occasionally find good fresh wakame at our local fish market. But there is also a funny (fairly pushy) old lady who sometimes comes by our neighborhood hawking hand-salted wakame. Even when I tell her we still have some, she insists I buy more. I'm not sure from what small seaside town she hails, but she has a thick country twang that is hard to understand. I suppose I should just buy her wakame when the opportunity arises, since she does not come that often and wakame keeps indefinitely in the fridge. Although I never came across it, I've read that salted wakame is available in some Japanese grocery stores in the U.S., and that a few fish markets are selling the fresh—in any case, the dried variety substitutes quite nicely.

miso soup with potato slivers and wakame SERVES 6

JAGAIMO TO WAKAME NO MISO SHIRU

1 small handful of wakame, dried or fresh

1 medium potato (4½ ounces/125 g)

Scant 1⅓ cups/300 cc Dashi (page 307)

2½ tablespoons organic brown rice miso

Rinse the fresh wakame, drain, and cut into bite-sized pieces (about 1½ inches/4 cm long); or rinse the salt from the salted wakame, soak for 10 minutes in a medium-sized bowl covered with cold water, drain, and chop into bite-sized pieces. Alternatively, soak the dried wakame in a medium-sized bowl for 20 minutes in cold water and chop if needed.

Peel the potato and slice into thin matchsticks. Pour the dashi into a medium-sized saucepan and drop in the potato slivers. Bring to a boil over medium-high heat, reduce to a gentle simmer, and cook about 5 minutes or so, until the potato is soft but not falling apart. Add the softened wakame pieces.

Measure the miso into a small bowl and dip a whisk into the miso to catch up all 3 tablespoons. Dunk the miso-covered whisk into the dashi and swirl it around in the soup liquid until the miso is well incorporated. Ladle the soup into small bowls (lacquer if you have them). Serve immediately, either before a meal or at the end with a bowl of rice.

VARIATION: Drop in a few small squares of tofu cut into a ⅓-inch (8-mm) dice from a quarter of a 10.5 oz (300 g) block of Japanese-style "cotton" tofu after adding the miso. Heat gently (and briefly) to warm the tofu squares.

Miso soup with clams is the most orthodox of all miso soups, and while often accompanying a sushi meal at sushi shops, it is also a well-loved home recipe. Usually miso soup is made by stirring miso into a dashi base; here, however, the clams exude their own liquor, so water (with or without sake) is the base. This soup relies on small clams for its presentation, so do not be tempted to make this with clams whose shells are larger than ½ inch (12 mm).

miso soup with small clams serves 6
ASARI NO MISO SHIRU

2 cups littleneck or Manila clams (*asari* in Japan), about 14 ounces (400 g)

½ cup (125 cc) sake

About 3 tablespoons mild-flavored organic miso (such as brown rice)

1 very thin scallion (or several chives), finely chopped

1 small bunch *mitsuba*, leaves removed (optional)

Scrub the clams in several changes of cold water to express some of the sand, then scoop them up and drop in a medium-sized saucepan. Pour the sake over the clams, cover, and bring to a boil over high heat. As soon as the clams start to open, add hot water to cover, replace the lid, and bring to a boil once again. Continue cooking until (almost) all the clams are open. (Some clams will never open—discard those.)

Dip a small whisk into the measured miso, drop the miso-covered whisk blade into the soup liquid and swirl to incorporate the miso into the soup. Ladle the soup, shells and all, into small lacquer bowls with lids (if you have them), and garnish with the chopped scallion or *mitsuba* leaves but not both. (More is not always better!) Serve immediately before a meal or at the end with a bowl of rice.

VARIATION: You can substitute teensy black freshwater mussels (*shijimi*) for the small *asari* or littlenecks, but these may not be available abroad. If you use *shimiji*, skip the sake-steaming step. Scrub and rinse the mussels, put them in a medium-sized saucepan with cold water to cover, place the lid on the pan, and bring to a boil just until most of the mussels have opened. Be careful not to overcook, since they will lose their flavor. Add the miso and green garnish following the directions above.

I have loved this soup since I first tasted it more than forty years ago, and my infatuation has not waned in the intervening years. This is Japanese cooking at its very best, with the crystal-clear flavor of the delicate fish broth and just a hint of aromatics such as finely sliced scallions or a couple of *mitsuba* leaves. Of course this soup is only good made from fresh, clean bones, so do take care to visit a fisherman or fishmonger before starting out. Also, I would not use bones from large oily fish such as those in the tuna family, since they tend to have a bigger flavors than you want—or maybe not. After all, in the end this is a personal decision. We typically make this fish broth after a trip to the fish market.

clear fish broth with chopped scallions SERVES 4

SAKANA NO ARAJIRU

2 cups (500 cc) very fresh bones and head from a mild-flavored fish, such as snapper or sea bream

Sea salt

1 thin *negi* (Japanese leek) or 2 thick scallions

1 (½-inch/12-mm) piece of ginger, peeled

1 small bunch *mitsuba*, leaves removed (optional)

1 very thin scallion or several chives, finely chopped

Strew the fish bones over a foil-lined cookie sheet and sprinkle very lightly with salt (just a hint of cooked salt is good enough to add depth of flavor to the stock). Broil both sides of the bones and head on the second rack from the top of your oven. Do not blacken, but make sure the natural oils of the fish have come out and the skin is sizzling.

As the fish bones and head are broiling, bring 4 cups (1 liter) of water to a boil in a medium-sized saucepan (large enough to hold the bones and head). Cut the *negi* or scallions into 2-inch (5-cm) lengths and the ginger into fine slices.

Plop the broiled bones into the boiling water along with the *negi* and ginger aromatics. Lower the heat and simmer gently for 30 minutes. Pour the soup through a fine-mesh strainer into a clean saucepan. Taste for salt and add a pinch or two if necessary. The broth should taste of the sea but not have an overpowering flavor profile. The salt should be a hint in the background. This is an elegant, mild broth that serves to refresh. Ladle into small beautiful bowls and drop in a few *mitsuba* leaves, if using, or a sprinkling of finely chopped very thin scallion or chives.

TOKANYA

I skirted the gray block wall along our driveway and rounded the corner onto the street in front of our house, barely making out the figures in the dim light of the lone streetlight. Only the flash of Tomori-san's camera illuminated the thickly braided straw ropes pounding on the pavement. *"Tokanya, waradepo yomochi kutte, buttatake!"* (Tokanya, straw gun, eat mochi in the nighttime, shoot!)

A car came up fast behind me and I yelled, "Car!" and stepped aside quickly as the driver did not show signs of slowing. The figures scattered but took up their cries right after *"Tokanya, waradepo yomochi kutte, buttatake!"* *Thwak.* The crack of the "straw gun" pounding the pavement wakes up the sleeping winter bugs and kills them (metaphorically). On the tenth day of the tenth month, we make "straw guns" called *waradepo* for Tokanya, an ancient farming rite to send off the rice field god to the mountains after the rice harvest. Friends come to help celebrate and we eat in the garden by torchlight.

I had just gotten back from a trip to the U.S. that morning, so Tadaaki was in charge with ex-student-babysitter-mother's-helper-good-friend Yoshie Takahashi as assistant. I set about unpacking with uncharacteristic haste and went upstairs for a second, only to come down and find a strange girl in the kitchen. Tadaaki has a fairly loose style at his events and gives little instruction to his helpers. I never did learn the girl's name, but she bumbled about (somewhat aimlessly) in our kitchen for a bit. Yoshie eventually showed up with another friend in tow, and at one point all three girls were stirring and skimming the soup together. I never have under-

stood why it takes so many people to do one task here. I guess it is the sense of camaraderie and group cohesion.

And I suppose as the wife I should have been the one feeling badly for not helping, but already the plan was out of my control, careening along without direction. Tadaaki tends to whoosh in, give a few minimal cooking commands, and then spin back off to the eggs, chickens, or deliveries. I am the opposite, completely controlling in the kitchen and not one to let people go willy-nilly. When I make the *kenchinjiru*, I like to slice the vegetables myself because I want them all to be the right size and thickness to cook at the same pace. Good enough is not where I look to end up. Each ingredient deserves to shine, so the finished dish should not be messed up by unwitting mistakes of well-meaning yet untutored assistants. But if the cooks at Chez Panisse could let me bump about in their kitchen that fall, I suppose I should be more forgiving (and flexible)—though I do relax the "rules" when it comes to little kids—but then we're just cooking for ourselves and not a crowd of thirty or forty hungry adults.

It used to be that the countrywomen all spoke the same language of food and knew how to prepare the same dishes. Today that's not true, since most young women do not learn to cook from their mothers and there are few farming families passing along traditions. Mothers (and even grandmothers) work, so supermarket prepared foods regularly appear on the table; and convenience store foods are eaten in the car on the way home or in transit to cram school (*juku*). After all, there is no mess in the kitchen if one eats in the car or reheats in the microwave.

I'm not a fan of convenience store or prepared food, but then our kitchen is never immaculate, so that's the trade-off.

Tokanya, *manju* stealing at Jugoya during the full moon, and even *mochi* making at New Year have all virtually died out in Japan. Our family never gave up on pounding *mochi* in the garden at New Year, but it wasn't until recently that Tadaaki revived Tokanya and Jugoya in our house. Having home businesses, trying to grow food for the family, and bringing up three small home-schooled sons stretched both Tadaaki and me to the thinnest point where sometimes I wondered when we would break. Yet somehow when I did not have energy, Tadaaki did, and vice versa, and so we survived those years. Unfortunately mushroom hunting and wild berry gathering in the mountains did not, though we did manage to keep river trips and fishing expeditions alive in the summer. I guess it was the cool water in the impossibly sweltering summers that pushed me to get on board those excursions. In contrast, climbing up the mountain with small babies did not seem as enticing (or practical).

All of this takes energy. And as I look around me, I realize that most (though not all) of our friends who are trying to live off the land or revive dying country customs are all transplants from the city (me included). I suppose we do not have the weight of generations past pulling us down, and I suppose we bring some naïve energy to the equation. But then I look at Tadaaki and our friend Suka-san carrying on the farming life, college degrees in hand—a new generation of farmers who choose the land because the land chose them. They both live and breathe farming in a way that we transplants will never be able

to, yet we transplants also bring a fresh wind to the area, and so our partnerships have a spirit of dynamism backed by mutual support and respect.

As I stood there on the street that night of Tokanya, I thought about how the old customs clash with the new. About the cars zooming down our neighborhood street no longer lined with old farmhouses—now razed for large prefab versions the younger couples favor. And about Tadaaki leading the kids and friends as they banged their "straw guns" on the pavement—as if they owned the street and the cars were the intruders. And I thought about the *shishimai* lion dancers who had come to celebrate the sending off of the rice harvest god and that we can do this because we do it together. We fight the fight to keep traditions alive because they are the heart of Japan and without them there is no life.

Traditionally this was a vegetarian soup made with root vegetables, tofu, *konnyaku*, and perhaps dried shiitake for depth of flavor. But we often make a broth from our Christmas duck carcasses for the *kenchinjiru* we serve at New Year because we have them. I add some sliced ginger and a few generous stalks of Japanese *negi* (substitute thick spring onions or thin leeks) to the duck bones and simmer the soup for a couple of hours or more. For a vegetarian broth, I would drop a generous piece or two of konbu into a large pot of cold water and bring it to a boil, then proceed to make the root vegetable soup.

country soup with vegetables SERVES 8
KENCHINJIRU

2 large carrots

2 burdock roots (*gobo*)

1 small daikon

4 taro roots (*sato imo*)

2 (10.5-ounce/300-g) blocks best-quality soft tofu (use *momendofu* in Japan)

4 pieces thin fried tofu (*usuage*), cut in half lengthwise, then crosswise into ¼-inch (6-mm) strips

4 tablespoons best-quality rapeseed oil

8 cups (2 liters) duck, chicken, or konbu broth, hot

1 (1-pound/500-g) block *konnyaku* (optional), see Note page 88

¾ cup (180 cc) organic soy sauce

7-spice powder (*shichimi togarashi*, page 7)

Scrub equal amounts of carrots, *gobo*, and daikon with a rough brush (*tawashi*). Slice into thin rounds, half-rounds, or quarters depending on the thickness of the roots. With the *gobo* you probably want to make diagonal cuts since they tend to be long and thin. The vegetables should be fairly uniform in thickness and size, as you will be cooking them together and most likely eating the soup with chopsticks. Peel and slice the same amount of taro root (*sato imo*) as you did for each of the other vegetables. Keep the daikon and taro each in separate bowls. Split the tofu in half horizontally, then into 4 pieces lengthwise and 6 pieces crosswise (creating 48 small cubes). If the *usuage* is not fresh, pour boiling water over it to remove oil and any odors—or maybe just skip it.

Film a small amount of oil in a large soup pot and sauté the sliced carrots and *gobo* for a few minutes before adding the sliced daikon. Stir and sauté a minute or so longer, then add the hot broth. Throw in the sliced taro, bring to a boil over high heat, and cook until the vegetables are getting soft but not falling apart (about 20 minutes or so).

Slide in the tofu, *usuage*, and *konnyaku*, if using (see Note), and simmer a few minutes more until heated through. Season with organic soy sauce to taste and serve with a bowl of white rice on the side. Pass the *shichimi togarashi* for those who like a little extra kick.

continued on next page

country soup with vegetables

NOTE: Fill a large pot halfway with water, toss in a small handful of salt, and bring to a boil. While the water is heating, tear the *konnyaku* into 1½-inch (4-cm) misshapen blobs (a little bigger than bite-sized). If using *mochi*, slice the *konnakyu* instead into thin (1½ by ¼-inch/4-cm by 6-mm) strips. Boil the *konnyaku* pieces over medium-high heat for 15 minutes, drain, and reserve.

MOCHI: Drop pieces of hot *mochi* into the soup and eat immediately.

During my first winter in Japan, my friends took me to a tiny little one-counter late-night eatery where we were served *yudofu*. I had previously only eaten cold tofu (almost daily), but was seduced by the warmth of the tofu and the simplicity of the garnishes in this dish. We don't make *yudofu* as often as other *nabe* (one-pot dishes), though I wish we did. I crave lighter flavors, but with a house full of teenaged boys and a farmer husband all looking for a little more "meat on the bones" in their dinner, I have to give in to their desires. Tofu is one of those heavenly foods that is best in Japan, but easily made at home—you just need a bit of patience and a tofu-making kit (see Resources) doesn't hurt. For $50 you can buy two—enough to make two large bricks of tofu (about the size of four pieces of the tofu sold in Japan).

You will need a portable tabletop gas burner to make this dish at the table.

simmered tofu with garnishes SERVES 4
YUDOFU

2 (10.5-ounce/300-g) pieces of Japanese-style "cotton" tofu, cut into 1-inch (2.5-cm) cubes

1 (1-inch/2.5-cm) knob of ginger, peeled and grated

2 or 3 thin scallions (with whites), cut into fine rounds

1 sheet of nori, crumbled or cut into fine slivers (about 1½-inch/4-cm) lengths

2 or 3 (6-inch/15-cm) pieces of konbu

Katsuobushi-Infused Soy Sauce (*Tosajoyu*, page 308)

Cooked Japanese rice, for serving

Divide the tofu cubes between a couple of small plates. Put the grated ginger, sliced scallions, and nori separately into three small bowls. Fill a flameproof casserole (*donabe*, page 15) one-third full with cold water, drop in the konbu, and bring to the table with the tofu and garnishes.

Slide some of the tofu pieces into the *donabe*. Bring to a gentle simmer on the tabletop burner set at medium heat. While the water is heating, heat the *tosajoyu* in a small pan on the stove over low heat.

Pour a little *tosajoyu* in a small bowl set in front of each person, and when the tofu has heated through, scoop some tofu into the bowl with the *tosajoyu*. Garnish to taste with ginger, scallions, and nori and eat. (Once all the tofu has been served, cook more.) Serve with a small bowl of Japanese rice on the side.

Monkfish (*anko*) is an exceptionally ugly fish, but it is also exceptionally delicious. The flesh is firm and flavorful and contains natural gelatins, so it holds up well in a *nabe*. If you are lucky enough to get a very fresh whole fish, check the liver (*ankimo*), and if it smells sweet, cook it separately. Remove any veins from the *ankimo*, lay it on a piece of foil, salt it, splash it with sake, wrap tightly, and let sit in the fridge for 1 hour. Remove from the fridge, rinse, and pat dry with a muslin towel. Wrap in heavy-duty plastic wrap and roll into an even cylinder. Twist the ends to close. Enclose the cylinder in aluminum foil and steam for 30 minutes. Chill before eating dipped in ponzu with squeezed grated daikon and red pepper. (This is known as *momiji oroshi*. Make 3 vertical holes in the top of the daikon and poke in 3 small dried chiles, then grate.) If the liver is small, simmer as is in the *nabe*.

You will need a portable tabletop gas burner to make this dish at the table.

monkfish nabe with mizuna SERVES 6
ANKO NABE

1 large bunch mizuna

12 to 18 enoki mushrooms, bottom ends sliced off

2 thick *negi* (Japanese leeks) or thin leeks, dirty (or sandy) bottoms removed

1 (10.5-ounce/300-g) block Japanese-style "cotton" tofu, cut into 8 pieces

2 or 3 (6-inch/15-cm) pieces of konbu

1½ pounds (750 g) monkfish, "bones" included

Country-Style Ponzu (page 309)

Cooked Japanese rice, for serving

Slice the root ends off the mizuna and cut the leaves crosswise into 2-inch (5-cm) bunches. Stack on a platter or in a basket with the enoki. Cut the *negi* or leeks into 2-inch (5-cm) lengths and heap with the mizuna and enoki. Put the tofu on a small plate. Fill a flameproof casserole or clay pot (*donabe*, page 15) one-third full with cold water, drop in the konbu, and bring to a boil over high heat.

While the water is heating, chop the monkfish (cutting the meat through the bones) into 1¾- to 2-inch (4- to 5-cm) rough pieces. Put the fish pieces into a medium-sized serving bowl and bring to the table with the vegetables and tofu.

Bring the casserole with hot konbu water to the table and set onto the gas burner. Ignite the burner and bring back to a boil, then reduce the heat to a brisk simmer. Drop some monkfish pieces into the casserole along with some tofu, *negi*, and enoki. Once the fish and vegetables are almost cooked, clear an area in the casserole by pushing aside the cooking vegetables and poke a handful of mizuna into the broth so it is completely submerged. The mizuna will cook quite quickly (since it is a salad green). Ladle out some of the *nabe* into each person's bowl, making sure that each ingredient made it into the bowl. Splash in a little ponzu to taste.

There will be a fair amount of bones, so prepare a bone bowl for the table. Make sure to finish all the fish and vegetables in the *nabe* before adding more. Serve with a small bowl of Japanese rice.

VARIATIONS: You can substitute any fish with firm flesh, any mild mushrooms, or any spicy greens. Adjust the cooking time according to the thickness of the ingredients. Instead of eating with a bowl of rice, some people (particularly ones drinking sake) like to add cooked rice to the pot of rich vegetable-infused fish broth (strained) at the end and eat as a savory porridge (Rice Simmered in Broth, page 163) to finish the meal.

SHISHIMAI

Our friend Harigaya-san lives up in the mountains near here with a group of young (and not so young) men and women who farm, hunt, and make musical instruments together. Harigaya-san is an ex-IT guy who chucked a life making money in Tokyo in favor of a life making computer music and furniture at the top of a winding road deep in the forest. He rebuilt an old Japanese mountain home, leaving the original open hearth (*irori*) cooking area and traditional wood-fired kitchen. That is where the whole crew now lives.

Harigaya-san and his eclectic bunch also play music and practice a type of "lion dance" (*shishimai*) together. They often come to our farm events or parties and perform their wild version of *shishimai*. Donning blue-and-white cotton *yukata* or a long green costume with white arabesque swirls and *shishimai* masks, they dance to invoke the gods and increase rice fertility on rice planting day. As Harigaya-san's flute music lilts over the rice fields, the workers feel a freshening wind and increase their pace, gaining energy from the quick

bursts of air Harigaya-san sends into his slender piece of bamboo.

I love that Harigaya-san's mountain group comes to our summer parties and dances their *shishimai* dance to express appreciation for the food. This primordial dance is far removed from the formalized version my kids learned and performed at the local shrine. This dance comes from the heart of the mountains and from the hearts of the dancers.

They set up their "stage" in the back portion of the yard under the chestnut tree, and we gather around as the drummers begin beating a deep, reverberating cadence. Harigaya-san joins in with sweet, haunting flute notes. The *shishimai* dancers duck behind trees and coyly feint, a grappling sort of "fight," sometimes lunging into the crowd, the masks biting at the heads of the watchers. The more intrepid kids hold their ground, while some hide behind their mothers. We don't censor here—Japanese love the phantasmagoric spirits that abound in old stories

and customs. With some reassuring words, the kids accept that they know the guy under the outlandish wooden mask and billowing green cloth garb. "It's just Adam," I say, for one of the dancers is an ex-teacher who is now practicing traditional Japanese carpentry and lives in the nearby foothills with his wife and baby.

As the dance ends and the musicians and dancers make their way back to the patio, guests once again, they leave the drums and cymbals for the kids to try. Four-year-old Minami jumps behind the biggest drum and throws herself into beating with joyous abandon. Kyo and Eric join on the smaller drums. Knowing the kids, my instinct is to worry about the drums, but I love the trust the musicians have and let it go. And it is a beautiful thing to see kids letting themselves get carried away by the beat.

Dusk approaches, and guests start to drift away, though some stay to help pack up the food and wash the plates. And while we finish our last glass of wine, two of the drummers perform a special fire dance as thanks to Tadaaki and me. With the insistent pound of the drums punctuating his moves, the first dancer, bare chest glistening in the firelight, swings two chains attached with round balls of fire in the darkness. He spins his chains round and round, painting circles of fire. I am mesmerized by the fire and wish for my camera but do not want to break the mood. The next dancer emerges from behind a tree and joins the first, who smoothly yields the "floor." This second dancer twirls his long pole with two burning cloth ends, sometimes tossing and catching the pole in the air. And the drum beats on. Powerful and elemental. Under the trees. In the dark. A moment in time never to be repeated and impossible to capture on film or paper.

When we were first married, Tadaaki loved to make fish *nabe* because they were easy and we always had lots of vegetables. After a while, I told him enough with the *nabe*, and we stopped eating them for a couple of years. Typically Shabu-Shabu (page 97) is prepared with beef, but one day Tadaaki had the inspiration to make fish shabu-shabu, perhaps because he knew I wasn't fond of oversimmered foods and we don't eat much beef. A brilliant idea, it became a favorite dish of the whole family. But this time around, we were careful not to overuse it, despite the fact that it was exquisite, a snap to throw together (especially if you use precut sashimi fish instead of curing kelp-wicked fish), and convivial to boot.

You will need a portable tabletop gas burner to make this dish at the table.

kelp-wicked red snapper shabu-shabu SERVES 8
MADAI KOBUJIME NO SHABU-SHABU

Kelp-Wicked Red Snapper (page 227)

16 shiitake mushrooms, woody stem bottoms removed

2 bunches bitter greens, such as mustard or turnip, cut into 2-inch (5-cm) lengths

2 (10.5-ounce/300-g) blocks Japanese-style "cotton" tofu, cut into 8 pieces

2 or 3 (6-inch/15-cm) pieces of konbu

Country-Style Ponzu (page 309)

Cooked Japanese rice, for serving

Remove the konbu from the prepared kelp-wicked fish and line two small plates with it. Slice the fish into ¼-inch (6-mm) thick pieces at a diagonal. Lay each sliced filet on top of the konbu-lined plates.

Arrange the vegetables attractively on a platter or basket. Put the tofu on two small plates. Fill a clay pot *(donabe)* or flameproof casserole one-third full with water and add the dried pieces of konbu (not the ones that were used to wick the fish). Take all the ingredients to the table and place the clay pot on the gas burner.

Start up the tabletop burner and bring the water to a boil. Add some of each kind of vegetable and several pieces of tofu. Once the vegetables are just cooked (the greens should still remain brightly colored), lower the flame. Ladle out some broth with a little of each kind of vegetable and a piece of tofu into a small bowl set in front of each guest. Flavor with a splash of ponzu to taste. Guests should grasp a piece of kelp-wicked snapper with their own chopsticks and swish in the simmering broth for a second or until no longer raw but still translucent in the center. (This swishing action sounds like *shabu-shabu,* hence the name.) Dip in the ponzu-flavored broth and eat the vegetables and tofu between bites of fish.

continued on next page

kelp-wicked red snapper shabu-shabu

Do not replenish the vegetables or tofu until guests eat all of the first batch (otherwise you'll end up with an unsightly mixture of gray vegetables and green). Serve with a small bowl of Japanese rice.

VARIATIONS: Any kind of pleasantly flavored white fish will work for this delicate *nabe*. Mizuna or even *mitsuba* would be excellent alternatives to the bitter greens, but they will cook much more quickly. In this case, begin by cooking just the shiitake and tofu, then add these tender greens several minutes later. Feel free to use another kind of Japanese-style or local mushroom in place of the shiitake.

Shabu-Shabu was the favorite dish eaten at the obligatory end-of-the-year parties (*bonenkai*) that I attended when first in Japan. One-pot cooking (*nabemono*) is ridiculously easy, so you have to wonder why these parties took place at restaurants. I didn't really think about it at the time because everything was new and I was just lapping up all there was to see, taste, and learn. The first time I had shabu-shabu was six months into my stay in Japan. I still wasn't accustomed to the fat surrounding the thinly sliced meat, so I picked off what I could. But that was a bit silly (and in retrospect, embarrassing), since the fat quantity was minimal and some is necessary for giving richness to this very simple but elegant preparation.

You will need a portable tabletop gas burner to make this dish at the table.

shabu-shabu SERVES 6

16 shiitake mushrooms, woody stem bottoms removed

¼ head napa cabbage, cut crosswise into 2-inch (5-cm) lengths

4 thin *negi* (Japanese leeks) or spring onions, cut into 2-inch (5-cm) lengths

1½ pounds (700 g) marbled sirloin, sliced sliced crosswise into ³⁄₃₂-inch (2.5-mm) thin sheets by a butcher (see Note)

2 (10.5-ounce/300-g) blocks Japanese-style "cotton" tofu, cut into 8 pieces each

2 or 3 (6-inch/15-cm) pieces of konbu

Country-Style Ponzu (page 309)

Cooked Japanese rice, for serving

Arrange the vegetables attractively on a platter or basket. Lay the meat slices on another platter or have the butcher slice them directly onto your own platter in his shop. Put the tofu on two small plates. Fill a clay cookpot (*donabe*) or flameproof casserole one-third full with water and add the konbu. Take all the ingredients to the table and place the clay pot on the gas burner.

Bring the water to a boil over high heat on the tabletop burner. Reduce the flame to a lively simmer, and add some of each kind of vegetable and several pieces of tofu. Once the vegetables are just cooked (the cabbage should be soft but not starting to discolor), lower the flame to a gentle simmer. Ladle out some of the broth with a little of each kind of vegetable and a piece of tofu into a small bowl set in front of each person. Flavor the broth in the bowls with a small splash of ponzu to taste.

Each person picks up a piece of sirloin with his or her own chopsticks and swishes it in the simmering broth for a couple seconds or until no longer raw but still slightly pink. Dip in the ponzu-flavored broth and eat with the vegetables and tofu. Do not replenish the vegetables or tofu until guests eat all of the first batch. Serve with a small bowl of Japanese rice.

VARIATIONS: I am particularly fond of peppery mizuna greens and bright *mitsuba* leaves—either would go well with the delicate meat. *Shimeji* mushrooms (or chanterelles!) would also be an excellent substitute for the more meaty shiitake.

NOTE: If you are able, prepare a platter for the butcher to lay the meat slices in an overlapping pattern. This will make serving much easier (and prettier).

大豆と卵子

4

soybeans and eggs

Next to rice, soybeans are the most important crop in Japan. Bring up the subject of foreign imports to a Japanese farmer, and you'll get an earful. Japanese soybeans are produced on a small scale and have a delicate soy aroma. Up to about thirty years ago, the typical Japanese farm family ate little meat or fish, so soy was a vital source of protein in their daily diet. Every family grew their own soybeans and made their own miso—some even made soy sauce or natto. Tofu making was usually left up to a local *tofuya* (tofu shop). In our area we are fortunate to have two top-quality tofu-making operations: Yamaki and Sannosuke. There is no reason for me to make tofu, but I did for this book, and was astounded at how well it turned out and how truly easy the process was. And although I have no real reason to make miso, my mother-in-law always did, so I will try my hand as well in order to pass that tradition on to my sons. The idea of growing or fermenting things such as miso, natto, or soy sauce is compelling at a very basic level. The more we can do, the more tightly woven becomes this version of farm life we are fashioning.

Not wanting to be a suburban slacker when we were first married, I jumped headfirst into cooking three meals a day for my constantly hungry farmer husband. But at the time our house construction was still in progress (we moved in despite the disarray), and I was also preparing morning and after-noon tea for the workers at 10 and 3. Not one to go just partway, I avoided the packaged snacks my mother-in-law had set out every day and made the workers homemade cookies, cakes, and little sandwiches to go with their daily green tea and tangerines. I quickly realized I couldn't handle making five meals a day, so Tadaaki was on his own for breakfast. Before I figured out it made more sense to make extra for dinner and eat the left-overs for lunch the next day, we often ate our farm eggs with pickles and rice at lunchtime because I was so enthralled with their exceptional flavor. And to this day, I prefer eggs at lunch rather than breakfast.

JAPANESE TOFU

Japanese tofu is like silky custard, with a back taste of fragrantly musky soy. To truly taste the nuance of tofu, you should try it without salt or soy sauce, but if you're just into eating it, go for the works. I like tofu with some freshly grated ginger, chopped scallions, shaved *katsuobushi*, and organic soy sauce.

When I first came to Japan in 1988, apartment deposits and nonrefundable key money had depleted my reserves. After buying rice, my dinner budget stretched just enough to buy one piece of tofu every day from the local shop, a few vegetables, and one can of beer. I ate rice crackers (*senbei*) with tea for lunch at the English school where I worked, one reason I don't like rice crackers anymore. Not unlike now, dinner was the high point of my day. The bus dropped me off near my house at around 9:30 p.m., so my dinnertime was close to 10. Once again keeping restaurant hours (as I had in my feckless twenties), I'd watch late-night cooking shows in Japanese while I ate my dinner. I didn't know what they were saying, but I got ideas from their methods. And that was my entrée into Japanese cooking.

The tofu shop down the street quickly became my special stop. The family was unusually friendly and interested in the foreign girl. We muddled along in a mixture of Japanese and English, but in the end they developed into my closest friends in Japan and stood in for my family at my Japanese wedding. Fate is a funny thing. The tofu shop family's last name was identical to my husband's: 八須—the same *kanji* characters and the same reading: Hachisu. The surname is uncommon and the characters even

more so, just another little piece of that red string that connected me together with two different 八須 families.

A couple of months after Tadaaki and I became engaged, my older sister Pam came for a visit—a response to my pleas to come vet the situation. Tadaaki and I were building a house together and a feeling of "there is no going back" had settled on me, causing me to experience a certain measure of panic. My mother had died a few months before I came to Japan, and I had uprooted myself to a totally foreign culture—not a good time to make life-changing decisions like marriage.

While Pam was visiting, we had any number of dinners out with friends. She still remembers the sea snails with visceral disgust, but not so the tofu. Perched on floor cushions in the cluttered tatami room adjoining the Hachisu family's tofu-making operation, we were served freshly made tofu and a few deep-fried tofu pieces (*atsuage*). Topped with chopped green onion, grated ginger, and bonito flakes, even Pam could not resist being seduced by the tofu.

After our marriage, I moved to my husband's hometown, Kamikawa ("God River") and in Kami-izumi ("God Spring"), the mountain town nearby, I found local organic tofu that defied description. The Hachisu tofu, though made from U.S. soybeans, had nonetheless been made from the heart. Loyalty is a strong bond, but distance made the decision uncomplicated. Tofu is perishable and best eaten the same day it is made. So the Touan tofu produced at Yamaki became our local favorite. And now I bring that tofu with me as gifts for the cooks and staff at Chez Panisse—in thanks for all the local meals they make for us when we're away from the farm.

Often described as bland, American tofu is primarily a meat substitute for vegetarian cooking and is not typically celebrated on its own. However, that is changing as local artisanal tofu is becoming more available in the U.S. But there is no comparison to Japanese tofu, glorious in its subtle elegance, slippery cool as it slides down your throat. Well worth the plane ticket to Japan.

Or just make your own with organic soybeans and spring water. It's easy.

Years ago, Tadaaki made tofu, and at the time it seemed to make quite the mess. That image stuck with me, so I was hesitant to dive into a tofu-making project the summer I was writing this book. A visit from my pal, Rachael Hutchins (of La Fuji Mama blog), and an e-mail from good friend Sylvan Mishima Brackett of Peko-Peko Japanese Catering convinced me to bite the bullet. Tadaaki kindly ordered a couple of wooden tofu forms for me on the Internet (see Resources), and, when I opened them up, I was assailed by the aroma of cut cypress and was thus galvanized to set up my tofu-making operation immediately. Touching and smelling the forms (and admiring how beautifully designed they were) spurred me on to embark on a process I had previously thought daunting but that ended up being surprisingly painless. And the tofu was excellent. Tofu is only as good as the soybeans and water you use, so keep that in mind.

homemade tofu MAKES 2 BLOCKS
TEZUKURI TOFU

1⅔ cups (300 g) small, flavorful dried soybeans

5 teaspoons liquid *nigari* (dissolved in ¼ cup/50 cc hot water)

1 large SoyaJoy wooden tofu form (optional but recommended, see Resources)

Soak the soybeans in 3 times their amount of the best-quality water you can find (5 cups/1200 cc) for about 8 to 9 hours in summer, 15 hours in spring, or 20 hours in winter. Soak time relates to ambient temperature. (Warm days need a shorter soak than cold days.)

Scoop one-third of the soybeans and soaking water into a blender, process on high speed for 2 minutes, and pour into a large mixing bowl. Repeat until all the beans have been processed. Bring 5½ cups (1300 cc) best-quality water to a boil over high heat in a medium-large, thick, well-insulated pot (such as cast-iron enamel). Add the ground soybean mixture and bring almost to a boil, stirring constantly, to ensure the bottom does not scorch.

Remove from the heat source and let the foam subside naturally (if it doesn't after about 10 or 15 minutes, proceed to the next step). Heat again slowly over low heat for 8 to 10 minutes.

While the soybean mixture is heating, set a fine-mesh strainer over a medium- to large-sized mixing bowl. Line the strainer with clean muslin cheesecloth. After the 8 to 10 minutes have elapsed, pour the hot soybean mixture through the muslin-lined cheesecloth. Twist up the free ends to squeeze out the excess liquid and let cool a bit for easier handling.

Wait about 10 or 15 minutes, then squeeze the muslin bundle to get the last remnants of liquid out of the solids. In the bowl you will have fresh soy milk ready to use for making tofu and in the muslin cloth you will have sparkling white fresh *okara* (soybean pulp). Transfer the *okara* to a plastic container and continue with your tofu-making operation. (Once cool, use *okara* immediately, or up to 2 days after, if kept chilled in the fridge. Otherwise, freeze for later use.) Stir-Fried Okara and Vegetables (page 111)

is the most common use of *okara*, but it also acts as a softening agent that sucks up excess fat when presimmering pork belly (page 286).

Rinse your heavy pot and pour in the freshly made soy milk you have just produced. Warm over low heat until the mixture reaches 175°F (80°C)—this will take up to 1 hour (or more), so bide your time. The skin that forms on top of the soy milk is *yuba* (page 7) and can be harvested by catching it up, slipping a chopstick end held horizontally to the surface of the soy milk—a bit tricky. The delicate *yuba* skin is rolled together and eaten with a dash of soy sauce or salt and dab of fresh wasabi, if you have it.

While the soy milk is heating, take out a large bowl, a flat wooden spoon, and the *nigari*. Once the soy milk reaches the desired temperature, pour it into the bowl. Dip the flat wooden spoon into the center of the bowl, rest the spoon against the bottom of the bowl, and pour the *nigari* against the spoon. Slowly stir the soy milk, making 2 wide revolutions ONLY, and pull the wooden spoon straight up out of the coagulating soy milk (so not to disturb the soft curds already forming).

Drape the tofu form with the muslin cloth included with the kit and set the form in a shallow pan. After 15 minutes, gently ladle in the coagulated soy milk, taking care not to disturb the curds. Fold the muslin cloth over the tofu on all sides to enclose, set the wooden top on the curds, and place a weight of about 1 to 1¾ pounds (500 to 800 g) on each and press down gently but firmly. Let the tofu sit for 30 minutes, then remove the weight, gently lift the muslin-wrapped tofu out of its form, and slip (unwrapped) into best-quality cold water for 30 minutes.

Unwrap the tofu from the muslin while still submerged in the water and carefully dislodge the tofu with a scraper and slide the cloth out. Dip your knife directly into the water and cut the tofu in half to form 2 blocks of about 10.5 ounces (300 g) each. Store the tofu in the fridge submerged in water in a plastic container. It will keep for several days.

VARIATION: Another form, such as a round sieve, can be used with some degree of success, though it will not be quite as aesthetically pleasing. In this case you would use a large-sized sieve lined with muslin in place of the rectangular form. Most people might be tempted to go this route, but the satisfaction will not be as great as when using a real tofu form. And consequently, you may just give up on making homemade tofu. As in many Japanese things, making blocks of homemade tofu does not require much hands-on time, just patience while it soaks, slowly heats, and drains.

One summer a few years ago, we decided to make lunches for the SSU! kids during the summer camps instead of having them bring their own from home. Summer is extremely busy for me because of the rampant weeds in the field demanding my attention and because I try to be a teacher for the camps (though I have since decided to leave that to younger, more energetic staff members or my son Christopher). The first time doing anything takes a bit of mind adjusting, and I had to scramble to think up some easy cold meals my assistant could put together during the camps. The farm stand down the street sells Yamaki tofu, *usuage* (thin deep-fried tofu sheets), and natto, and so my tofu lunch was born. I call it tofu composé in the spirit of salade composée (composed salad). This is a wildly popular lunch at my school, though perhaps not strictly orthodox Japanese.

tofu composé SERVES 4
TOFU COMPOZE

A seasonal Japanese salad of your choice with Miso Vinaigrette (page 301)

2 blocks best-quality tofu (each about 10.5 ounces/300 g)

1 (3-ounce/80-g) package natto (optional)

4 Half-Boiled Eggs, halved (page 45)

Sea salt

Japanese Mayonnaise (page 312, optional)

Grilled Tofu Pouches with Ginger and Scallions (page 46, optional)

About ⅓-inch (1-cm) knob ginger, peeled and grated

1 thin scallion (including whites), finely chopped

⅛ cup (30 cc) large *katsuobushi* flakes (*hanakatsuo*, page 6)

Organic soy sauce

Make the Japanese salad of your choice. I like to use julienned celery or carrots, or just plain lettuce—usually dressed with miso vinaigrette. (Since you are already using soy sauce on the tofu I would avoid a soy sauce dressing, but it's not out of the question.)

Remove the tofu from their tubs, slice each one in half, then each half into quarters, and set a quartered half-block of tofu in the middle of each of four dinner plates. The tofu is positioned in the center in order to keep the soy sauce pooled up and leave space for the other components of the plate that should be placed around the perimeter.

If using, dump the natto into a medium-sized soup bowl and whip with chopsticks to create a creamy mass of beans encased in sticky threads. Add the enclosed flavor packets (most likely dashi with soy sauce and a little mustard) and mix well to incorporate. Do your best to scrape a quarter of the natto on each plate.

Set 2 egg halves on each plate. Pinch a little sea salt over the eggs and add a dollop of homemade mayonnaise between the halves, if you are using it.

If you have located some good-tasting *usuage* (tofu pouches), by all means use (and garnish at the same time as the tofu). Dab some grated ginger on the tofu pieces; sprinkle with chopped scallions, *katsuobushi* flakes, and drizzle with soy sauce. Strew a little chopped scallions over the eggs and natto for color and flavor pop.

Serve the prepared salad on the plate in the (hopefully) remaining free spot.

NATTO

With its pungently funky aroma and slimy threads that you can never seem to wash off, natto may not appeal at first glance (or first whiff). I first became aware of natto at the Palo Alto sushi bar (Sushiya) I frequented in California. Toshio Sakuma (now of Kaygetsu) was the chef, and his owner-partner ran an English school in the Japanese countryside near Kumagaya city. It was through Toshi-san that I learned of the teaching job I eventually took, thus irrevocably changing the course of my life.

Toshi-san served oozing conical rolls of natto to only the most intrepid customers (not me). It almost seemed a gross-out contest, or a way to prove who had the most hair on his chest. And yes, most of the natto-eating customers were male. To be fair, I never did sample the natto roll at Sushiya, so could not attest to its taste. For the most part, I was put off by the drama and the overflowing too muchness of it all. I really can't say for sure when I had natto for the first time in Japan—obviously not an earth-shattering milestone. But I liked it.

These days, even in Japan, natto will most likely be sold in small foam packs along with a teeny plastic package of hot mustard or wasabi and another of dashi-infused soy sauce. Organic natto is available in Japan, but is not particularly common. In the U.S. most natto is sold frozen, though Japan Traditional Foods, a small company in Sebastopol, California, is making local, organic natto; their products can be bought via the Internet (see Resources).

Natto packed in straw can still be found in some regional areas of Japan. However, the natto we buy is made by our local tofu maker, Yamaki

Jozo, and is packed in paper-thin pine wrapping (*kyogi*). When you first unfold the *kyogi*-encased natto, the fermented beans seem fairly inert, almost dormant (which I suppose is an accurate assessment). But once you plop the small flat mass of beans into a bowl and begin to whip it with chopsticks into a creamy frenzy of sticky threads, the natto comes alive—though actually since natto is fermented soybeans (inoculated with a "good" bacteria, *Bacillus natto*), technically it is always alive and will continue to ferment slowly, even in the fridge. Like most fermented foods, natto has a long shelf life (probably well beyond the date stamp). But like most fermented foods, the taste will become more pungent over time; if any sourness develops, toss it.

I'm always surprised when food people don't connect with natto's wild funk but absolutely fascinating flavor profile. One year I brought a selection of organic natto along with the Yamaki tofu to the Chez Panisse cooks. A bunch of us collaborated on an eclectic East-meets-West kind of Japanese dinner at my friend Sharon Jones's house in North Berkeley. Her son Nico simmered up *buri daikon* with his home-cured pancetta in place of the yellowtail and Sylvan Mishima Bracket from Eat Peko Peko was directing us all. Christopher and I made *kyuri momi* (Salt-Massaged Cucumber with Miso and Sesame, page 175). We also contributed the deep-fried tofu (*usuage, atsuage,* and *ganmodoki*) hand-carried from Japan, which was grilled over the fire outside. And I whipped up some natto for everyone to taste. The cooks wandered by and scooped the natto onto a small square of nori before rolling up and popping into their mouths. No one really loved it—maybe natto is best experienced first in Japan—another reason to come.

To understand *ganmodoki* (especially if you have never eaten one or even seen one), imagine tofu that has been squeezed to express excess water. Into that tofu you have perhaps added some finely chopped or very finely julienned pieces of mild but aromatic vegetables, maybe some chopped mushroom or softened konbu left over from making dashi . . . and a bit of salt. To bind this mixture, you can add some "mountain yam" (*yama imo*) ground into a viscous mass on a metal or ceramic-toothed grater (*oroshigane* or *oroshiki*, page 14). But to keep this simple, you need to understand that you can forgo all of the extra ingredients and fashion *ganmodoki* from squeezed tofu. From there commence. Pound up some aromatics and mix into the tofu. Or add some ground roasted sesame seed. Experiment—but first get the squeezing, shaping, and frying technique down. Also, the *yama imo* does help bind, so if possible, try to track that down at a Japanese grocery store or Asian farmers' market.

tofu and vegetable "croquettes" MAKES 9
GANMODOKI

2 (10.5-ounce/300-g) pieces Japanese-style "cotton" tofu (page 7)

1 small (3 ounce/90 g) scrubbed carrot, finely chopped

2 tablespoons (⅝-inch/1½-cm long) slivered konbu left over from making dashi (or soaked in sake)

2 tablespoons finely chopped burdock root (*gobo*) or 2 tablespoons finely chopped *shimeji* mushrooms

2 tablespoons grated *yama imo* (page 364, optional)

½ teaspoon sea salt

Rapeseed oil for deep-frying

FOR SERVING

1⅔ cup (400 cc) Tempura Dipping Sauce (page 311)

Place the tofu on a cutting board propped up on one end, angled into the kitchen sink for draining. Lay another chopping board or plate on top of the tofu to press out excess water for 1 hour. Squeeze the tofu by small handfuls and drop into a medium-sized mixing bowl.

Add the chopped carrot, dashi- or sake-softened konbu, *gobo* or *shimeji*, grated *yama imo*, if using, and salt to the tofu and mix well by squeezing the mixture with your hands to amalgamate. Smooth into small (about 2¾-inch/7-cm-diameter) patties with cupped hands.

Line a cookie sheet with thick sheets of newspaper, cover with paper towels, and set next to the burner where you will be frying. Heat 2 inches (10 cm) of oil in a wide, deep saucepan over medium-high heat until hot but not smoking. When the oil is ready, gently slide 4 or 5 tofu patties, one by one, into the oil and deep-fry slowly until golden brown and buoyant. The oil bubbles will be quite lively at first but will subside (thus signaling that excess moisture has left the *ganmodoki*—about 6 minutes). Skim the cooked *ganmodoki* out of the bubbling oil and drain on the paper towel–lined newspapers.

These are absolutely delicious hot but also good the next day recrisped in a small amount of rapeseed oil, covered, over low heat. Serve the *ganmodoki* in a saucer with a small ladle of tempura dipping sauce (*ten tsuyu*) spooned over.

VARIATION: I also like *ganmodoki* drizzled with a little soy sauce, grated ginger, and finely chopped scallions.

I became close friends with the local tofu shop family soon after I arrived in Japan and visited the shop every day to buy tofu. The mother of the family, Mitsu-san, gave me cooking advice, all the while giggling shyly with her hand held up to her mouth. To this day, she remains one of the kindest and most giving persons I have ever met in Japan (or anywhere). Mitsu-san handed me a bag of *okara* one day and tried to explain how I should prepare it. I (sort of) understood. It was a big bag, so I ended up with enough *unohana* to last me a week. After this daunting experience, I didn't make it again until there were family members around to help me eat it. Some of the older Japanese farm women love to make a very sweet version of *unohana* and serve it to guests with green tea. I prefer my version because it is not too wet or too sweet, and the vegetable-to-*okara* ratio is higher than usual.

stir-fried okara and vegetables SERVES 4

UNOHANA

⅔ pound (300 g) soybean pulp (*okara*)

4 tablespoons rapeseed oil

1 small to medium carrot (4½ ounces/120 g), scrubbed and julienned

¼ small burdock root (*gobo*) (3½ ounces/90 g), scrubbed and julienned

½ *negi* (Japanese leeks) or 2 thick scallions (white part with a little green), julienned

3 tablespoons *Tosajoyu* (page 308) or soy sauce

1 tablespoon sake

Sea salt, optional

Parch the *okara* in a dry wok or large frying pan over low heat, stirring with a flat wooden spoon, until dry and fluffy (about 3 minutes).

Wipe the pan clean and heat the oil in it over medium heat. Throw in the julienned carrot and *gobo*. Stir continuously with a flat wooden spoon for a few minutes until the vegetables are just starting to get soft. At this point, add the julienned *negi* or scallions and continue stir-frying for a couple of minutes more to wilt the *negi*.

Add the soy sauce and sake, and stir-fry over low heat for a couple of minutes more to let the vegetables soak up some of the soy sauce flavor. Dump in the parched *okara* and toss to blend. Turn the stir-fried *okara* and vegetables into a medium-sized bowl and serve with a sprinkling of salt, if needed. It can also be refrigerated overnight and eaten as a chilled side dish or as an interesting addition to a *bento* lunch.

VARIATION: If you prefer a wetter style of *unohana*, you could add a cup or so (300 cc) of dashi (page 307) to the stir-fried *okara* and vegetables at the end and simmer over low heat, stirring occasionally, for an additional 15 minutes.

In the West, it's a given that eggs and bread go well together, but I'd have to say that rice goes even better. When I first came to Japan, I tried not to eat any Western food and owned only chopsticks. I drank green tea with my breakfast instead of coffee and ate rice with eggs. I had not eaten much rice growing up, so was struck by how well the eggs went with the rice. After a bowl of rice with an egg (cooked or not), my body felt clean inside. The hot rice cooks the egg just a smidge, but essentially it is raw, so do not attempt this method unless you are able to buy your eggs directly from a local farmer. Knowing your egg source and how the chickens live assures you that the eggs can be safely eaten uncooked without qualms.

raw egg on hot rice SERVES 4
TAMAGO-KAKE GOHAN

2 cups (500 g) cooked Japanese rice (hot!)

4 very fresh large farm eggs, at room temperature

Organic soy sauce

For each serving, scoop about ½ cup (125 cc) or more rice into a small bowl. Break the egg over the steaming grains and splash in a little organic soy sauce. Mix with chopsticks. Eat every grain of rice. Lick the bowl if you like.

VARIATION: If you don't find the idea of eating raw eggs appealing, you can make a couple of Japanese-style fried eggs to eat on top of the rice. Heat a teaspoon or two of rapeseed or sesame oil in a small frying pan over high heat with 1 small dried chile torn into 3 pieces. Break 2 farm-fresh eggs into the hot oil, reduce the heat to low, cover, and cook until the white is set but the yolks are still runny. Loosen the eggs from the pan with a spatula and set on top of a small bowl of rice. Drizzle with soy sauce and eat for breakfast (or lunch).

FARM EGGS

The first time I had a real egg was in Hanover, New Hampshire. I had come out for the summer to help my mother through chemotherapy by doing what I know best: searching out the most vibrant local organic ingredients and cooking food to heal body and soul.

My mother, a professor of medieval English at Dartmouth, was a strongly independent woman who didn't care much for following proscribed social conventions (sometimes bumping heads in the conservative, right-wing community where I grew up). And even in New Hampshire, she stood out as an original.

"Here racky-racky-racky," she would call, shaking a food bowl standing out on the front porch of her little house in the woods. She was calling the raccoons. Who feeds the raccoons? Aren't they pests? But she thought they were cute, and Isabelle the cat (about the same size and just as furry as the raccoons) liked to stare at those masked creatures through the dining room glass doors.

I spent that summer antiquing with my mother in Vermont and New Hampshire, and, under tents set out in fields, we'd bid on the only ratty pieces we could afford. It was fun but in a way depressing to see how little remained from our short American history. Fighting a 3-percent chance to survive single-cell lung cancer can make you bold in ways you never knew. And under those auction tents no smoker was safe from my wispy-haired mother tapping him on the shoulder to tell him that she had lung cancer and to please put out the cigarette. I was embarrassed but proud.

After that initial taste of "real" egg from the Hanover Co-op, I suspected even better was out there. Every Saturday I visited the Norwich Farmers' Market several minutes due west of

Hanover on Route 5 South to stock up on the glorious vegetables heaped on tables set out in a loose circle around the Vermont-green meadow. I scooped up home-baked whole grain breads and fished through freezers of local winter lamb to select hunks for stews and soups.

And I bought eggs, for eggs were what my mother craved every morning.

To this day, eggs are also my soul food—you know, food that leaves you feeling deeply warm and comforted. I suppose that is what most people call comfort food. And when I'm away from the farm, I miss Tadaaki's eggs with their orangey yolks that pop up pertly from the viscous (never watery) whites. And I miss the familiar taste of home that I get from our eggs, for eggs take their nuanced flavors from what the chickens eat. Tadaaki feeds his chickens a combination of corn, seaweed, crab shells, and greens, and the resulting eggs are mild but with their own subtly original flavor profile: uniquely ours, uniquely Tadaaki's.

The Japanese name for this omelette translates as "rolled egg with dashi," but we don't use dashi. Our eggs are so good alone, they don't need much more than a touch of soy sauce and sugar to heighten their natural sweetness. Restaurants do not always have access to the freshest farm ingredients, so some dashi is used to help mellow the flavors of food. Farm households have boldly flavorful food at their fingertips, thus don't need to fiddle so much coaxing out the so-called umami, that ephemeral taste sought after these days in the cooking world.

A rectangular Japanese egg pan makes this recipe easier, but it isn't essential.

rolled egg "omelette" SERVES 4
DASHI-MAKI TAMAGO

6 medium-small eggs, at room temperature

1 tablespoon organic soy sauce

½ tablespoon organic granulated sugar

Rapeseed oil

Briskly whisk the eggs, soy sauce, and sugar in a small bowl with chopsticks.

Heat a rectangular Japanese egg pan over medium-high heat. Pour a little oil on a folded-up paper towel so it seeps into the middle of the folds but is not saturated. Wipe the pan with oil. Give the eggs a quick mix to freshen and redistribute the sugar and soy sauce, then pour one-fourth of the mixture into the pan, tilting the pan to cover all the free surfaces of the bottom with egg. When the egg is set on the bottom but still runny on top, tip the pan toward you and gently roll the egg in the direction of the handle, using your chopsticks. This takes practice, so hang in there. You will get it.

The idea is to keep building up the egg roll with about three more additions of egg mixture. The first roll will provide the core around which the second semirunny egg layer will be rolled. This will in turn create a pleasing circular pattern in the cooked omelette.

Rub the pan with the paper towel swab, making sure to get the portion under the omelette roll still in the pan. Leaving the first rolled omelette in the pan, pour another one-fourth of the egg mixture (stirred once with your chopsticks before using) into the oiled pan and tip the pan to cover the whole bottom surface of the pan evenly. Be sure to lift up the cooked roll of egg to allow the raw egg mixture to run underneath it.

When the bottom is set but the top is still runny, roll the cooked egg away from you so that it gathers up the semicooked egg layer on its rolling path. Repeat these steps two more times with the remaining one-fourth portions of the egg mixture.

Dashi-maki tamago is often eaten with grated and squeezed daikon drizzled with soy sauce. We don't; our eggs are just too good on their own.

VARIATION: You can make a rough approximation of the above rolled omelette by using a large, well-seasoned frying pan. In this case, you should add the egg mixture all at once after wiping the pan generously with oil and cook over medium-high heat. Use a heatproof rubber spatula or flat wooden spoon to nudge the egg mixture into a mass in the center of the pan while rolling and tipping the pan to let the raw egg mixture run to the outside. When the egg is about three-quarters of the way cooked, roll the omelette to one corner, tip the pan toward the flame, and gently brown the surface. The key here is not to overcook the egg—the inside should be runny like a French omelette. It may not end up a traditional *dashi-maki tamago*, but we ate these slightly sweet soy sauce–flavored omelettes for lunch often when we were first married and didn't have anything planned. Some pickles and a bowl of rice complete the meal.

This very thin egg "pancake" is useful and almost needs no recipe. We use the thick ribbons in Country Sushi Rolls (page 146), whereas thin threads are pretty strewn on salads, hot rice, or even on top of sushi rice in a bento box along with pickled things that keep well at room temperature.

golden egg ribbons MAKES ONE PANCAKE
USUYAKI TAMAGO

1 large egg, at room temperature

Rapeseed or sesame oil

Whisk the eggs lightly with a fork or chopsticks but do not overbeat.

Heat an 8-inch (20-cm) large round well-seasoned (or nonstick) frying pan over high heat. Pour a little oil on a folded piece of paper towel and rub the entire surface of the pan, even going up the sides.

Pour the eggs into the pan, lift it off the heat, and roll/rotate the pan so the mixture covers the entire bottom surface. Try not to go up the sides, because you will end up with lacy edges. This action is similar to making a crêpe, but the egg "pancake" should be slightly thicker than a crêpe for ease of handling. Flip the egg onto a cutting board and cut into ¾-inch (4-cm) wide ribbons or cool, roll, and slice into very thin threads.

The thick ribbons can be used to stuff sushi rolls, and the thin threads to garnish salads or bento box meals.

We order *tamago dofu* every time we go to Soba Ro or Soba Ra, our favorite restaurants here in Japan. Kanchan, the chef-owner, uses Tadaaki's eggs, so that of course contributes doubly to our enjoyment of the dish. The name *tamago dofu* ("egg tofu") refers to its square tofu blocklike shape and delicate texture. We love this dish so much that we make it at home—especially in the winter during the holidays, when we can find some decent crab. It may not be Dungeness crab, but nonetheless works well with this savory egg custard preparation. I also recommend doubling the recipe and making two.

egg custard squares
with crab and spinach SERVES 4
KANI NO TAMAGO DOFU

4 large eggs, at room temperature

¾ cup (150 cc) Hot Noodle Broth, cooled (page 311)

½ cup (125 cc) very small enoki mushrooms

½ cup (125 cc) blanched, squeezed spinach leaves

½ cup (125 cc) fresh crabmeat

¾ cup (150 cc) Noodle Dipping Sauce (page 310)

Smoothly line an 8 by 4-inch (20 by 10-cm) loaf pan with aluminum foil. Fill a wide, deep saucepan or wok one-third full of water and bring to a simmer. Set a steamer basket on top of the simmering water.

Beat the eggs in a medium-sized bowl with chopsticks or a whisk until amalgamated but not frothy. Stir in the cooled hot noodle broth and pour through a fine-mesh strainer into a clean bowl. (Kanchan strains the mixture three times, but at home once is enough!)

Place the enoki mushrooms in a strainer and pour hot water over them to cook slightly, then squeeze out the excess water with your hands. Roughly chop the spinach leaves and strew in the bottom of the loaf pan. Sprinkle in the crab and enoki on top of the spinach.

Pour the egg mixture into the pan and place in the steamer. Steam over low heat, covered, for 30 minutes, or until set. Test by jiggling the pan a little or inserting a bamboo skewer into the center of the savory custard.

This can be eaten hot, but it is easier to serve cold (and we prefer it cool and slippery). Cool to room temperature, then chill at least half a day. Chill the noodle dipping sauce as well.

Cut into 8 squares and serve each person 2 squares on a small saucer with a spoonful or so of the cold noodle dipping sauce. Encourage people to pick up their saucers at the end and drink the "soup."

VARIATIONS: Substitute any mild mushroom for the enoki, any blanched squeezed greens for the spinach, or shredded chicken for the crab. Omit the crab for a vegetarian version.

I have always had a great fondness for *chawan mushi*, but for many years did not make it often since I felt constrained by the idea of the one ginkgo nut, the one little piece of chicken, and the *mitsuba* sprig. I often prefer vegetarian versions because the chicken doesn't always add much to the equation, and the ginkgo nut ... well, who really has ginkgo nuts hanging around. .... *Chawan mushi* should be served immediately, steaming hot, but it is also refreshingly tasty served chilled the next day if you omit the asparagus.

egg custard pots
with asparagus and peas SERVES 4
ASPARA TO GURIIN PISU NO CHAWAN MUSHI

1 teaspoon sea salt

1⅓ cups (300 cc) Dashi (page 307)

3 large or 4 small eggs,
    at room temperature

2 teaspoons sake

2 or 3 thin stalks asparagus

2 tablespoons freshly shelled
    green peas

Zest of 1 small yuzu or half a
    Meyer lemon, slivered (optional)

Sprinkle the salt over the dashi and warm slowly to dissolve the salt. Let cool or use warm, but it should not be hot. Break the eggs into a medium-sized bowl and gently whisk with a fork to homogenize the whites and yolks. Whisk in the dashi and sake lightly to avoid creating foam. Pour through a fine-mesh strainer into a clean bowl.

Break the hard bottoms off the asparagus stalks by grasping both ends gently in either hand and bending the stalks to allow their natural breaking point. Slice diagonally into ½-inch (12-mm) pieces. Drop about 1 tablespoon of the cut asparagus into each of 5 *chawan mushi* pots or Japanese-style handleless teacups (that hold about ¾ cup/180 cc). Distribute the fresh peas evenly into each cup and portion out the dashi-flavored egg mixture among the cups by pouring a bit at a time into each one. Leave at least 20 percent of the cup unfilled, as the custard will puff up a bit.

Place the custard-filled cups in a bamboo or metal steamer set over a large pan of simmering water. Steam over low heat for 15 minutes, or until set. Garnish with a speck of slivered yuzu zest if you like. Serve immediately because the green of the asparagus will slowly leach into the pristine custard.

VARIATIONS: Substitute any small pieces of crisp seasonal vegetables (such as green beans) in place of the asparagus and peas. Mushrooms can also add an earthy note.

Using citrus shells is a little tricky, but the presentation is worth a bit of uncertainty in the cooking process. This is a gorgeous dish that can be prepped ahead of time and cooked at the last minute.

egg custard with flowering mustard in sour orange halves SERVES 4

NANOHANA NO NATSUMIKAN CHAWAN MUSHI

1 (2-ounce/60-g) chicken breast filet (*sasami*)

1 teaspoon sea salt

1⅓ cups (300 cc) Dashi (page 307)

3 large or 4 small eggs, at room temperature

1½ teaspoons mirin

5 sour oranges (*natsumikan, daidai, amanatsu,* or Seville)

12 (1-inch/2.5-cm) sprigs flowering mustard or tender rapini

Sprinkle the chicken breast filet with ¼ teaspoon of salt, and drop into a heavy resealable plastic bag. Press out the excess air, seal, and refrigerate for at least an hour if not overnight.

Add the remaining ¾ teaspoon of salt to the dashi in a small saucepan. Warm slowly over low heat to dissolve the salt. Let cool or use warm, but it should not be hot. Break the eggs into a medium-sized bowl and gently whisk with a fork to homogenize the whites and yolks. Whisk in the dashi and mirin lightly to avoid creating foam. Pour through a fine-mesh strainer into a clean bowl. Finely grate the zest of 1 sour orange directly into the custard and stir.

Slice the tops off the 4 other oranges and scoop out the pulp and juice into a bowl. Strain and use for something else. Leave a thin layer of pulp so the egg custard will not be in direct contact with the bitter white pith.

Cut the chicken breast filet into ½-inch (12-mm) pieces and distribute evenly among the 4 prepared sour orange shells. Nestle 3 flowering mustard sprigs in with the chicken pieces.

Place the custard-filled citrus halves in a bamboo or metal steamer set over a large pan of simmering water. Portion out the egg mixture among the halves by pouring a bit at a time into each one. Since the citrus halves are porous, you can fill them to the top.

Steam over low heat for 30 minutes or until set.

Serve immediately on a pottery plate with a small wooden or lacquer spoon.

VARIATIONS: Substitute any small pieces of crisp green vegetables or blanched greens in place of the mustard flowers. Omit the chicken filet for a vegetarian version.

5

noodles and rice

MEN AND YAKUMI: NOODLES

MESHI: RICE

For the most part, dried noodles have replaced homemade udon or soba in the Japanese family kitchen, but udon is such an easy dough to master on a beginning level that I encourage you to take the plunge. Tadaaki was always the noodle maker in our family, while I was in charge of the dipping sauce and garnishes. But as Tadaaki got busier, he taught Christopher how to crank the heavy iron and brass Japanese noodle-rolling machine that we clamp on the counter. The only skill required for using the cranking machine is that you must tighten each side of the rollers evenly, other-wise your noodles will not be of even thickness. Years ago I would make the noodles occasionally, but I developed a phobia for the noodle-rolling machine after a memorable ravioli-making extravaganza undertaken when pregnant with Christopher. Now older and wiser, I have licked the noodle machine (or perhaps have found more personal balance), and making homemade noodles is one more job I share with Tadaaki.

In our area of Saitama prefecture, farmers grew wheat for their nightly noodles, not buckwheat. But as a young farmer, just home from university, Tadaaki was excited to pave his own way and to create his own style of farming—not just follow his father's methods or what had always been. Tadaaki butted heads with his father on many of his life choices; farming was no different. As a postwar farmer, Tadaaki's father had enthusiasti-cally bought into the use of chemical fertilizers and pesticides touted in the name of "agricultural medicine" (*noyaku*) by Japan Agriculture (via the U.S. government). Tadaaki refused to use chemicals on the fields and joined a natural farming group headed by a local folk hero farmer, Kazuo Suka (father of our friend Toshiharu Suka). And Tadaaki also began growing buckwheat to make soba because he liked soba. That's the kind of guy he is—if he wants to eat it, he's going to grow it and make it by hand. Tadaaki no longer grows buckwheat but still grows the traditional wheat—perhaps because wheat has so many more uses.

Making soba noodles at home is not always easy. In Japan, the finest soba flour is ground from the very innermost kernel of the buckwheat. (In the U.S., the whole seed is used—the flavor is exceptional, but the texture too rough for top-quality soba noodles.) Also the ratio of buckwheat flour to wheat flour is crucial. Essentially you want to have as close to 100 percent buckwheat as possible, with the wheat flour only added as a sort of binding agent for ease of handling and to prevent the noodles from falling apart when boiled. It is traditional to make soba on December 31 for the first soba of the year (*toshikoshi*). In the Hachisu house, Tadaaki's brother, Sumito, often volunteered to be the soba maker (before he got married and had kids), and still sometimes does. More often than not, though, the soba does not get made (though our middle son, Andrew, tried his hand a couple of years ago). Some things have to give. These days we concentrate our energy into gathering the family together and putting beautifully delicious food from our fields on the table. Soba is still a favorite noodle of our family, so when we want to eat it, we go to Soba Ro or Soba Ra—two restaurants owned by our good friend Kanji Nakatani—where they get it right each and every time.

A typical farm family in Saitama, my husband's family ate udon noodles every night, but pearly white rice was still king. *Meshi* = rice = food in Japanese. That tells you right away how important rice is to the Japanese meal. Despite bread slipping into the Japanese diet, most Japanese still feel that without rice or noodles, there is no meal. For many years after Tadaaki and I were first married, my mother-in-law was confounded that I did not serve rice with my Western meals when Japanese guests came for dinner. Each time we had this conversation, I patiently explained that I would be preparing plenty of food and we certainly would not be needing rice. Without fail, she always offered to make rice "balls" (*onigiri*), and I always declined the offer, though sometimes she still did, much to my chagrin.

SUSHI

Most Japanese farm families didn't eat much sushi. Or if they did, it was ordered from the local sushi shop for special guests. Nowadays generic sushi is available at convenience stores, supermarkets, and chain restaurants. And sushi-in-the-round is rapidly replacing traditional sushi restaurants—by using lower-quality fish—often frozen, imported, or farmed. Undeniably artisanal sushi shops run by experienced and skilled sushi masters have become high-end drinking spots for those who can suffer the tariff. Still, I find it heart breaking that single-owner *sushiya* are dying at an alarming rate. They just can't survive. Even upscale Tsukiji fish market–based small chain *sushiya* are closing up shop. Why?

It's all about value. I'd rather go to a good sushi shop once a year than a mediocre one once a month. But then I'm crazy for sushi—and not just any sushi. I recharge my psyche by sitting at the blond wood counter in front of a glass case of raw fish, picking out and eating each selection two pieces at a time, slowly and lovingly savoring each bite as I flip the sushi, fish side down, onto my tongue.

I came to Japan in 1988 for two reasons: to learn Japanese and to experience sushi in the land of its origin. So, fresh off the plane, I was obsessed with finding a real *sushiya*. Armed with the characters for sushi and some pointers from Japanese coworkers, I ventured out on the town but was totally baffled by the split curtains hanging in front of each storefront (be it a restaurant or not). I blundered up the stairs into someone's house and the surprised but kindly grandmother directed me to a nearby drinking spot that also served food, where I managed to order some grossly oversized slices of yellowtail sashimi, salt-pickled napa cabbage, and a beer. At least I snared some raw fish. A couple of nights later, tired of the sickly smell of summer festival food, I stumbled upon a hole-in-the-wall shop with a fish tank out front.

I slid open the wood and glass door, and as I poked my head through the indigo-dyed curtain (*noren*), the owner's head jerked up in surprise. Nonetheless, he was welcoming and patient as I tried to order familiar sushi. That was when I still thought sushi was all about the little dishes that California shops serve or that salmon roe (*ikura*) demands a quail egg yolk (the master got a good giggle out of that one). Perhaps the quail yolk softens the acrid salty taste of not-so-fresh *ikura*, but it certainly adds nothing to firm eggs freshly nudged from their sac and sprinkled with a bit of sake, salt, and grated yuzu zest (page 26). These eggs burst one by one as you squeeze them between your tongue and the roof of your mouth. These eggs don't need the quail yolk because they're that good.

Tadaaki had not often eaten at a *sushiya*, so I initiated him into the dos and don'ts of sushi protocol. Don't put wasabi in the soy sauce dish because it leaves an unsightly muddy mess. Pick up the sushi with your fingers and flip it upside down, dip one little corner of fish into the soy sauce, then pop the whole piece of sushi into your mouth, fish side down. This sequence is crucial to immediately get the full fish taste, followed by a flash of hot wasabi and the satisfying finish of vinegared rice. And never let stray rice grains escape into your soy sauce dish (very bad form).

In Japan, sushi is all about the impeccable fish. It's all about simplicity. Fish + vinegared sweet rice = sushi. That's enough. It's delicate, it's subtle . . . there is ritual. Sushi is not about monster rolls or mayonnaise. Sometimes we should just accept something as it was meant to be and not insist on pushing and prodding it to be exactly how we think it should be. And sometimes giving in is a relief.

Simmered *gyoza* are one of my earliest Japanese food memories (if you don't count the sukiyaki savored as a young girl at Sakura Gardens in Palo Alto—with its raised tatami-matted rooms, shoji doors, and servers in kimono—a rare treat for our family of six wild children). I first had *gyoza* (or so I thought) at a little Japanese coffee shop opposite my (at the time) favorite sushi bar, Onna no Shiro, by the gates of Grant Street in San Francisco. By then I had already gone down the rabbit hole for sushi, and I fell in love with those *gyoza* as well. But the coffee shop closed early, and in those days I never got out to eat until late, so did not eat them as often as I'd like until I arrived in Japan and began haunting the ramen shops.

About twenty years ago, we had a party at our house for my husband's karate group. One sensei had a small factory and employed Chinese workers, whom he brought along to the party. And at this party they taught us how to make *gyoza*, Chinese style (simmered instead of steam-fried). At that time I remembered a bunch of us from Stanford hanging out at the house of my roommate, Diana Hu, in Palo Alto making boiled pot stickers, known in Japanese as *sui gyoza* ("water" *gyoza*). I love how life comes full circle sometimes. In our house, this is how we make *gyoza*.

simmered gyoza SERVES 6
SUI GYOZA

GYOZA SKINS

¼ teaspoon sea salt

1 cup (150 g) good-tasting all-purpose flour (page 10), plus more for sprinkling

GYOZA FILLING

1 cup (¼ pound/100 g) finely chopped napa cabbage

2 teaspoons fine sea salt

½ pound (225 g) headless unpeeled Gulf shrimp

⅔ pound (300 g) thinly sliced pork shoulder meat or fine-ground pork

2 tablespoons sake

1 tablespoon soy sauce

1 heaping tablespoon grated ginger

2 or 3 finely chopped garlic chives (*nira*)

Bring ½ cup (125 cc) of water to a boil over high heat in a small saucepan and stir in the salt to dissolve.

Measure the flour into a medium-sized mixing bowl. Using a pair of long chopsticks, mix the still very hot salt water into the flour in small additions until the dough holds together. Knead until smooth and pliable—it should be softer than your earlobe. Shape into a ball, wrap with plastic, and let rest while you prepare the filling.

Fill a medium-sized heavy pot about halfway with water and bring to a boil.

Meanwhile, make the filling: Put the napa cabbage in a bowl that can hold about 2 or 3 cups (500 to 750 cc). Sprinkle with the salt and massage in well but don't overwork it. Let sit 10 minutes before squeezing very well to express every bit of liquid you possibly can.

Remove the shrimp meat from the shells and hand chop finely. Scrape into a large mixing bowl. Finely hand chop the pork shoulder and add it to the shrimp. Mix in the squeezed napa cabbage, sake, soy sauce, grated ginger, and chopped garlic chives. Knead gently until the filling mixture is smooth and well amalgamated.

Roll the dough on a floured surface into a long cylinder 2 inches (5 cm) in diameter. Pinch off 1-inch (2.5-cm) pieces of dough and roll into 4-inch (10-cm) circles. Flour and stack as you go.

Rice vinegar

Soy sauce

Rayu (Chile-Infused Sesame Oil, page 315)

(Stuffing the *gyoza* goes a lot quicker if you have help, so try to enlist family members.) Fill a small bowl of water halfway with cold water and set it next to you. Place a wrapper in your palm and spoon a little dollop of filling right above where the middle crease would be if you folded the round into a half-moon. You want to get as much filling as you can in and still close the *gyoza* well—about a teaspoon or so depending on your *gyoza* skins. Dip your index finger into the cold water and run it along the half circle where your filling is. Close the circle by folding over the front flap and making ¼-inch (6-mm) pleats at ¼-inch (6-mm) intervals as you adhere it to the wet edge, all the while curving the back dough into the pleated front. Sound complicated? I admit it does, but all I can say is that it is easier than it sounds, and ultimately, even if you just make a smooth-edged half-moon, it will still be delicious (especially with homemade wrappers from artisanal flour).

Plop as many *gyoza* as can comfortably cook in your simmering pot of hot water (they should not be crowded when they rise to the surface). Cook, gently stirring to avoid sticking, at a lively simmer on medium-high heat until the *gyoza* rise to the surface. Cook a few minutes longer, then scoop a few *gyoza* and a very small amount of the hot water broth (just to keep the *gyoza* warm) into small rice bowls. Serve with a bowl of rice on the side. Unlike steam-fried *gyoza*, this dish makes a satisfying supper, especially if served with a daikon, carrot, or napa cabbage salad.

Each person should drizzle a little each of vinegar, soy sauce, and *rayu* to taste into a small soy sauce dish and dip the *gyoza* in the mixture before eating.

VARIATIONS: The balance of shrimp to pork can be adjusted according to your taste. And the garlic chives (*nira*) can be omitted, since they are quite pungent and may linger on your breath until the next day.

RAMEN

Like sushi, ramen is one of those foods for which there is no substitute. When you crave it, you've got to have it. When I first came to Japan, we'd stop off at the ramen shop after a night out. These days, we go for lunch.

Our local shop, Momotaro Ramen, with its white plastic siding and red *noren* entrance curtain flapping in the breeze, doesn't look like much on the outside . . . but what ramen shop does? As you enter, you feel a blast of warm air from the open kitchen with steam billowing out from vats of boiling water, frying vegetables, and sizzling *gyoza*. I prefer cooking at home, but a bowl of ramen hits the spot when we're in the mood. And it's just down the street.

The master at Momotaro coaxes every essential flavor component from chicken and pork bones to create a complex soup that serves as the base for all of his ramen dishes. It is satisfying and delicious, the best classic ramen I've ever tasted. Recently though, I got a tantalizing taste of the very unusual Ivan Ramen at a Japanese food event held at the Culinary Institute of American in Napa. The noodles were homemade, the broth bright and fresh feeling (unusual for ramen soup's typical deep-flavor paradigm), but most surprising were the bits of tomato confit floating in the broth. "Strange," I thought at first glance; "inspired," I realized after my first bite. The line had been long, but I would have queued up for more had they not run out. I kept thinking about that ramen and vowed to make my way to Ivan Ramen as soon I got back to Japan. As luck would have it, I did not have to wait that long, for later that night I stumbled upon Ivan boiling up his startlingly tasty, springy-textured ramen noodles, and I got to eat my own whole bowl.

Who would have thought the huge difference those homemade noodles would make?

(So ridiculously obtuse of me, since we only eat homemade pasta at home, never dried.) In Japan, the focus is on the soup—a ramen shop is only as good as its soup—but the noodles are all basically the same. I never absolutely loved the noodles, but it never occurred to me a shop might break out of the mold and serve excellent noodles from flour that has its own intrinsic taste. I suppose it takes a foreigner to think outside of the cultural box sometimes.

When I had first arrived in Japan I watched cooking shows on TV and bought some Japanese cookbooks. I was determined to only eat Japanese food and did not even own a fork. I cooked a lot and invited friends as well. Never verbalized, but as time wore on, I realized that of course my guests really wanted to eat "my food," not Japanese food when they came to our house. And so when we were married, I took a back seat on the Japanese meals and became Tadaaki's kitchen assistant. But as the years passed, the lines began to blur until Tadaaki was cooking Western and Japanese and so was I. We were just cooking "our" food.

I deeply believe that it is important to first understand the origin and heart of the food culture before putting your own touch on it. That is how I approached Japanese food and that is how I imagine Ivan Orkin of Ivan Ramen has done it. Ivan, a graduate of the CIA at Hyde Park married to a Japanese woman, has found his cooking niche in Japan. His shop is a couple of hours away by train, so I still haven't gotten there, but in a certain sense we are part of the same community, and it is comforting to know he's there, making a stand for good food in a city that probably has more little restaurants than any other city in the world.

Tadaaki usually makes the ramen at our house, but I go for a simpler method and have slashed and burned his here. David Chang's it is not, but we cannot all follow the Momofuku ramen method, so keep in mind the basic idea and experiment from there.

I like to make stock from the leftover bones of chickens I have roasted whole, stuffed with garden thyme branches and quartered lemons. Our chickens are so sublime that I add nothing but water along with the thyme sprigs and drippings off of the cutting board. I tried to cook the soup all night, but the gas alarm company called my mother-in-law in the middle of the night, and she crept upstairs to wake my husband. He has now nixed the overnight cook method. This deeply flavorful chicken soup makes an unforgettable ramen broth for homemade ramen (though not strictly orthodox). Also a dab of any reserved pan juices in each bowl adds extra complexity to the homemade ramen.

ramen at home SERVES 4
TEUCHI RAMEN

BROTH

2 small carrots, cut into 1-inch (2.5-cm) lengths

2 small *negi* (Japanese leeks) or spring onions, cut into 1-inch (2.5-cm) lengths

1 (¾-inch/2-cm) knob fresh ginger, peeled and finely sliced

4 free-range chicken thighs, bone-in (or 8 wings)

1 teaspoon sea salt

2 tablespoons best-quality rapeseed or sesame oil

NOODLES

2 tablespoons sesame oil

2 cups (300 g) good-tasting all-purpose flour (page 10)

2 large eggs, at room temperature

2 egg yolks, at room temperature

Start the ramen soup early in the day or at least several hours before dinner.

Heat the oven to 450°F (235°C). Put the carrots, *negi*, ginger, and chicken thighs in a cast-iron pan and sprinkle with the salt and oil. Smoosh the oil around to coat all the chicken and vegetables and roast for 30 to 45 minutes in the middle of the oven.

Scrape the roasted chicken and vegetables and all of the pan drippings into a large heavy pot with 4 quarts (4 liters) of cold water and bring to a boil over high heat. Lower the heat and simmer, covered, for 1 hour. Uncover, pull out 2 thighs, place in a medium-sized bowl, and ladle a bit of broth over to allow the meat to cool gently. Simmer the stock, uncovered, for 1 hour more. If you are in a hurry, use half the amount of water and cook in a pressure cooker. (In Japan, meat is usually not sold on the bone, so Tadaaki uses chicken wings. N.B.: Most ramen shops use pork bones as the base to their broth, though chicken bones and dried fish usually play some role as well.) After the chicken meat has cooled for a half hour, shred, moisten with a ladle of broth, and reserve. When the stock is done, strain into a clean saucepan and keep warm over low heat.

continued on next page

ramen at home

TOPPINGS

4 Half-Boiled Eggs (page 45)

1 small bunch boiled, squeezed, and chopped bitter greens (bok choy or *komatsuna*, page 171)

3 tablespoons finely chopped *negi* (Japanese leeks) or scallions

1 sheet nori, cut into eighths

Rayu (Chile-Infused Sesame Oil), for serving (page 315, optional)

Yuzu Kosho, for serving (page 316, optional)

FLAVORINGS

Miso

Soy sauce

Sea salt

Prepare the ramen noodle dough by mixing 2 tablespoons of the sesame oil into the flour with your fingers until crumbly. Add the eggs and egg yolks and stir with your hand until just incorporated. Knead on a clean, flat surface for 5 minutes until pliable but stiff. Let the dough rest while you prepare the ramen toppings.

Fill the largest stockpot you own with hot water and bring to a boil over high heat.

Roll out the ramen noodles following the udon noodle method (page 134), but roll them a little thinner than the ⅛ inch (3 mm). Cut them on the linguine setting of a pasta machine (or by hand). Slice into 9-inch (22-cm) lengths with a pizza cutter, flour well, and toss to distribute the flour. Leave on the workspace, but do not clump into a mass.

Take out one large soup bowl per person and add seasoning to each bowl according to each person's desire: 1 tablespoon miso, 2 teaspoons soy sauce, or ½ teaspoon salt. Mix a little broth in to melt the salt or emulsify the miso. Distribute the reserved shredded chicken pieces among the bowls along with the small amount of broth in which it was cooled.

Boil the noodles for 2 minutes and right before the noodles are done, add 2 or 3 ladlefuls of broth to the bowls. Set a large strainer in a bowl and after 2 minutes has elapsed, scoop the noodles out of the boiling water with a small fine-mesh strainer and drop into the large strainer. Divide the noodles among the bowls filled with soup and quickly add 2 egg halves, a dollop of greens, and a piece of nori before sprinkling liberally with the *negi*. Serve immediately. If you are doubling (or tripling) the recipe, do not be tempted to cook more than 4 portions at a time. Continue cooking more noodles, but the first four people served should dive in, otherwise the noodles will inflate beyond control!

If added spice is desired, drizzle soy sauce or miso ramen with *rayu* and dab salt ramen with *yuzu kosho*.

VARIATIONS: You can also substitute semifresh ramen noodles (sometimes found at Japanese or Chinese grocery stores) or dried. Follow the directions on the package for cooking. They will not be as good.

Tadaaki was always the noodle maker in our house. When I developed this recipe for an article I wrote a few years ago, I had Christopher roll out the noodles because I was busy (and a bit intimidated). I promised him he only had to roll enough for us to shoot the photo for the article, so he obliged. But at the end of the shoot, I was left with the rest of the dough and no Christopher. He showed me how to adjust the pasta machine, and I discovered how simple making noodles is. And my noodles turned out to have the perfect thickness.

udon noodles SERVES 6
TEUCHI UDON

½ tablespoon salt

3⅓ cups (500 g) organic, unbleached cake or pastry flour

1⅔ cups/400 cc Noodle Dipping Sauce (page 310)

Garnishes (suggestions follow)

Dissolve the salt in ⅔ cup (160 cc) water. Measure the flour into a large mixing bowl. Add the salt water and mix until the dough holds together. Knead until smooth and pliable, then transfer to a heavy plastic bag. Pat the dough out to a 2-inch (4-cm) thick rectangle and knead further by rhythmically and firmly treading on the dough. Remove the dough from the bag, fold in thirds, and repeat the treading process a few times. (Or process with a metal blade in a food processor until the dough is crumbly and knead by hand.) Udon dough, like pasta dough, is dense and semidry, otherwise it will stick when rolled.

Roll out with a pasta machine, making rectangles about 2 feet (60 cm) long by ⅛ inch (3 mm) thick. Cut the noodles on the thin linguine setting and cut in half horizontally for 1-foot (30-cm) lengths. Flour the cut noodles as you finish each batch so they will not stick together.

Alternatively, roll out into a rough oblong shape on a counter surface with a 30-inch (75-cm) long dowel 1½ inches (3 cm) in diameter. Roll from the center out, periodically rolling the dough around the dowel to keep from sticking on the counter. When the dough has reached the desired thickness, roll it around the dowel, slide the dowel out, and gently flatten the roll of dough to cut. Slice into ⅛-inch (3-mm) wide strips with a broad-bladed, razor-sharp knife.

continued on next page

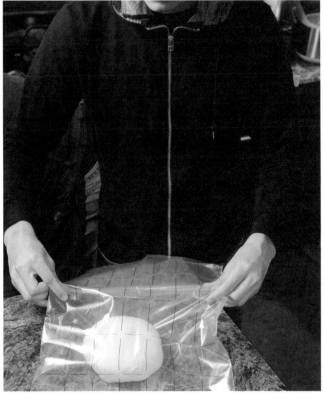

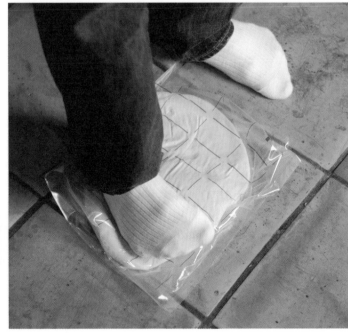

udon noodles

Fill a large stockpot with hot water and bring to a boil. Set a large mixing bowl in the kitchen sink and fill with cold water. Scoop up half of the raw udon and boil for 2 to 3 minutes, depending on thickness. The noodles should be softer than pasta but not mushy. Plunge the noodles into the bowl of cold water and refresh under cold running tap water. Shake off and swirl the small bunches into 3 attractive piles arranged on a dinner plate. Cook the rest of the udon in the same fashion.

Dip the udon noodles in a small bowl of dipping sauce (*tsuyu*) with flavor garnishes (*yakumi*). Slurping is de rigueur in Japan.

FLAVOR GARNISHES (*YAKUMI*): Use finely slivered citrus peel, finely chopped fresh green chile, slivered fresh ginger, torn *sansho* leaves, a chiffonade of shiso leaves, or finely chopped scallion or chives. Each diner sprinkles the desired garnishes into a small bowl of dipping sauce.

Although soba is a challenge to make at home, it is certainly not impossible. Dried soba makes an admirable alternative as long as you choose the best-quality buckwheat noodles you can find. I prefer organic and also tend to select packaging that looks artisanal or aesthetically pleasing, with the perhaps naïve idea that packaging and contents relate.

soba with walnut dipping sauce SERVES 6
KURUMI SOBA

½ cup (125 cc) whole fresh walnuts

1 pound (500 g) dried soba

1⅔ cups (400 cc) Noodle Dipping Sauce (page 310)

2 tablespoons finely sliced rounds of scallions, mainly white part

Fill the largest stockpot you have with hot water and bring to a boil over high heat.

Grind the walnuts in a *suribachi* or mortar until powdery but not pastelike.

Follow the directions on the package, but in general, soba takes about 4 to 5 minutes of cooking to become the right texture of soft with a little bite.

While the noodles are cooking, place two large mixing bowls in the kitchen sink (if two fit—otherwise use just one bowl) and fill with cold water.

When the noodles are cooked, scoop them out of the boiling water and immediately plunge them into the first bowl of cold water to take the intial heat off. Swirl once and scoop into the other bowl. (You can skip the second bowl dip if you want, but this is Tadaaki's method.)

Refresh under cold running tap water. Shake off and swirl small bunches of soba into several attractive piles on a flat bamboo noodle basket set over a dinner plate to catch the drips. (If you don't have a basket, put the noodles directly on the plate or on a lacquer tray.)

Serve with a small bowl of dipping sauce flavored with a heaping teaspoon of ground walnuts and a healthy sprinkling of scallions.

The Austrian owner and her Japanese husband of the English school where I worked served *somen* to me for lunch one day my first summer in Japan, and I was entranced by the ice-cold noodles and fresh-flavored garnishes. Years later, I participated in a *nagashi somen* party put on by some of the mothers at Sunny-Side Up! A narrow, canted trough from gray plastic piping was set up, with one end elevated above shoulder height and the other end about waist level. They fed a hose into the top of the trough and placed a bucket at the bottom end. Everyone received a ladle of dipping sauce in their bowl, along with some garnishes, and then stood on either side of the trough. Someone dropped the *somen* into the top of the trough so it sped down the watercourse, careening along toward the waiting bucket. The trick was to catch up a dollop of *somen* from the cold water, plunk it in the bowl of sauce, and eat. Loads of fun . . . but a bit hard to get full, all things considered.

somen with ginger, myoga, and scallions SERVES 6
SOMEN

3 *myoga* (page 366), cut lengthwise into fourths

2 tablespoons finely sliced rounds of scallions, mainly green part

1 tablespoon finely slivered fresh ginger

1 pound (500 g) dried *somen*

1⅔ cups (400 cc) Noodle Dipping Sauce (page 310)

Fill a large stockpot with hot water and bring to a boil over high heat.

Set each quarter piece of *myoga* (one of the cut sides down) on a cutting board and cut into thin lengthwise slices with a razor-sharp knife. Mound the *myoga* slices in a small bowl and bring to the table with the scallion rounds and slivered ginger.

Place a large mixing bowl in the kitchen sink and fill with cold water. Drop the *somen* into the boiling water and cook for about 2 minutes, or according to the package directions.

As soon as the noodles are done, scoop them out of the boiling water and slide them into the bowl of cold water. Start running more cold water into the bowl and hold onto the *somen* so it won't run out of the bowl. When the noodles have cooled, turn off the tap.

Grab the *somen*, one handful at a time, give it a shake, and set the swirls on a bamboo noodle basket or plate. Bring the *somen* to the table. (If you are using a noodle basket, you will need to set the basket on top of a dinner plate to catch the drips.)

Serve with a small bowl of dipping sauce. Sprinkle a bit of the *myoga*, ginger, and scallion into the dipping sauce, plunk in some *somen*, and slurp.

ON WASHING RICE

Have you ever read something that you pretended to understand but really didn't?

The Heart of Zen Cuisine was one of the first books I bought in Japan, and I learned how to wash rice from this book. Or at least I thought I did.

The author had a beautifully soft style when describing food and cooking. In essence, she told the reader to concentrate on the task at hand and immerse oneself in the process. I would stand in front of my stainless steel sink in my new tatami-matted apartment, and reaching down into the rice would focus very intensely (too intensely) on the grains as I swished them around in the cold water. My back would hurt a little because the sink was deep and the counter 4 inches (10 cm) lower than Western standards. But I was not deterred, I knew I could get this concept. I really wanted to be "Zen"—you know, one with my rice. But I was trying too hard. Even then I knew it was an act.

One thing I've learned while living in Japan is that good things take time. And I don't mean that it takes two hours to make a sensational dinner. I mean that it takes years to get to a "destination," and the journey in itself is essential. Maybe I never got the idea of Zen, but then again, maybe I did.

Don't get disheartened when I tell you it probably took me another ten years before I really was focusing on the task at hand. Cooking is one of the most soothingly therapeutic occupations we can do when not hurried. But so often our minds are elsewhere as we go through the motions, not thinking of the food in front of us that we are chopping or stirring into yet another meal. I notice my cooking students mixing dough completely disengaged from what they are doing, chatting across the counter with other students equally distracted from their tasks. They are often completely unaware of what is happening in the bowl before them. Now, I counsel, pour yourself into the bowl and put your love in the food. Use a light hand with a powerful spirit.

It used to be that our teenage son Andrew was in charge of washing the rice—a task he performed with a singular lack of enthusiasm. But one day a few years ago, Tadaaki and the boys were off doing pottery, so I made the rice. Andrew and I share a common trait: We both tend toward the slapdash. When under the gun, my cooking usually involves a lot of swearing, spilling, and blood. I'm no less focused, but "in the zone," so stay out of my way. It's dangerous. My food may not be pretty, but it definitely is gorgeous. I splash the plates with vividly colored vegetables, not unlike an edible canvas.

With a singular lack of enthusiasm, I went out to our dusty storage house (where mice lurk in the corners) and scooped out some rice from a 25-kg sack. I brought the rice into the house and set about washing it. I felt the grains bounce off my hand as I scrubbed them. The cool water slipped against the grains and through my fingers as the rice sent soft little currents up my arm. I thought about how those grains got to be in my sink. I remembered planting that very rice by hand the year before—squelching around in the mud. I thought about the work it takes to grow each grain of rice. And I felt the energy that my farmer husband had put in, helped along by the sun, soil, and water. I felt how beautiful each little grain was—so simple and perfect, but so hard to produce. Each little grain so precious.

And that night when Tadaaki took his first bite of rice, his eyes widened in surprise and he asked me what I had done to make the rice taste so good. What had been my special touch? I told him I had put love into it.

Most Japanese who cook will make at least one pot of rice in their rice cooker every day. Inevitably the repetition of the task of washing the rice will lead to some feeling of disassociation or the desire to hurry through the task. Rice washed lackadaisically will lose a bit of spark. The rice will not be bad but it also will not be great. It's worth giving the rice some attention while you wash it and perhaps one more clear water rinse before cooking.

plain rice MAKES 4 CUPS (1000 CC)
GOHAN

2 cups (500 cc) Japanese-style short-grain rice

Measure the rice into a rice cooker receptacle or a heavy, medium-sized saucepan. Fill the receptacle or pan to the very top with cold water and pour off any debris or little bugs floating to the top (don't be squeamish; better bugs than chemicals). Scrub the rice in your fist to dislodge extra bran. Fill with cold water repeatedly, pouring off the water each time until the water runs clear. Drain one last time and pour 2 cups (500 cc) cold water into the rice, sloshing around the sides a little to dislodge any grains sticking to the sides of the pan. If possible, let sit for 30 minutes before cooking.

Cook in a rice cooker by selecting the correct setting. Or cook in a heavy, covered saucepan on the stove. Bring the rice to a boil in the covered pot (bubbly steam will escape around the edges of the pot lid). Turn the heat down immediately to the lowest setting and cook slowly until you hear little crackles when you lower your head close to the bottom of the pan (but be careful not to burn your ear!).

Let the rice sit for 5 minutes, then fluff with chopsticks to aerate (a paddle can easily smash the rice). In cool weather, it is best to store leftover rice overnight at room temperature, since refrigerating will cause the rice to harden.

RATIO: rice : water—1:1

After Tadaaki graduated from college, he returned home to live with his parents and work with his father as is the custom for the son designated to take over the family business. A naturally curious guy, Tadaaki was interested in trying new foods and experimenting with different eating styles. He decided to replace his daily white rice with brown rice but found himself losing his appetite at an alarming pace as each day passed. For this reason, we do not eat as much brown rice in our family as I would like. The method here follows the traditional Japanese way of making rice. For fried brown rice, I often boil the rice like pasta in plenty of water so that the brown rice is drier and easier to fry.

brown rice MAKES 4 CUPS/1000 CC
GENMAI

2 cups (500 cc) Japanese-style
  short-grain brown rice (*genmai*)

Measure the rice into a rice cooker receptacle or a heavy, medium-sized saucepan. Fill the receptacle or pan to the very top with cold water and pour off any debris. Briefly scrub the rice between both of your palms and fingers and rinse once more. Drain, then measure 3 cups (750 cc) water and add to the rice. Soak for 30 minutes before cooking to absorb some of the soaking water.

Cook in a Japanese rice cooker by selecting the brown rice (玄米) setting, though be aware that this cooking cycle takes appreciably longer than the normal one. Or cook in a heavy saucepan on the stove as described on page 143.

Let the rice rest for 5 minutes, fluff with chopsticks, and serve. To store leftover rice, try to avoid chilling it. It can be stored in small containers in the freezer and reheated for later use.

RATIO: rice:water—1:1.5

VARIATION: For a more pilaf style, toss the brown rice into a large, heavy pot of boiling water and cook for 30 minutes. Drain, return to the pot, cover, and let rest for 20 minutes before using.

The first time I tasted hot sushi rice was at a sushi counter in Tokyo's Tsujikji fish market. It was an eye-opener. The sushi master had just run out of rice and an assistant brought a steaming batch of freshly made *sumeshi* in a wooden tub. By the time the master had patted out our sushi, the rice had cooled enough not to cook the fish but was still pleasantly warm in contrast to the cold fish. Delicious.

sushi rice MAKES 6 CUPS/1500 CC
SUMESHI

3 cups (750 cc) Japanese-style short-grain rice

2 tablespoons sake

1 (6-inch/15-cm) piece of konbu

6 tablespoons rice vinegar

3 tablespoons organic granulated sugar

2 teaspoons fine sea salt

Wash the rice according to the method for Plain Rice (page 143). Add 3 cups (750 cc) filtered water to the washed rice, remove 2 tablespoons of the water, and replace them with the sake. Slip in the konbu and let sit for 30 minutes. Cook the rice following the method for Plain Rice (page 143) or on the sushi rice (すしめし) setting of a rice cooker.

Measure the rice vinegar into a small bowl and stir in the sugar and salt. Set aside to dissolve while the rice is cooking, stir occasionally if you think about it.

Five minutes after the rice is done, discard the konbu and dump into a wide wooden tub (*handai*) or onto a large wooden cutting board. Sprinkle the prepared sushi vinegar over the rice and aerate the rice carefully with a flat paddle by cutting into the rice grains and lifting them up from the bottom (similar to folding in egg whites) while fanning the rice with a flat Japanese fan or a piece of cardboard with your other hand (the definition of a chew-gum-and-walk kind of operation, so enlist a helper.) Do not smash! The idea here is to cool the rice quickly in order to facilitate the absorption of vinegar into the rice grains. It will take several minutes for the steamy rice to come to body temperature. Cover with a damp cloth until ready to use. Do not store in the fridge.

RATIO: rice : water—1:1

On trips back to the United States, I never liked the airline food (who does?). And after my first son was born, I realized bringing my own food was the only option if I wanted to stay one step ahead of the inevitable travel cold brought on by sleep deprivation and lowered resistance. Traveling with one baby is exhausting; I ended up traveling with three. And the food I brought with us kept me going.

My mother-in-law, like many older Japanese farm women, has a bent back, so it was hard for her to hold babies. But she is an expert at making country sushi: *inarizushi* and *inaka zushi*—a traditional meal she prepared for special days. So I enlisted her help in making our lunches for the plane. She was ecstatic to be useful to her son's stubbornly independent foreign bride (me) and whipped up several boxes each time we went—enough for about eight people, but we did our best to finish. You eat both *inarizushi* and *inaka zushi* with your hands— no need for soy sauce—but a hot towel is recommended for wiping fingers. Clean tasting and slightly sweet for a needed energy boost, these two country styles of sushi are typically made ahead of time to be eaten later in the day. They are excellent choices for travel lunches or bento boxes. (In the countryside, we call these rolls *inaka zushi*, but they are probably known best as *futo maki*.)

You will need a bamboo sushi rolling mat for this recipe.

country sushi rolls MAKES 6
INAKA ZUSHI

1½ cups (200-g package) salted jellyfish (*kurage*, page 11)

1 tablespoon dark sesame oil

½ teaspoon red pepper flakes

3⅓ cups (800 cc) Noodle Dipping Sauce (page 310)

1 tablespoon unhulled sesame seeds, roasted

Sea salt

6 dried gourd strips (*kanpyo*, page 11)

½ small burdock root (*gobo*), cut into 3 by ¼-inch (7.5-cm by 6-mm) batonettes

2 medium carrots, cut into 3 by ¼-inch (7.5-cm by 6-mm) batonettes

Soak the jellyfish in a large bowl of cold water for 1 to 2 hours. Rinse out the excess salt in several changes of cold water, then drain and squeeze. Heat the sesame oil with the red pepper flakes in a small saucepan over medium-high heat until they turn bright red. Toss in the drained jellyfish, increase the heat to high, and sauté for a minute or so. Be careful not to burn it! Add 2 tablespoons of the noodle dipping sauce and simmer for 5 minutes on medium-low heat to reduce most of the liquid. Roast the sesame seeds in a small dry pan, shaking over medium-high heat until they start to pop. Toss them into the jellyfish.

While you are soaking the jellyfish, massage some sea salt into the *kanpyo*. Fill a medium-sized bowl with cold water and soak the *kanpyo* for 20 minutes to reconstitute. Drain and squeeze, then cut into manageable lengths of about 4 inches (10 cm) or so.

Fill a medium-sized saucepan three-quarters full with water, salt lightly, and bring to a boil over high heat. Drop in the *gobo* batonettes and simmer briskly for about 2 minutes until half done (they should just be starting to soften). Scoop the *gobo* out with a small strainer and set over a bowl to drain. Follow this same process to cook the carrot for about a minute or so in the same water used to boil the *gobo*.

Rice vinegar

6 sheets nori

6 cups (1500 cc) Sushi Rice (page 145)

1 tablespoon finely julienned ginger

2 Golden Egg Ribbons (page 116)

When the carrot pieces are half done, drain. Dump the simmering water, add the remaining noodle dipping sauce (after you have taken out 2 tablespoons for seasoning the jellyfish), and return the drained carrots and *gobo* back into the saucepan along with the reconstituted *kanpyo*. Place some parchment paper or a drop-lid (*otoshi buta*, page 15) on the surface of the vegetables and simmer until they are soft; cool in their broth.

Pour a little rice vinegar into a small bowl and set it next to where you will be making the sushi rolls. Place a bamboo sushi-rolling mat on your work space, the side with the flat rolling bar should be closest to you. Lay one nori sheet on top of the mat, shiny side down (with the grain going crosswise). Scoop a cup and a half (250 g) of sushi rice onto the sheet of nori, dip your fingers in the rice vinegar (splashing vinegar up to your palms), and spread the rice evenly to the edges, including the rolling end, but leave a 1¼- to 1½-inch (3- to 4-cm) border at the finishing end. Lay a few pieces of each of the above ingredients about a third of the way up from the bottom of the rice parallel to the rolling edge. But easy does it, as this roll can get quite large. It shouldn't be much more than 2 inches (5 cm) in diameter when done. Roll tightly and firmly away from you one rotation, and squeeze gently with both hands along the roll. Pick up the edge of your rolling mat and continue to roll to the end. Lift up the mat-enclosed roll, adjust the mat, and smooth the roll into an even cylinder. Wrap each roll separately in parchment paper, then plastic wrap and serve anytime that day (or the next). To serve, unwrap each roll, dip a razor sharp knife in rice vinegar, and cut the sushi rolls into 8 thick rounds.

When Baachan brings over a plate or two of her sushi, I find myself reaching for these silky little pillows of rice before the country sushi rolls packed with simmered vegetables. There is something about the squishy, slightly sweet deep-fried tofu wrapping that is immensely appealing (and almost addicting).

stuffed tofu pouches SERVES 6
INARIZUSHI

10 pieces *usuage* (deep-fried tofu, page 7)

2⅔ cups (600 cc) Noodle Dipping Sauce (page 310)

Rice vinegar

6 cups (1500 cc) Sushi Rice (page 145)

Fill a medium-sized saucepan three-quarters full of water and bring to a boil over high heat. Slap the *usuage* against the counter to help pop the two sides apart (this was traditionally the kids' job) and drop in the boiling water for 1 minute to remove the excess oil. Drain in a fine-mesh strainer. When cool enough to handle, cut in half crosswise.

Bring the noodle dipping sauce to a simmer over medium heat in a medium-sized saucepan and slip in the *usuage* halves. Lay some parchment paper or a drop-lid (*otoshi buta*, page 15) on the surface of the *usuage* and simmer gently on low heat for 5 minutes, occasionally switching the bottom ones to the top to ensure even flavoring. Remove from the heat and cool in the liquid.

Pour a little rice vinegar into a small bowl and set it by your workplace. Pluck a seasoned *usuage* half out of the pan and pry it apart to create a pocket. Place it in your palm, dip your free hand in the vinegar, and grab a small handful of sushi rice (a heaping ⅓ cup/75 g). Press the rice gently into a compact oval, but do not squeeze. Stuff the rice inside the *usuage* pouch, tucking one edge of the ends over the other to close up the opening. Arrange on a plate as you go and cover with plastic wrap until serving. These keep for at least a day, unrefrigerated, in cool weather.

I first ate hand-rolled sushi for dinner at a friend's family home on Christmas Eve. I loved the idea that you could just eat and eat and eat (and not worry about the bill). Tadaaki used to pass by the fish market every Saturday on the way home from egg deliveries, and *temaki zushi* was our Saturday dinner for years. These days Tadaaki's delivery schedule has changed, so we make sushi at home when we have the whim but perhaps less regularly than before.

hand-rolled sushi SERVES 4 TO 6
TEMAKI ZUSHI

About 2 pounds (1 kg) assorted fish, cut for sashimi

3 tablespoons finely chopped scallions or chives

2 tablespoons freshly grated ginger (if squid or shiny silver fish are included)

2 tablespoons freshly grated wasabi

12 shiso leaves

20 sheets (or more) nori, cut into quarters

Soy sauce (as needed)

6 cups (1500 cc) Sushi Rice (page 145)

A small handful of sprouted daikon (optional)

Arrange the sashimi fish attractively on a plate with some green leaves or julienned vegetables to keep the fish apart (see pages 228-229). Mound the chopped scallion and grated ginger in a free spot on the perimeter of the sashimi plate and dab some wasabi in a free corner. Put the shiso leaves and nori separately on small plates. Bring all these plates to the table.

Set a medium-sized plate and a small saucer in front of each person and pour a little soy sauce into the saucer. Put the sushi rice in a medium-sized serving bowl with a rice paddle and bring it to the table.

Make your own hand-rolled sushi by laying a piece of nori, shiny side down, across your palm, then spreading some sushi rice on the nori. (Better not to go hog wild here because the roll will quickly become too awkward to eat if overstuffed.) Using chopsticks, pick up a couple of pieces of sashimi and drape them over the rice. Scrape some wasabi across the nori and sprinkle the fish with chopped scallion or top with a fresh shiso leaf, or daikon sprouts, if using. You don't need all three, since the idea is not to include everything but the kitchen sink. Roll up the nori square straight (not cone fashion), dip in the soy sauce, and eat. This is a well-loved family meal in Japan and often the answer for how to eat fairly good sushi on a budget.

Besides curry rice, this is my youngest son Matthew's favorite dish and he requests it often. *Cha* means "tea" in Japanese, so *chazuke* by nature (if not the name alone) signals a dish involving tea (in this case, green tea). But we don't drink green tea, so it's not something we have lying around—and typical farming families had drank up their tea at tea break. Tadaaki makes a light dashi, then flavors it with soy sauce. I prefer the clean taste of salt. Either way, no tea. Also we only use beautifully fresh sashimi-cut fish garnished with the nori and green onion to surprise your tongue. Good for breakfast, a light lunch, or a starter before dinner.

yellowtail sashimi on hot rice with broth SERVES 4
BURI CHAZUKE

1⅓ cups (300 cc) Dashi (page 307)

½ teaspoon fine sea salt

2 cups (500 cc) hot Plain Rice (page 143)

16 slices yellowtail sashimi (*buri* or *kampachi*)

4 teaspoons chives or thin scallion tops, chopped into fine rounds

¼ sheet nori, snipped into fine threads (about 2 teaspoons)

Heat the dashi with the salt in a small saucepan over low heat to dissolve. Keep warm.

Scoop the hot rice into four small bowls with a rice paddle. Lay 4 slightly overlapping sashimi slices over the rice in each bowl. Sprinkle with chives and cover with enough salted dashi to almost reach the top of the rice (about ⅓ cup/85 cc). Sprinkle with nori threads and serve immediately.

VARIATIONS: Substitute salmon, sea bass, flounder, or similar sashimi-grade cuts for the yellowtail. Add a little slivered yuzu or Meyer lemon zest with the chopped chives.

I never was a big fan of fried rice because it can end up a bit greasy and a little too heavy on the rice component. But one night in Berkeley, I stopped by Michelle and Rayneil De Guzman's house for an early dinner with their darling little toddler, Renato. Rayneil (of Filipino heritage) put together a light version of fried rice that converted me. Rayneil cooks in the Café at Chez Panisse, so his cooking reflects both his heritage and his training: very eclectic and always delicious. I never say no to an invite to dinner at the De Guzmans', and, more often than not, just invite myself. Inspired by Rayneil, I thought a summer vegetable version of fried rice (*chahan*) would be both fresh and light. I was not wrong. In the summer, when vegetables are coming out of your ears, it's fun to see how many you can get on the plate. This particular fried rice is irresistible because it packs so many of those wonderful summer vegetables into the dish and thus yields a very bright version of a dish that can quickly become overly brown or too oily. If you have any tofu hanging around, cut it into small ½-inch (12-mm) squares and strew over the rice before garnishing with the green aromatics. The cold silky tofu juxtaposes well against the hot rice.

fried rice with corn and peppers SERVES 6
TOMOROKOSHI TO PIMAN NO CHAHAN

4 cups (1000 cc) Plain Rice (page 143)

3 ears corn

About 5 tablespoons organic rapeseed oil

1 large onion, cut into ¼-inch (6-mm) dice

Fine sea salt

1 tablespoon finely chopped ginger

½ tablespoon finely chopped garlic

2 small mild Japanese red peppers or 1 large Western, cut into ¼-inch (6-mm) dice (1 cup/250 cc)

4 eggs, at room temperature, beaten with ¼ teaspoon sea salt

3 tablespoons soy sauce

3 tablespoons finely chopped *negi* or scallion, including the white part, for garnish

3 tablespoons finely slivered shiso leaves, for garnish

While the rice is cooking, prepare the vegetables.

Set each corncob in a large bowl and cut the kernels off the cob with a sharp knife. After all the kernels are removed, go over the cob with the back of the knife to get the juicy corn "meat" still adhering to the cob. Break up the kernel clumps with your fingers and measure—you should have about 1½ cups (750 cc).

Heat 2 teaspoons rapeseed oil in a large, well-seasoned wok or frying pan over medium heat. When hot, add the onion and a large pinch of salt. Sauté while stirring gently with a flat wooden spoon to distribute the oil. After a couple of minutes, toss in the chopped ginger and garlic. Stir for a minute or two more and scrape into a bowl big enough to house all of the fried rice vegetables as they are cooked.

Wipe the pan and heat 2 more teaspoons of oil over medium heat. Throw in the peppers and a pinch of salt. Lower the heat and stir-fry for a couple of minutes, stirring constantly. The peppers should just lose their raw edge but should not really be cooked at this point. Dump in the corn kernels, and add another teaspoon of oil and a large pinch of salt. Stir gently to distribute. Cover and cook for a minute or two more over low heat, until the corn and peppers have softened but still have a slight crunch. Push the cooked onion aside and add to the bowl.

Wipe the pan again and heat 1 tablespoon oil over high heat. Add the salted eggs and cook quickly, while continually scraping the bottom of the pan to incorporate the cooked egg layer into the raw egg mixture on the surface. Remove the cooked eggs to another medium-sized bowl while still slightly runny.

Turn the cooked rice onto a flat wooden basin (*handai*) or large wooden cutting board and cut into the rice with a rice paddle, spreading out the rice to aerate and release steam. Wash the wok or frying pan and heat 2 tablespoons oil (in the clean pan) over high heat.

Dump the rice into the pan and sauté for several minutes, stirring constantly with a flat wooden spoon, turning the bottom layer up over the top layer to ensure even cooking and to dry out the rice. When all the rice has met the oil and has been seared by the bottom of the pan, stir in the soy sauce. Sauté for a few more minutes to evenly distribute the soy sauce. Once the rice is evenly colored by the soy sauce and no white remains, stir in the cooked vegetables. As soon as the vegetables are well incorporated into the rice, turn off the heat and add the cooked egg, cutting it up with the flat edge of the spoon as you distribute it into the fried rice.

Scoop a few large spoonfuls onto a plate and sprinkle with finely chopped *negi* and shiso threads. If additional salty flavor is needed at the table, opt for fine sea salt over soy sauce.

VARIATIONS: If you don't have any red peppers to create the arresting yellow-red-green color trilogy, you could optionally add 1 cup (250 cc) of ¼-inch (6-mm) diced fresh tomatoes that you have quickly sautéed in ½ teaspoon rapeseed oil with a pinch of salt. Alternatively, you could skip the sauté and strew the chopped fresh tomatoes on top of the fried rice before serving. Folding the quickly sautéed tomatoes into the fried rice will result in a slightly wetter dish. Either way, sprinkle with the shiso and green onion before serving.

RICE PLANTING

You plant rice in bare feet. When you take your first step into the rice paddy, your toes curl to get some purchase. It's like sticking your feet into cornstarch gloop. Every time you take a step, the wet mud does not want to let you go—the suction effect makes each and every step a concerted effort. Also, you must step slowly and carefully, walking in others' footsteps, so not to create more holes in the rice field, which has been carefully leveled. At this point there is about a ½ inch (1 cm) of water covering the field. Trying not to think about the leeches that live in the muddy water, you separate a seedling from the dripping bunch you are carrying, and holding it gently, almost like a calligraphy brush, you flip your wrist as you insert the seedling straight down into the mud. The seedling should not be planted too deep; the roots should just break the mud's surface. It's slow going, but when that last row is planted and you look out over the scores of other rows, that is a mighty feeling of accomplishment.

Tadaaki used to plant the rice with a machine, but the machine left so many seedlings floating on top of the water that he had to go over the whole field to fix the missed plantings. When the boys were small, Tadaaki worked on the rice field with his father, but in the intervening years

the boys and I began to help. A couple of years ago Tadaaki decided to plant the rice by hand with the help of Slow Food friends from Tokyo who were hot to try their hands at "real farming." He made *doburoku* (homebrewed sake—strictly illegal) and invited more friends. Cooking lunch and dinner for thirty plus takes time, so I often don't make it to the field anymore. But I can see the satisfaction on the faces of the exhausted workers as they trickle in for dinner after a trip to the local hot spring for a bath to wash off the mud, and often wish I could.

By 7:30 the workers, ice-cold beers in hand, are gathered around our dinning room and kitchen tables, grabbing up handfuls of fresh-picked edamame from steaming bowls. The beer is a welcome relief after a day of planting in the hot sun, and the edamame a summer given. Tadaaki drags out the big pottery urn full of *doburoku* and starts passing cups around. *Doburoku* has a pleasant overtone of flowers, but it can be disconcerting to have bits of rice floating around in your drink. New friends are made and old friends rediscovered. Our guests have worked on the land and now they are eating the food that came from that land. They eat with gusto and great interest, and lively conversations spill out as we mill around. For that evening we are a close community brought together by the shared labor and the shared food. And it feels good to be connected.

Our meat shop had a fire and was closed for a couple of months and I felt less than inspired when faced with the choice of supermarket meats. One day I needed a fresh new idea to liven up the SSU! school lunch and was moved to re-create a dish I had loved at a now defunct organic cafe run by our dear friend Matsuda-san (the mayonnaise maven). I had always wondered what happened to the chef who, like Matsuda-san, had a innate feeling for creating interesting and delicious food from local ingredients and the organic vegetables that Matsuda-san grew. Later, I discovered her waitressing at another local organic café that serves uneventful pizza. What a waste!

natto fried rice SERVES 6
NATTO CHAHAN

4 cups (1000 cc) Brown Rice (page 144), boiled pilaf style (see variation)

5 tablespoons rapeseed oil

1 large carrot, peeled and diced

3 small onions, diced

1 (1-inch/2.5-cm) piece of ginger, peeled and finely chopped

Fine sea salt

2 *usuage* (deep-fried tofu pouches), cut into ½-inch/12-mm dice (optional)

3 eggs, at room temperature, beaten with ¼ teaspoon sea salt

2 tablespoons soy sauce

2 (3-ounce/80-g) packages natto, well aerated and seasoned with the accompanying sauces (page 7)

4 to 6 tablespoons Japanese Mayonnaise (page 312)

4 to 6 tablespoons finely chopped scallion, including white part

While the rice is cooking, heat 1 tablespoon rapeseed oil in a large, frying pan over medium heat. When hot, add the carrot, onions, ginger, and ¼ teaspoon salt.

Stir-fry for a couple of minutes, stirring constantly with a flat wooden spoon. Cover and cook for a few more minutes, until the vegetables have just softened but are not completely cooked through. The carrot should still have a bit of snap. Scrape into a medium-sized bowl.

If using the *usuage*, wipe the pan one more time and heat 1 tablespoon oil over high heat. Throw in the *usuage* and ¼ teaspoon salt. Toss quickly over high heat; pop a piece in your mouth to make sure the surface has crisped a little but has not toughened. Transfer to a small to medium-sized bowl.

Wipe the pan again and heat 1 tablespoon oil over high heat. Add the salted eggs and cook quickly, while continually scraping the bottom of the pan to incorporate the cooked egg layer into the raw egg mixture on the surface. Remove the cooked eggs to another medium-sized bowl while still slightly runny.

Dump the cooked brown rice into a large bowl. Heat the remaining 2 tablespoons oil in a large, heavy pot over high heat. Add the rice and sauté for several minutes, stirring constantly with a flat wooden spoon, turning the bottom layer up over the top layer to ensure even cooking. When all of the rice has been heated up, stir in the soy sauce. Sauté for a few minutes more to evenly distribute the soy sauce, then stir in the cooked vegetables and *usuage* (if using). Once mixed in, turn off the heat and add the cooked egg, cutting it up with the flat edge of the spoon as you distribute it into the fried rice.

Scoop a few large spoonfuls onto a plate and add a few dollops of whipped natto. Spoon a little mayonnaise on top of the natto and sprinkle with scallion. If additional salty flavor is needed at the table, opt for fine sea salt over soy sauce.

Serve with a leafy green salad dressed with Miso Vinaigrette (page 301).

My mother-in-law made *sekihan* every farm holiday (when she wasn't making country sushi rolls). She would pack it in lacquer boxes, lay some leaves from our nandina berry shrub (pictured on the cover), and include a small paper-wrapped packet of roasted sea salt and sesame seeds. She would bike over (even then, a little wobbly) and deliver these boxes to us at our former house a few blocks away (now the site of my little school, Sunny-Side Up!). In those days I was less accustomed to having food show up on my doorstep, but always welcomed those lacquer boxes of *sekihan*. I liked the sharp taste of salt on my tongue and the way the beans rolled against the pleasantly sticky rice. I also liked that (in my mind) it went with any food and that it kept for a day or so. Sometimes I felt boxed in a corner if presented with perishable extra food when I already had a tableful. I've progressed from that brash young farmwife who chaffed at country customs, and have learned to receive graciously. While writing this book, I realized that my mother-in-law had not made *sekihan* in a few years—maybe not even since she began eating dinner at our house every night (after my father-in-law died). Like so many customs, the making of *sekihan* almost slipped away unnoticed, but now it is Tadaaki's aunt Katchan or I who make the *sekihan* and pack it in the lacquer boxes. And someday it will be our sons.

red bean rice MAKES ABOUT 7 CUPS (1750 CC)
SEKIHAN

½ cup (125 cc) azuki beans

3¾ cups (900 cc) glutinous rice
  (*mochi gome*)

2 tablespoons fine sea salt

4 tablespoons unhulled
  sesame seeds

Starting the day before, soak the azuki for about an hour or so. Drain, add cold water to cover about 2 inches (5 cm) above the beans, and bring to a simmer over medium-high heat. Reduce the heat to low and continue simmering until cooked halfway. Drain the beans and reserve the pink simmering liquid. Once the beans have cooled, chill them in the fridge to use the following day but be sure to take them out a couple of hours before cooking so they can return to room temperature.

Wash the glutinous rice until the water runs clear and soak overnight in a medium-sized bowl with the cooled bean simmering liquid. This soak is essential because the bean liquid imparts a lovely pink hue to the rice.

Fill a wide, deep, slope-sided pan or wok half full with water and bring to a boil over high heat.

Drain the *mochi gome* and mix it with the half-cooked beans in a medium-sized bowl until the beans are well distributed into the rice. Line a steamer basket with a thin muslin cloth and dump in the rice and beans. Poke a 2-inch (5-cm) hole in the center of the rice with your finger to give the rice space to expand. Fold the edges of the cloth in loosely (leaving a small air vent in the center to allow steam to escape) and cover. Set the steamer basket above but not touching the boiling water.

Steam over high heat for about 15 to 20 minutes, until there is a strong blast of visible steam rising from the rice (signaling that, not just the steaming water, but the rice itself has taken on intense heat). Uncover the steamer and open the muslin cloth. Sprinkle a little bit of water on the surface of the rice and beans (*uchi mizu*), rewrap (leaving a vent hole), and re-cover. Do this two or more times. It will take from 30 to 40 minutes for the rice to steam. As the rice steams, the hole you poked will swell and almost disappear. Check the doneness by inserting a chopstick into the rice. If you feel resistance or roughness, the rice is not yet done; if the chopstick slides in nicely, the rice is done. Of course, this is subjective. Some people like a bit of bite to their grains, and some people prefer them quite soft. Use your best judgment by tasting it.

While the *sekihan* is cooking, roast the sea salt over low heat in a small pan to remove any lingering dampness. Scrape into a small bowl. Toast the sesame seeds over medium-high heat, shaking the pan, until they pop. Add to the salt in the bowl and combine with a small spoon.

When the rice and beans are finished cooking, dump them into a large, shallow wooden tub (*handai*, page 16) or the back of a wide wooden cutting board. Cut, spread, and fluff with a rice paddle to cool.

Pack in lacquer boxes and, if you have them, set a small sprig of leaves snipped from a nandina shrub on top of the rice as a natural preservative. (Katchan also dusts a minute amount of sugar over the *sekihan* to help keep it soft.) Serve sprinkled with toasted sesame seeds and roasted salt. Keeps at room temperature for a couple of days, depending on the weather.

Calling these rice "balls" is a bit misleading, since *onigiri* are usually triangular in shape. Although *onigiri* are now sold alongside sandwiches in the local convenience shops, in years past, they were *the* easy, well-balanced meal. There are any number of fillings that can be used, ranging from fish to pickles to preserves. (Convenience store onigiri wrappings are cleverly designed; the nori stays crisp until unwrapped, and the unwrapping sequence has a fascinating choreography.) Though if you don't mind taking about thirty seconds to pat an *onigiri* together and another to wrap up a piece of nori separately, you can make your own and avoid the convenience store ones (that, despite the ingenious wrapping, inevitably contain MSG and preservatives).

salty salmon rice balls MAKES 8 TO 10
SHAKE ONIGIRI

4 small salmon filets, weighing
  2½ ounces (70 g) each

2 teaspoons fine sea salt,
  plus extra for the rice balls

4 to 5 sheets nori, cut in half

4 cups (1000 cc) Plain Rice (page 143)

Sprinkle the salmon on both sides with about ½ teaspoon salt from about 1 foot (30 cm) above the fish. Seal tightly in a zippered plastic bag, roll, and refrigerate for at least half a day or overnight. (The longer it cures, the saltier the salmon becomes. This is purely a matter of taste, but typically, the salmon is quite salty.)

Once the salmon is sufficiently salted, cook it under the broiler on a rack set over a pan in the second shelf slot from the top of the oven. Broil for 10 minutes, skin side up, and 5 minutes, skin side down. Remove from the broiler and peel off the skin. Check for any bones and remove those as well. If the idea of adding some crispy skin to the salmon meat sounds good to you, broil the skin for 4 minutes in the top rack of your oven, until it has brown splotches and the skin fat is sizzling.

Crumble the salmon meat into a medium-sized bowl, finely chop the extra broiled salmon skin if you are using it, and fold into the salmon.

Set out four small rice bowls at your workplace, along with a small bowl of water (for your fingers) and a small saucer of salt. Lay your nori out on the workplace or a board, shiny side down. Line each rice bowl with plastic wrap, dip your finger into the water and smooth it around the plastic (to help the salt adhere), then sprinkle in a little salt. Scoop out a scant cup of hot, aerated cooked rice (150 g) and plop it into one of the rice bowls. Do the same for the other three. Poke about a tablespoon or two (to taste) of salty salmon into the center of the rice and smooth the hot rice around the salmon by enclosing it with the plastic wrap. Shape the *onigiri* by cupping the rice ball in one hand and cupping your other hand on top to encircle. Squeeze together repeatedly to make a compact triangular ellipse. Unwrap from the plastic, and set each one in the middle of the top half of one of the nori strips. Fold the bottom half of the nori over the rice ball and tuck the free corners over the exposed rice. These are best eaten right away, steaming hot, but are also good at room temperature: In this case, just leave them in the plastic and wrap in the nori right before eating so the nori stays crisp.

OTHER FILLINGS: *Umeboshi* (pitted or not), *katsuobushi* mixed with soy sauce, and steamed cod eggs are all good substitutes for the salmon. My favorite, however (to which I am fairly addicted), is line-caught canned tuna smashed with pasteurized mayonnaise and a splash of rice vinegar to taste (finely chopped green onion is also nice but optional).

VARIATION: When Christopher was little, I started making him what I called "*onigiri dango*" for some reason (*dango* are usually round balls, but these were cigar-shaped). I cut the nori into 4 pieces, spread a little rice on the rough side, sprinkled it with salt, and rolled it up straight (not like a cone). This style is very easy for small children to eat and also readily portable if you pop them in a plastic container or wrap in plastic. Add a little filling, and they will be even better!

Years ago my friends and I often went to a yakitori restaurant on Friday nights and, after eating our fill of the various barbecued meats on a stick, we would order *yaki onigiri* (grilled rice balls) to finish off the night. Sitting at the counter, sometimes the smoke drifts your way, but you can also talk to the master and observe his cooking techniques. I was always mesmerized by how long it took the rice balls to become thoroughly crusty and how patient the master was with the process. He did not just grill the two flat sides of the *onigiri*; he also grilled each of the three narrow widths of the triangular form. Finally, he brushed the *onigiri* with soy sauce and cooked them just a tad more—I suggest using miso because it's a little easier to handle.

miso-grilled rice balls MAKES 8 TO 10
MISO YAKI ONIGIRI

4 cups (1000 cc) Plain Rice (page 143)

About 3 tablespoons organic miso

4 to 5 sheets nori, cut in half

Make the rice balls following the method for Salty Salmon Rice Balls (page 160), but omit the salmon and the salt.

Cook the *onigiri* on both sides over a low-ember charcoal fire or on a mesh rack set directly over the lowest flame of a gas stove. Rubber-tipped tongs are useful turning implements, but the real key to making great *yaki onigiri* is patience. Wait until each side has formed a thick crust before turning (turn too soon and you risk the whole thing falling apart).

Once the *onigiri* are well crisped, smear about ½ teaspoon miso on both sides (only on the crusty areas) and sear just a bit more to seal. Set the cooked *yaki onigiri* in the center top portion of a half-sheet of nori, fold the bottom portion up over the *onigiri*, tuck in the side flaps, and eat hot.

On the eve of my wedding I went with my two closest friends, Aino and Kinuyo, to a *fugu* (blowfish) restaurant to commemorate the last night before being married. I remember that night vividly for several reasons. Despite the high-ticket meal, I was nervous about not eating or drinking too much lest any excess pounds or fatigue show up on my wedding photos (or render my tight wedding kimono even more constricting than it already was). I had not planned on drinking alcohol but could not resist a few sips of sake in which broiled *fugu* fins had been warmed. The handling of *fugu* is strictly controlled in Japan, and the master of the restaurant was required to undergo rigorous training and certification before being allowed to serve the potentially lethal fish. The broiled fins released a trace amount of poison into the sake, just enough to titillate (and make our tongues pleasantly numb) as we flirted on the edge of danger. I also remember the gorgeous plate of sashimi that the master arranged in the shape of a chrysanthemum, but I will never forget the *ojiya* he served after we finished our pot of *fugu nabe*. He skimmed out the last lingering vegetable bits and fish bones, scooped in some cooked rice, and simmered the whole affair for several minutes. A small bowl of the rice simmered in savory *fugu* broth was all we needed before heading back out into that icy December night.

rice simmered in broth SERVES 4
OJIYA

1 cup (250 cc) leftover cooked Plain Rice (page 143)

3 cups (750 cc) strained stock left over from a *nabe* (one-pot dish) or homemade stock

2 tablespoons finely chopped green onion

1 tablespoon roughly crumbled nori

Soy sauce or sea salt

Add the rice to the hot stock and simmer over medium heat, stirring occasionally until the savory gruel is creamy (the amounts are flexible—"about" is good enough). It will take 15 minutes or so, depending on the amount of rice and stock and the level of the heat.

Serve in small bowls with a sprinkling of chopped green onion and nori. Season with soy sauce or salt to taste. Eat with a spoon.

RATIO: rice : water—1 : 3

VARIATION: The one time I ever used powdered chicken stock is when I made *ojiya* for the boys when they were sick (with a raw egg stirred into the hot rice after taking the pot off the heat). My supply of powdered stock dwindled, however, and I never replaced it. So when Matthew came down with a cold and requested *ojiya*, I discovered that I could make a beautifully spare, soothing *ojiya* by simmering a small amount of cooked rice and water (1 : 3) with a heaping tablespoon of shaved *katsuobushi* in a small pan over medium-low heat, stirring. Once the rice was creamy, I dropped in a pitted *umeboshi*, torn into pieces, and served it with a sprinkling of snipped nori threads and a few drops of soy sauce. Matthew ate that *ojiya* for breakfast, lunch, and dinner over the course of three days. I guess it was good.

When Kanchan cooked the first soba dinner at Chez Panisse, he served mushroom rice made from local hedgehog mushrooms and Tadaaki's rice (brought from Japan). The cooks fashioned the cooked mushroom rice into torpedo-shaped rice balls and served them at room temperature with seared, shrub-raised beef (page 270). There are so many beautiful mushrooms, unique to each locale, that I would just use what grows near you rather than trying to force the recipe by using imported Japanese mushrooms.

mushroom rice SERVES 4 TO 6
KINOKO NO TAKIKOMI GOHAN

2 cups (500 cc) Japanese-style short-grain rice

1 tablespoon sake

2 tablespoons soy sauce

1 cup (250 cc) local, flavorful mushrooms, roughly chopped

2 tablespoons roughly crumbled nori

A few sprigs fresh *sansho* leaves, picked off the stem (optional)

Wash the rice as described in the method for Plain Rice (page 143) and drain. Add 2 cups (500 cc) cold water, and let sit for 30 minutes. Before cooking, remove 3 tablespoons of the soaking liquid and replace with the sake and soy sauce. Stir in the mushrooms to distribute evenly. Cook according to the directions for Plain Rice (page 143).

When done, let rest 5 minutes, aerate with chopsticks, and serve in small rice bowls sprinkled with the crumbled nori and a few *sansho* leaves, if using. Alternatively, form into triangular rice balls (*onigiri*, page 160), cover with plastic wrap, and eat later (wrapped in nori). Avoid refrigeration.

VARIATIONS: Depending on the mushrooms (such as large ones like shiitake), you could slice them into ¼-inch (6-mm) pieces instead of chopping them. In this case, however, I would cut the stems off and chop those separately rather than leaving them intact (shiitake stems are tasty but woody, so I always remove them from the caps).

RICE CROPPING

Cropping rice by machine is faster but less viscerally satisfying as grasping a handful of vibrant stalks top-heavy with plump rice grains, and stroking a sickle gently but firmly across the base of the clump in a fluid upsweeping motion. *Inekari*, literally, "rice cutting," has become a sort of cult cool thing for city people to do. It's a way to get in touch with the land through the heart and soul of Japan: rice. With the reconfiguration of Japan's rice fields in the eighties, most fields are cropped and sown by machine. By hand means you need a lot of hands, and these days the cooperative neighborhood spirit is petering out along with the small family farms. Inspired by a second year of hand-planting veterans who wanted to return to help crop what they had sown, Tadaaki threw caution to the wind and didn't reserve the rice-cropping machine a few years ago.

The whole affair ended up spread out over two days, involving lunch and dinner for the cropping crews, then breakfast for the late night revelers who slept over. I was exhausted more from the cooking than the cropping I missed. My mother-in-law thought we should buy rice balls (*onigiri*) from the local convenience store for lunch. She didn't see the irony. Instead, I served rice with local tofu, our late cherry tomatoes, and hard-boiled eggs from our farm with a dollop of homemade mayonnaise.

The first crew arrived from Tokyo at lunchtime on Saturday and got the whole field cut by dusk. The cutting process is hard on the back, but there is immediate gratification since the work goes fast and you can quickly see the results of your labor. The next step, tying the stalks, was slow going and didn't get finished even with fifteen people working from morning to night the next day. The workers all went back to their lives, but Tadaaki and Christopher returned to the field the following week to complete the job. Andrew and Matthew, newly in school, somehow escaped the bulk of the cropping and were noticeably absent. Christopher, on the other hand, stood in for Tadaaki and instructed the neophytes (including me) on all aspects of rice cropping. On Sunday, we had mainly local people who knew what they were doing, as well as some mothers and kids from the school. The mothers worked diligently, while the "wild ones" ran around the field chasing frogs. A few of the more enterprising kids actually got into ferrying tied rice stalks to the drying poles, although most of them just ended up accidentally scattering the straw piles. Despite the craziness, kids should be there so they know the work that goes into their bowl of rice even if they aren't doing the work.

I only came for a short time. It felt wrong not to be part of the cropping, and I wanted to share in the bond of collective labor, but the cooking had to get done. Christopher made it look so easy. The first crew had cut small bunches of rice stalks and laid them down on the field in a crosshatched V formation the day before. The second crew was using last year's straw (minus the rice) to tie the top of the rice stalks so they could be draped over a couple of horizontal 40-meter-long iron poles set up as drying racks. The straw kept breaking, and frustrated, I figured out that if I pulled some straw to the left and some to the right I could elongate my makeshift tie. This little trick showed me how working with imperfect natural tools fostered problem solving. And I felt the satisfaction of having made that discovery.

Why grow rice if it's so much trouble? Good question. In recent years before he died, Tadaaki's father had wanted to stop. But for Tadaaki, growing the family's rice is elemental to his existence. If he didn't grow our rice, it would be like giving up on life. Money doesn't matter as long as we have our own rice. That is what gives meaning to his life as a farmer. Traditionally, the main farm household (*honke*) provided rice and vegetables for extended family members who had moved to the city. But now there are less and less farmers and more and more people in cities. Most Japanese still feel in their bones that Japan should be sustainable, yet they continue to buy foreign fruits and vegetables at the supermarket. Probably because they're there.

6

vegetables

Japanese farm food originates from the vegetables growing in a farm family's fields. Homegrown rice or homemade udon noodles made from homegrown flour were the meal—the food that sticks to your ribs. Vegetables provided the bright note of variety to the table, often the same few vegetables prepared in different ways. In my husband's childhood, his family basically only ate what they grew, though they sometimes could have air-dried fish (sent to them from an aunt living at the seaside) or the occasional egg from the chickens they kept (most of the eggs were sold to supplement the household income). It is important to understand how truly simple Japanese vegetable preparation methods can be, so I have created a chart for Vegetables by Method (page 368) where you can easily see at a glance all the different ways you might be able to make broccoli, daikon, or whatever vegetable you happen to have. I encourage you to go out to your local farmers' market and buy with your eyes and mouth rather than rely on an arbitrary menu culled from a cookbook. Look at the vegetables, choose ones that scream "buy me," and then go home and decide what to cook.

Japanese country cooking involves a finite number of preparation methods, which can be applied to any number of vegetables, but I have included a couple of examples of each main preparation method (blanched with soy sauce or dashi dressing; blanched or salt massaged with sesame-miso dressing; blanched with tofu-miso dressing; salads; stir-fried with miso, soy sauce, salt or *shottsuru*; deep-fried; or simmered). The recipes in this chapter are organized as such, with many followed variations, so feel free to experiment. Study the Vegetable by Methods chart on page 368—you will clearly see the logic and versatility of using your own local vegetables. Each meal I make begins with the vegetables I have in the field or on my kitchen counter. I touch the vegetables to get a feel for how they should be prepared. Try it—you may surprise yourself.

WASHING AND STORING VEGETABLES

Every farmer knows that many vegetables keep longer if stored with dirt still clinging to their roots. Once washed, vegetables begin to degrade from the water seeping into their cell walls.

Whenever possible, I always avoid washing vegetables. Perhaps this is easier for me because often the vegetables come from our fields. Lettuces can be tricky, but if they are cut just above the soil line, unwanted dirt can be avoided. Peel off the outer layer of green onions and snap off the root end, leaving all the dirt and strawlike strands in the field. Of course all root vegetables need to be washed (or peeled) eventually, but whenever possible, store potatoes, onions, and garlic in a dark, cool place in a cardboard box or paper bag.

Carrots, radishes, turnips, and daikon need to have their tops lopped off before storing (otherwise the leaves suck some vital energy from the roots, quickly rendering them droopy). Since it is probably impractical to have bags of dirt-encrusted vegetables in the refrigerator and you are most likely going to use the vegetables fairly soon, it makes sense to wash and dry these root vegetables that are eaten fresh (as opposed to those stored like potatoes or onions) before packing them in large resealable plastic bags. Just be sure to towel them dry.

Lettuce should be cut off of its root, otherwise the leaves will wilt. Most

Japanese preparations require boiling the greens with the root end intact to keep the leaves and stems aligned, so keep that in mind when storing greens destined to be used for Japanese recipes.

Greens most likely will be steam-sautéed or boiled, so ultimately, introducing a bit of water right before cooking won't affect the outcome of your dish. However, lettuce is generally dressed with an oil-based vinaigrette of some kind, and you know what they say about oil and water. Any water particles will hinder the oil from grabbing onto the lettuce. Certainly you can wash, spin, and pat dry, but perhaps an easier method would be to take off the outer leaves, cut off the stem end, and be done with it (wipe off any residual dirt with a damp kitchen towel).

If you really think about it, other than dirt, what can you possibly wash off with a cold-water bath? Not much.

Komatsuna is the most popular and versatile bitter green that we have in Japan. It also is available almost year-round. It has mildly bitter wide green leaves and juicy stems that turn translucent when boiled or steam-sautéed. *Komatsuna* does not wilt in the way that spinach does, so it retains a bit of that leaf crunch and shines with simple treatments such as a sprinkling of shaved *katsuobushi* and drizzled with soy sauce or soy sauce–flavored dashi. Mustard or turnip greens also work well here. I particularly like the fresh balance of dashi with bitter greens. When using dashi, you are going to be more generous with the drizzle than with soy sauce, so the greens are beautifully cloaked in the stock.

bitter greens with dashi SERVES 6
KOMATSUNA NO OHITASHI

2 small bunches (about 1⅓ pounds/600 g) bitter greens (*komatsuna*, turnip, mustard)

⅓ cup (75 cc) Dashi (page 307)

2 tablespoons soy sauce

2 tablespoons freshly shaved *katsuobushi* or 3 tablespoons *hanakatsuo* (page 6)

Bring a large pot of hot water to a boil and place a large bowl of cold water in the kitchen sink. Hold the bunches of greens by their tops and lower the stems into the boiling water. Count to ten or twenty (depending on the thickness of the stems), then drop the greens into the pot and cook an additional 1 to 3 minutes. Scoop out the greens with a strainer and dump them immediately into the cold water. Turn on the tap and plunge your hands into the water, lifting the greens up directly into the stream of cold running tap water to cool them. Pull out a few connected strands and squeeze down the length of the greens to express the excess water. Lay the greens on a cutting board, cut off the end tips, and slice into 2-inch (5-cm) lengths.

Squeeze the greens one more time and arrange the cut clumps attractively on a medium-sized saucer with the cut sides facing up. Season the dashi with the soy sauce, pour over the greens, and sprinkle with the shaved *katsuobushi* right before serving.

VARIATION: Also nice with some slivered citrus peel (such as yuzu or Meyer lemon), though in this case, I would cut back (or omit) the *katsuobushi*.

Like a refrigerator in a well-used kitchen that yields odds and ends to be incorporated into the next meal, so does a field reproduce seeds from past seasons. Volunteers sprout up in the late summer or early fall, little bonuses to bridge the gap through less-prolific seasons. I love that the field hands us a present so selflessly because the field is our partner. And we may not tend her perfectly, but she is forgiving if treated gently, respectfully, and with love. These turnip greens are native to our fields and are really a mix of reseeding turnip, mustard, and *komatsuna*. Here we just splash them with soy sauce rather than making the traditional soy sauce-flavored dashi for *ohitashi* (boiled and squeezed greens).

turnip greens with soy sauce SERVES 6
KABUNOHA NO OHITASHI

1 large bunch (about 1 pound/450 g) turnip greens (or mustard, bok choy, *komatsuna*)

2 tablespoons freshly shaved *katsuobushi* or 3 tablespoons *hanakatsuo* (page 6)

2 tablespoons soy sauce

Bring a large pot of hot water to a boil and place a large bowl of cold water in the kitchen sink.

Line up the turnip greens so the stems are all at the same end. Grasp the whole bunch of turnip greens and lower the stem ends into the boiling water for a count of 10. Drop the greens into the water and boil for about 1 or 2 more minutes. Scoop the greens out of the water with a strainer and plunge the strainer of turnip greens in the bowl of cold water to cool. Add cold water if the water loses its chill.

Pull the turnip greens out of the water by the root ends, squeeze, cut into 2-inch (5-cm) lengths, and stack attractively in a couple of small bowls for the table. Serve with the shaved *katsuobushi* and a generous dose of soy sauce right before eating.

Kyuri momi along with *abura miso* are, hands down, the quintessential summer dishes of any farm family. My husband calls them his soul food. In the middle of summer we can't even give away the slender cucumbers and eggplants. Everyone grows them, so summer means eating eggplant and cucumbers in a myriad of ways. They're said in the same breath: *nasu/kyuri*.

Before my mother-in-law lived under the same roof, I would stop her at our door when she tried to drop off big bags of each. Somehow I thought of the field as my own private vegetable shop. I could saunter over and pluck a bit of this or that for any meal. I didn't know that you have to pick the whole row every two days, otherwise the plants stop producing. We wait all year long to eat cucumbers and eggplant and revel in them when we have them in abundance, eating them at every meal.

salt-massaged cucumber with miso and sesame SERVES 6
KYURI MOMI

1¾ pounds (800 g) Japanese cucumbers (7 or 8 small)

½ tablespoon fine sea salt

4 tablespoons unhulled sesame seeds

3 tablespoons brown rice miso

2 tablespoons rice vinegar

6 shiso leaves

Slice the cucumbers into paper-thin rounds and toss with the salt in a medium-sized bowl. Let sit 10 minutes.

Toast the sesame seeds over medium-high heat in a dry frying pan until they are fragrant and start to pop. Grind the sesame seeds with a *suribachi* (Japanese grinding bowl) or mortar until most of the seeds have broken down and are almost pastelike. Add the miso and rice vinegar and blend until creamy.

Squeeze the cucumbers by handfuls to express the water, then add to the sesame-miso mixture.

Stack the shiso leaves, roll into a cigar shape, and slice into fine tendrils; toss gently but well with the cucumbers.

RATIO: sesame:miso:vinegar—4:3:2

VARIATIONS: If you can find them, use young *sansho* leaves sliced from the stem instead of shiso. Or add finely slivered ginger to the cucumbers or ginger juice (grate ginger and squeeze out the juice in your fist) to the dressing.

You may not think that cauliflower is a particularly Japanese vegetable and you would almost be right. Tadaaki of course grows it because he has a foreign wife and he knows I like it. But these days, many of our organic grower friends are planting and selling cauliflower successfully. Broccoli has been a mainstream Japanese vegetable for many years now, so it makes sense that cauliflower would be easily accepted once the foreignness of it wore off. Cauliflower makes a tasty tempura, but I find the sesame-miso combination in this dish particularly well suited to cauliflower, almost more so than the classic version with spinach.

cauliflower
with miso and sesame SERVES 6
KARIFURAWA NO GOMA-AE

1 large head cauliflower
   (about 1½ pounds/700 g)

4 tablespoons unhulled
   sesame seeds

3 tablespoons brown rice miso

2 tablespoons rice vinegar

¼ teaspoon fine sea salt

Bring a large pot of hot water to a boil and place a medium-sized bowl of cold water in the kitchen sink. Slice off the cauliflower head from the stem and pare small florets off of the perimeter of the stem. Cut any tender stem pieces into halves or quarters, about the same size as the florets. Slide the cauliflower into the boiling water and cook for 3 minutes. Lift the florets out with a strainer and dump them immediately into the cold water. Turn on the tap, place the strainer on top of the cauliflower so the pieces do not float out of the bowl, and run cold water directly on top to cool. Scoop the cauliflower out of the water with the strainer and pour the bowl water out into the sink. Set the strainer back on top of the bowl to drain.

Toast the sesame seeds over medium-high heat in a dry frying pan until they are fragrant and starting to pop. Grind the sesame seeds with a *suribachi* (Japanese grinding bowl) or mortar until most of the seeds have broken down and are almost pastelike. Add the miso, rice vinegar, and salt and blend until creamy.

Empty the drained cauliflower florets into the grinding bowl and fold gently to distribute the sesame-miso paste. Scrape down the sides and serve as is in the *suribachi*.

RATIO: sesame : miso : vinegar—4 : 3 : 2

VARIATIONS: A few slivers of yuzu or Meyer lemon peel will add a bit of unexpected sparkle to the rich sesame paste.

top: broccoli with tofu and yuzu,
page 182

• 177 • VEGETABLES

One night, Tadaaki packaged up some eggplants (peeled in alternating strips) in plastic wrap and popped them in the microwave for 2 minutes before slicing them and tossing with ground sesame seeds, miso, and vinegar. He added a secret note: fresh *yuba* (tofu skin) from Yamaki, our local tofu maker. You can omit the *yuba*, but perhaps a little squeezed tofu might be nice. I love the texture of steamed eggplant, slippery and juicy, and of course not oily. Plastic wrap keeps the eggplant juices from running off, thus intensifying the flavor of the dish. If you have one, use a bamboo steamer to soften the eggplants.

steamed eggplant
with miso and sesame SERVES 6
NASU NO GOMA-AE

1¾ pounds (800 g) Japanese eggplants (7 or 8 small)

4 tablespoons unhulled sesame seeds

3 tablespoons brown rice miso

2 tablespoons rice vinegar

A 2½-ounce (70-g) package *yuba* (optional)

Fill a deep frying pan or wok with water and bring to a simmer over high heat. The pan should be large enough to be able to set a steamer over but not in the simmering water.

Slice off the eggplant peel at 1-inch (2.5-cm) intervals. Enclose each eggplant tightly in plastic wrap and place in the steamer. Cook for 10 minutes, or until the flesh is soft when gently squeezed. Remove the steamer from the heat and cool the eggplants in the plastic wrap.

While the eggplants are cooling, toast the sesame seeds over medium-high heat in a dry frying pan until they are fragrant and starting to pop. Grind the sesame seeds with a *suribachi* (Japanese grinding bowl) or mortar until most of the seeds have broken down and are almost pastelike. Add the miso and rice vinegar and blend. Mash in the *yuba*, if using, or squeezed tofu described in Broccoli with Tofu and Yuzu (page 182).

Unwrap the eggplants and slice in half vertically. Lay, cut side down, on a cutting board and slice lengthwise again into about 4 or 5 long pieces (about ⅜ inch or 1 cm thick). Toss the eggplant pieces with the sesame-miso in the grinding bowl with gentle fingers. Be sure to distribute the *goma-ae* dressing well, but try not to smash or overwork the eggplant pieces.

RATIO: sesame : miso : vinegar—4 : 3 : 2

The traditional version of this dish uses sesame (*horenso no goma-ae*) and is a wildly popular dish in *izakaya* drinkeries as well as on the farm. I have sampled *horenso no goma-ae* in the United States but did not like those versions much. The mistakes most commonly made (in my mind) were not toasting or grinding the sesame seeds enough and oversweetening. Winter is spinach season here, and when in season, spinach is naturally sweet so it needs no added sugar. The juxtaposition of sweet greens against the salty, vinegary walnut-enriched dressing is perfectly balanced and perfectly delicious.

spinach with walnuts and miso SERVES 6
HORENSO NO KURUMI-AE

3 small bunches spinach (about 1½ pounds/675 g), if possible with pink bottoms intact

5 heaping tablespoons whole walnuts (about 1¾ ounces/50 g)

2 tablespoons brown rice miso

1½ tablespoons rice vinegar

Bring a large pot of hot water to a boil and place a large bowl of cold water in the kitchen sink. Grasp the spinach in two hands near the tops and lower the thick stems (and pink bottoms) into the boiling water. Count to ten, then drop the spinach into the pot and cook an additional minute. Scoop out the spinach with a strainer and dump immediately into the cold water. Turn on the tap and plunge your hands into the water, lifting the spinach up directly into the stream of cold running tap water to cool them. Lay the spinach bunches out on a cutting board, cut off the bottoms, and reserve for a different salad of your choice. Slice the stems and leaves into 2-inch (5-cm) lengths. Squeeze the spinach by handfuls to remove as much water as possible.

Grind 2 tablespoons of the walnuts with a *suribachi* (Japanese grinding bowl) or mortar just until the nuts have been smashed and resemble finely chopped nuts. Scrape into a small bowl and reserve. Drop the remaining 3 tablespoons walnuts into the grinding bowl and smash well until the oil has exuded from the walnuts and a rough paste has formed. Add the miso and rice vinegar to the mortar and blend until creamy.

Squeeze the spinach one more time for good measure and gently fold into the dressing by scooping from the bottom of the *suribachi* to dislodge the dressing and scissoring the greens with your fingers to distribute the dressing evenly. Sprinkle in the reserved crushed walnuts, toss once or twice, and serve in the *suribachi* or an attractive pottery bowl.

RATIO: walnuts : miso : vinegar—10 : 4 : 3 (about)

Shira-ae depends on great tofu, so find the best-flavored one available. In the U.S., I've often found that the softer tofus have a creamier texture reminiscent of Japanese tofu and no unpleasant soy aftertaste. *Shira-ae* marries particularly well with bitter-flavored vegetables; the addition of sliced dried persimmons or even slices of fresh, firm Japanese persimmons introduces a bit of sweetness. Come early spring, our fields are full of flowering greens such as mustard, turnip, bok choy, and *komatsuna*. The tops have formed green clusters of small buds before they burst into flower. The window is short (maybe two or three weeks, depending on the weather), so I go to the field often and cut as many tops as I can pile in my basket for dinner (or Sunny-Side Up! lunch). You can find these flowering tops in Asian farmers' markets, but a thin-stemmed rapini also substitutes nicely.

mustard blossoms with smashed tofu SERVES 6

NANOHANA SHIRA-AE

1 (10.5-ounce/300-g) piece Japanese-style "cotton" tofu

1 large bunch (about 1 pound/450 g) flowering mustard tops (or other bitter greens)

2 tablespoons unhulled sesame seeds

2 tablespoons brown rice or barley miso

2 tablespoons *warisu* (page 307) or rice vinegar

Place the tofu on a cutting board propped up on one end, angled into the kitchen sink for draining. Lay another chopping board or plate on top of the tofu to press out the excess water for 1 hour.

Bring a large pot of hot water to a boil and place a large bowl of cold water in the kitchen sink. Grasp the flowering greens in two hands near the tops and lower the thick stems into the boiling water. Count to ten, then drop the greens into the pot and cook an additional 1 to 3 minutes. Scoop out the greens with a strainer and dump them immediately into the cold water. Turn on the tap and plunge your hands into the water, lifting the greens up directly into the stream of cold running tap water to cool them. Lay the greens on a cutting board and slice into 2-inch (5-cm) lengths. Squeeze the greens by handfuls to express the excess water.

Toast the sesame seeds over medium-high heat in a dry frying pan until they are fragrant and just start to pop. Grind the sesame seeds in a *suribachi* (Japanese grinding bowl) or mortar until most of the seeds have broken down. Add the miso and *warisu* to the mortar and blend. Squeeze the handfuls of tofu to express any lingering moisture and add to the dressing. Continue grinding to emulsify all the ingredients until creamy. Gently fold in the cooked and squeezed mustard tops. Serve in an attractive pottery bowl.

RATIO: sesame : miso : *warisu*—1 : 1 : 1

VARIATIONS: Also nice with peppery cresslike greens in place of mustard or some slivered citrus peel (such as yuzu or Meyer lemon) to add a bright note to the tofu. A couple of dried persimmons (*hoshigaki*) or several unsulfured dried apricots sliced into small strips complement any bitter greens and will add a slightly sweet note to the dish.

Tofu paired with ground seeds and earthy, salty miso make an absolutely phenomenal combination. Creamy and nutty, with a slight vinegar edge, *shira-ae* is the consummate foil for bitter greens but also tasty on crucifers like broccoli or cauliflower. Best the first day and fine the next.

broccoli with tofu and yuzu SERVES 6
BUROKKORI NO SHIRA-AE

1 (10.5-ounce/300-g) piece Japanese-style "cotton" tofu

3 medium-sized heads broccoli (about 2 pounds/900 g)

2 tablespoons unhulled sesame seeds

2 tablespoons brown rice or barley miso

2 tablespoons rice vinegar

¼ teaspoon sea salt

Zest of 1 small yuzu or ½ Meyer lemon, slivered

Place the tofu on a cutting board propped up on one end, angled into the kitchen sink for draining. Lay another chopping board or plate on top of the tofu to press out excess water for 1 hour.

Bring a large pot of hot water to a boil and place a medium-sized bowl of cold water in the kitchen sink. Slice off the thick stems of broccoli and pare around the perimeter of the stem to free the little florets. Cut the tender stem into half or quarters so the pieces will cook at the same pace as the florets. Drop the broccoli into the boiling water and cook for 3 minutes. Scoop out the broccoli florets with a strainer and immediately plunge them into the cold water. Turn on the tap and press the strainer gently on top of the broccoli so it will not flow out of the bowl. Run additional cold water to cool. Lift the broccoli out of the bowl with the strainer and dump the water from the bowl into the sink. Set the strainer back on top of the bowl to drain.

Toast the sesame seeds over medium-high heat in a dry frying pan until they are fragrant and just start to pop. Grind the sesame seeds in a *suribachi* (Japanese grinding bowl) or mortar until most of the seeds have broken down. Add the miso and vinegar to the mortar and blend. Squeeze handfuls of tofu to express any lingering moisture and add to the dressing with the salt. Continue grinding to emulsify all the ingredients until creamy. Gently fold in the cooked broccoli florets with most of the yuzu slivers. Serve in an attractive pottery bowl strewed with the remaining yuzu peel.

RATIO: sesame : miso : vinegar—1:1:1

VARIATIONS: Substitute cauliflower or green beans for the broccoli.

THE JAPANESE FARMER

Our friends Junko and Toshiharu Suka are real farmers. Like many farm couples, they don't get out much to socialize because they are too busy running the farm. That's a bit how our life goes, though I jump on the plane every once in a while to play at being a social animal in the outside world.

Every Christmas Day, however, the Suka family comes to dinner. They make it late—but usually catch the tail end of our traditional gougères and champagne starters. And by dessert, Suka-san is usually falling asleep at the table. Most farmers get up at 5 a.m. to start the day, so 9 or 10 o'clock is pushing the envelope (especially after a few glasses of merlot).

One Christmas a few years ago, I asked Suka-san, a "natural farmer," how he could keep on farming year in year out (while not making pots of money). "When people love to eat my vegetables, it makes me happy and gives me energy to keep on growing things" was his response. It was at that moment I realized the farmer puts the same love into the field that we cooks put into our food. It's that alpha factor, along with great ingredients, or heirloom seeds and rich, loamy earth, that will push the food to the extraordinary.

Suka-san's father started natural farming (*shizen noho*) vegetables almost fifty years ago—way before anyone else in the Kanto (Greater Tokyo) region. In Kansai (Kyoto-Osaka-Kobe), however, Masanobu Fukuoka, of *The One-Straw Revolution* fame, was practicing his own version of natural farming. (My husband, Tadaaki, often says that Suka-san's father is the Masanobu Fukuoka of Kanto.) Put simply, natural farming is a farming practice that goes further than the no chemical pesticides or fertilizers of organic farming. Natural farming never uses animal or bird fertilizers on the fields. The followers of this method of farming believe the animal or bird fertilizers upset the natural nitrogen balance of the field and also that they leach into the taste of the vegetables.

I'm not genetically hardwired for Japanese farm life, but my husband is. Day in and day out, he jumps out of bed before 6 a.m. and doesn't finish work until after 7 p.m. And he whistles when he cooks dinner, even after a thirteen-hour workday. Japanese farmers have a strength of character and ability to work selflessly that way exceeds what I learned growing up in the suburbs of San Francisco. And maybe that is what draws young Japanese people to the farm, or Westerners to Japan—this desire for a deeper sense of what it means to be unfettered by all the trappings and complications of modern urban life. Maybe getting one's hands dirty and being part of mind-numbing work quiet the soul. Maybe that is what people need.

While I do thrive on the simplicity of our life, for me, farming will always be about playing a role, and one I'm not especially good at. I'll never be a real farmer because in the end, I don't have that requisite strength of character and in the end I'll slack off when I don't feel like doing the work. I'm selfish like that. Well, I'm a town girl. What else is there to say?

My sisters and I were in charge of the vinaigrette for our family salad. We never measured but always tasted. I continued following that approach well into my adult life, but now as I develop Japanese recipes, I have started to measure. And I derive great comfort from discovering the logic of ratios in all of these salad dressing variations. Ultimately it's up to you to figure out how much dressing to make and to hold yourself back from drenching the salad. I've been using an extremely bright organic rapeseed oil and recommend tracking some down. And buy the best soy sauce or rice wine vinegar you can.

heirloom red lettuce salad with soy sauce SERVES 6
SHOYU-FUMI MURASAKI RETASU SARADA

3 small heads heirloom red lettuce (such as oak leaf)

1 tablespoon soy sauce

1 tablespoon rice vinegar

2 tablespoons rapeseed oil

Tear off the outer discolored or saggy leaves of the lettuce and lop off the stem end with a sharp knife about 1 inch (2.5 cm) from the bottom (this helps remove unwanted dirt). If possible, don't wash the lettuce— just wipe any clinging dirt with a damp towel.

Cut the lettuce crosswise into 3-inch (7.5-cm) wide pieces (or leave whole if the leaves are beautifully perfect and not too long).

If the lettuce is gritty, fill a large basin or sink with cold water and drop in the sliced-up leaves. Gently swirl the lettuce in the water to dislodge any dirt. Let the dirt settle for a couple of minutes, then lift out a few handfuls of lettuce at a time and toss into a salad spinner (if you are using the kind with a center plunger, be sure to mound the leaves to the outer edges so they will not be smashed in the center). Spin several rotations, dump the accumulated water, and spin again. Turn onto a clean dish towel and continue spinning the rest of the lettuce. Distribute the leaves evenly on the towel, cover with another clean dish towel, and roll loosely. Refrigerate for up to 1 hour. If not using right away, slip the leaves into a large resealable plastic bag and carefully squeeze out the air (without smashing the lettuce) before returning to the fridge.

When ready to serve, remove the lettuce from the fridge and make the dressing. Whisk the soy sauce and vinegar together in a small bowl before drizzle-whisking in the rapeseed oil to emulsify. Take care to rewhisk the vinaigrette if you do not dress the salad immediately after making. Spoon enough well-emulsified dressing on the salad to film the leaves and gently toss with light hands. Save any extra dressing in a jar in the refrigerator. It keeps for several weeks.

RATIO: soy sauce : rice vinegar : rapeseed oil—1 : 1 : 2

VARIATION: Serve the salad on individual plates with two halves of Half-Boiled Eggs (page 45) alongside. Spoon a dollop of Japanese Mayonnaise (page 312) on the eggs and sprinkle with chopped chives.

When tomatoes first appeared on the shelves of the local vegetable shops, they were invariably underripe, to the point of being almost green. But Japanese liked them that way, astringent and crisp. As Japanese traveled abroad, however, they began to prefer a riper, sweeter tomato. Still today, tomatoes are sold perhaps less ripe than you would typically find in Western countries. But it makes sense if you think about it. I prefer a slightly underripe tomato for Japanese-style salads. Also, it is important not to toss the salad, and instead drizzle the dressing on top of the tomatoes. Spooning the dressing components on separately allows more control over the flavors. I also love tomato wedges (or cherry tomato halves) drizzled with miso dressing.

tomato wedges drizzled with soy sauce SERVES 6
TOMATO SARADA SHOYU-FUMI

4 to 6 medium-sized slightly underripe organic tomatoes

Organic rapeseed oil

Organic soy sauce

Organic rice vinegar

Several chives (or a couple of thin scallions), cut into fine rounds

10 shiso leaves, cut into threads

Right before serving your meal, core the tomatoes and slice into 6 thick wedges. Arrange 4 to 6 tomato wedges on individual plates (or in the corner of a larger dinner plate that you will use to serve the rest of your meal). Drizzle with a little oil, followed by soy sauce, and finish with a few drops of vinegar (this is a light dressing that just kisses the tomatoes and is not meant to drench them or overpower their innate tomato-ness). Sprinkle with the chopped chives and strew with the shiso threads. Serve immediately.

VARIATIONS: Substitute a firm, brightly flavored variety of cherry tomatoes and cut them in half before dressing. Also wonderful with Miso Vinaigrette (page 301) spooned over the tomatoes. In this case, you may want to be more generous with the dressing—I would maybe even use a couple of teaspoons (or more) of dressing for 4 tomato wedges or 8 small cherry tomatoes.

Japanese love carrots, but for the most part prefer them cooked. I am a salad maniac and think carrots go superbly with Japanese-style dressings. The citrus balances well with the sweet carrots, while the addition of a little heat from the *negi* and spicy-fresh taste from the *mitsuba* make an irresistible combination. This is an eye-catching salad that has a wonderful symmetry of flavors.

carrot and mitsuba salad with citrus SERVES 6

NINJIN SARADA KANKITSU-AE

3 cups (750 cc) julienned carrots

2 tablespoons julienned *negi* or scallions (white and light green parts)

¼ teaspoon fine sea salt

2 tablespoons mild citrus juice (yuzu, Seville orange, Meyer lemon)

2 tablespoons rapeseed oil

Handful of *mitsuba* leaves (substitute lovage, cilantro, or chervil)

Place the carrots and *negi* in a large bowl and sprinkle with salt. Gently toss. Measure the citrus juice into a small bowl and whisk in the oil. Pour over the carrots and onion and mix lightly to distribute the vinaigrette. Add the *mitsuba* leaves and toss once.

Serve on gorgeous small plates that show off the bright colors of the salad. Be sure to serve from the bottom, since the dressing quickly drips down, and prop up a few *mitsuba* leaves on the individual plates to add a bit of pop.

RATIO: citrus juice : rapeseed oil—1:1

VARIATIONS: Substitute julienned daikon or turnip with a small handful of chiffonaded bitter green tops instead of the green onion and *mitsuba*.

When our boys were small, the field was often off our radar, so Tadaaki sometimes missed planting lettuce seeds. Some years we didn't have lettuce. Around that time, Matthew was turning one year old, so I took the boys to France. It was in the Dordogne, at the Dubois farm, that I discovered winter salads such as cabbage, chicory, and savoy cabbage. Napa cabbage (*hakusai* in Japan) is the one winter green we always seemed to have because Tadaaki's father was diligent about growing it in those days. I'm particularly fond of this version with the citrus and toasted sesame. I wouldn't normally pair sesame and citrus, but somehow it works, though I'd use a mild citrus that can marry well with the sesame.

napa cabbage salad with sesame seeds SERVES 6
GOMA NO FURIKAKE HAKUSAI SARADA

Half a napa cabbage,
    sliced vertically through the head
    (about 1⅓ pounds/600 g)

½ tablespoon fine sea salt

2 tablespoons mild citrus juice
    (yuzu, Seville orange, Meyer
    lemon)

2 tablespoons rapeseed oil

1 tablespoon unhulled
    sesame seeds

Slice the cabbage crosswise into fine strands and toss lightly in a large bowl with the salt.

Measure the citrus juice into a small bowl and slowly whisk in the oil to emulsify. Pour over the cabbage, mix gently to distribute the dressing.

Toast the sesame seeds over medium-high heat in a dry frying pan until they are fragrant and start to pop. Toss into the salad and serve immediately.

RATIO: citrus juice : rapeseed oil : sesame seeds—2 : 2 : 1

I don't really use that much daikon for some reason, though I do love it raw in a salad or simmered in broth. The crunch of the raw is so compelling (yet the meltingly soft, but somehow juicy texture of simmered daikon is pretty alluring as well). The leaves add an essential pop to what can be a fairly bland root. I prefer the hotter varieties, called *karumi daikon*, but these may be difficult to find abroad. *Karumi daikon* is native to northern areas, so although Tadaaki does grow it here in western Saitama, it often loses some of its natural punch in our milder climate. Grated *karumi daikon* is unforgettable served with freshly pounded *mochi* and soy sauce. The gooey, hot *mochi* makes an ideal contrast with the spicy grated daikon.

daikon and daikon leaf salad SERVES 6
DAIKON TO DAIKON-BA SARADA

1 medium-small daikon,
  preferably a "hot" variety
  (about 1⅓ pounds/600 g)

1 tablespoon sea salt

2 small or 1 medium yuzu
  (substitute Meyer lemon)

2 tablespoons organic miso

2 tablespoons organic rice vinegar

4 tablespoons organic rapeseed oil

2 tablespoons slivered *negi*
  or scallions

Slice the daikon into manageable lengths. Cut those pieces in half vertically and slice lengthwise into fine slabs. Lay those slabs flat on the cutting board and slice into fine julienned strands about 1½ inches (4 cm) long. Put the julienned daikon into a medium-sized bowl as you go. Chop a large handful of the most tender leaves medium-fine and add to the julienned daikon. Sprinkle with the salt and massage in gently. Let sit for 10 minutes.

Pare off the yellow zest of the yuzu (or Meyer lemon) peel (avoiding the white pith) with a sharp knife. Stack roughly and slice into fine slivers. Muddle the miso with the vinegar and whisk in the oil until emulsified.

Squeeze the daikon and daikon leaves in handfuls and drop into a clean bowl. Toss with the yuzu peel and *negi*. Give the dressing a quick whisk and fold into the daikon right before serving.

RATIO: miso : rice vinegar : rapeseed oil—1:1:2

THE KITCHEN GARDEN

Tsugumi picks up the offending piece of green bean, pokes it out toward me, and declares, "I don't need the green one!"

Tsugumi is my six-year-old student at Sunny-Side Up!—the English immersion preschool/kindergarten I run in the Saitama prefecture countryside. I have made breaded pork cutlets (*katsu*) for lunch, and served alongside is a small pile of my husband's first-of-the-season green beans that we picked that morning. I boiled the beans for exactly two minutes and drizzled them with organic Japanese rapeseed oil and a sprinkling of salt. I know they are beyond delicious—they will knock her socks off.

"Just try one, please, Tadaaki grew them for you!"

Screwing up her face, Tsugumi pops a small segment in her mouth. Slowly she chews, then, her whole face alight with pleasure, bursts out, "They're yummy! They're so, so, sooooo yummy!" And she promptly goes back for more. In fact, she ends up going back eight times, each time receiving a little pile of those magnificent beans. Tsugumi was converted.

The cutlets are homemade, not bought prefried at the meat shop or supermarket. I start with best-quality, butcher-cut pork chops and roll them in homegrown wheat flour before dipping in a bowl of whisked up free-range eggs collected that morning from my husband's chicken coops. Oh, and I pat them in homemade panko (dried bread crumbs) and fry them in more of the bright-flavored organic rapeseed oil that I drizzled on the beans. That's the school lunch at SSU!

A lot of people think I'm crazy to cook for my students every day—especially since I use the best stuff around to make the lunches. But there is something magical about seeing the kids' faces light up and hearing their joyous cries of "Thank you for cooking! It's so yummy! I love you Nancy!" Who wouldn't want to cook for them and who wouldn't want to give these kids something wonderful to eat each and every day?

I realized it wasn't enough just to cook for them, so a few years ago, we started a kitchen garden. Now even the little ones have jumped into the fray. In the morning, when I call out, "Who wants to help cook?" I get about ten miniature assistants climbing up on the stools around the table anxious to help peel potatoes or smash organic canned tomatoes. And the two-year-olds are the most enthusiastic of the bunch—though I'm looking for a knife that can cut vegetables and not fingers. They still manage to cut themselves with the peelers sometimes, but I tell them, "Don't worry about it, it's just a little blood. I cut myself all the time!" And they keep peeling.

The kids are no less enthusiastic in the field. Once we cured them of their initial instinct to run, they got right into the planting. Of course everyone wanted to do it, but with a little bribery we managed to get them to wait their turn. Grubby little hands shot out, and each kid got a sprinkling of seeds. No surprise, the seeds were sown too densely, resulting in lots of overcrowding. We've been practicing with birdseed for the spring plantings. Also, some ruthless thinning will be helpful. The preschoolers (and some elementary kids) love to try anything and everything in the field. They smell the wild fennel and bite into it, exclaiming that it tastes like toothpaste. Arugula is "spicy" and the lettuce is "yummy." Trying new tastes in the field is always an adventure.

A lot of people (my husband included) thought I was even crazier to start a school garden. But you know, there is something so basic and so elemental about growing food. And this is something every child should learn. When you grow it, it just tastes better.

What Suka-san told me about getting the energy to keep on farming from people loving to eat his vegetables really stuck with me. It made me realize that farming is a lot like cooking. And that is what I'm trying to show the kids at Sunny-Side Up! through the garden. Love goes into the field as we grow our vegetables, and love goes into the food as we cook the lunch. The kids understand that very simple but essential idea. We don't need to teach this, they just get it through experiencing the seed-to-table process. And even if all the kids don't yet eat their vegetables—they want to—and will be able to soon. The ones who go for seconds are proud and tell me how many times they have gone back to get more. The others who clean their plates turn it toward me for inspection and a few words of praise, which I give gladly. "Good job!"

When you cook a lot, you end up with little odds and ends of vegetables or sauces. I love creating new dishes from the bits and pieces and also being able to incorporate those serendipitous little leftovers into a new menu. This salad is the result of one of those days. I was making lunch at the school and had only a few of each kind of vegetable. A bit of tofu left over from lunch the day before sparked the inspiration of strewing some diced tofu on top of the chopped salad before dressing. The cold, custard texture played off well with the miso vinaigrette and bright summer vegetables.

chopped summer salad with miso SERVES 6

MISO-AJI NATSU YASAI SARADA

1 medium red or orange tomato, cored

1 Japanese cucumber, unpeeled

4 small green peppers, cored and seeded

2½ ounces (75 g) "cotton" or silk tofu

1 tablespoon organic miso

1 tablespoon organic rice vinegar

2 tablespoons organic rapeseed oil

6 shiso leaves, cut into fine threads

Chop the tomato, cucumber, and green peppers into ¼-inch (6-mm) uniform dice and scrape each one into the same medium-sized bowl. Do not toss. Cut the tofu carefully into ½-inch (12-mm) squares.

Muddle the miso with the vinegar and whisk in the oil. Right before serving, toss the vegetables, then spoon onto individual plates (or onto a larger dinner plate that you will use to serve the rest of your meal). Drizzle with the miso dressing, drop a few cubes of tofu on top, and strew with the shiso threads. Serve immediately.

This is a riff off the classic bistro fare of leeks vinaigrette. Miso-mustard is a standard Japanese dressing, and I paired it with the leeks because it made so much sense. Japanese "leeks" (*negi*) have a long season in our area and are easy to grow, so I use a lot of them. They are lovely in stews because they become silky when simmered. Purists might say that this dish is not strictly traditional Japanese, but in spirit I think it is.

steamed "leeks" with miso-mustard SERVES 4 TO 6

NEGI KARASHI-MISO

6 (½-inch/12-mm) thick *negi*, spring onions, or thin leeks, cut into 2-inch (5-cm) lengths

1 tablespoon hot Dijon mustard (preferably Edmond Fallot)

3 tablespoons brown rice miso

3 tablespoons organic rice vinegar

Separate the green tops of the *negi* from the white bottoms and place the bottoms in a bamboo steamer set over a pot of boiling water. Cover and steam for 4 minutes, then add the green tops and steam 4 minutes more. Remove the steamer cover and rest the container over a large bowl to cool (and catch any drips).

Muddle the mustard, miso, and rice vinegar together in a small bowl. Transfer the *negi* to a suitably beautiful bowl, fold the dressing in gently, and serve with salt-broiled fish such as herring (page 237).

RATIO: mustard : miso : rice vinegar—1 : 3 : 3

I used to say I don't like brown food, an unfortunate attitude given that most Japanese country food is flavored with miso or soy sauce and therefore cast with a brownish hue. But one night Christopher urged me to try the *abura miso* Tadaaki had just finished tossing together in his wok. I yielded to pressure and picked up a few slices with my chopsticks. They were hot, creamy, and subtly salty. In this archetypal summer dish, the miso's haunting salty/sweet character combines well with the melting eggplant, and the sake serves to give balance. No sugar is necessary because the vegetables are flavorful and naturally sweet. And as Christopher predicted, I couldn't stop scooping up more and more mouthfuls.

stir-fried eggplant and ginger with miso SERVES 6
NASU NO ABURA MISO

2 tablespoons best-quality miso

1½ tablespoons sake

1 pound (450 g) Japanese eggplants (4 or 5 small)

6 tablespoons rapeseed or cold-pressed sesame oil

2 whole dried red peppers, torn in half

1 tablespoon slivered ginger

1 tablespoon finely sliced shiso leaves

Muddle the miso with the sake in a small bowl. Slice the eggplant down the middle lengthwise, then diagonally crosswise into slightly less than ½-inch (1-cm) slices.

Heat the oil with the dried red peppers in a large wok or skillet over medium heat until the peppers turn bright red. Throw in the ginger and eggplant pieces and toss gently for several minutes, until the eggplant slices are shiny and soft. Add the miso-sake mixture, and stir gingerly to evenly coat the slices without smashing or breaking them. Sprinkle in the shiso leaves, toss once, and serve while still blisteringly hot.

RATIO: oil : miso : sake—6 : 2 : 1.5

Tadaaki grows several different heirloom varieties of kabocha squash. Some are good for roasting and some become silky sublime when simmered or steam-braised (such as in this method). Miso goes particularly well with kabocha, but it's a delicate balance. Too much miso or too much cooking and the dish will not be as spectacular. You don't want the kabocha falling apart, or the miso flavor too strong.

sake-steamed kabocha
with miso SERVES 6
KABOCHA NO ABURA MISO

3 tablespoons best-quality miso

6 tablespoons sake

1⅓ pounds (600 g) kabocha squash
    (½ medium, seeds scooped out)

3 tablespoons rapeseed
    or cold-pressed sesame oil

2 whole dried red peppers,
    torn in half

Muddle the miso with 3 tablespoons of the sake in a small bowl. Peel the kabocha slightly, depending on the toughness of the skin, and slice into ⅛-inch (3-mm) thick pie-shaped wedges. (I cut the kabocha in half from stem to stern, then again crosswise, and cut the thin wedges from those pieces.) Any long pieces should be cut in half crosswise, since they should be able to be eaten in one bite, no longer than 2 inches (5 cm).

Heat the oil with the dried red peppers in a large wok or skillet over medium-low heat until the peppers turn bright red and become aromatic. Throw in the kabocha and toss to coat the pieces with oil. Splash in the remaining 3 tablespoons of sake, and toss once to distribute. Cover and cook, stirring occasionally, for about 6 minutes, until the kabocha slices have softened through to the skin. Add the miso-sake mixture, stirring carefully to evenly coat the slices without smashing or breaking them. Serve hot, at room temperature, or cold the next day in a bento.

RATIO: oil : miso : sake—1 : 1 : 2

VARIATION: Cook firm, ripe winter Japanese persimmons using this same method for an unusual but intriguing combination. After peeling and coring the persimmons, slice into wedges as if for apple pie, about ¼ inch (6 mm) on the thickest part. The persimmons should retain a slightly firm center, so do not steam them as long as the kabocha. Crisp, yet soft is the texture you are looking for.

Beans and peas require forethought. They need to be planted in the late fall to be cropped in the early spring. More often than not, we miss the window. We are imperfect farmers. But we are lucky because our eighty-five-year-old citrus grower friend Mochizuki-san sends us a variety of spring peas. One day a small box of snap peas arrived, and I happened to be craving miso that day. So, what better combination? The fresh bright, crunchy peas worked well against the earthy miso and the heat of the chiles. Also the oil contributed to the shiny look of the dish. We didn't have leftovers that night, though this dish would be a wonderful addition to a next-day bento.

stir-fried snap peas with miso and red pepper SERVES 6

SNAKKU ENDO NO ABURA MISO

1½ tablespoons best-quality miso

2¼ teaspoons sake

1½ pounds (700 g) snap peas

2 tablespoons rapeseed or cold-pressed sesame oil

2 whole dried red peppers, torn in half

1 tablespoon slivered ginger

Muddle the miso with the sake in a small bowl. Top and string the snap peas by grasping the top and pulling down the straight side of the pea.

Heat the oil with the dried red peppers in a large wok or skillet over medium heat until the peppers turn bright red. Throw in the ginger and snap peas. Toss gently for several minutes, until the peas' color has brightened and they are no longer raw. Add the miso-sake mixture, and smooth around the peas with the back of a wooden spoon to coat evenly. Serve immediately, as the peas will quickly lose their vibrant green color.

RATIO: oil : miso : sake—3 : 2 : 1

VARIATIONS: Substitute snow peas, haricots verts, or 2-minute blanched green beans for snap peas. Whole okra is also nice, as are wedges of juicy new onions or summer green peppers. Cook just long enough so no longer raw, but leave slightly crunchy.

The classic *kinpira* is made from burdock root (*gobo*) and carrots. *Gobo* is not commonly available in the U.S. and can be woody if not fresh, so if you can find it, check for telltale signs such as brown discoloring and be sure to scrub the skin well with a rough brush. Since we (or our friends) don't often grow *gobo*, I don't use it much. We do grow carrots, but they never seem to get big enough for stir-frying. However, our good friend Suka-san grows the best carrots I have ever tasted in my life. Suka-san's family keeps their own seeds, and have been growing those "flavor bomb" carrots for over forty years—so they've had some time to get it right. Carrots are one of our most staple vegetables since they store well and have an almost yearlong growing season. Leftover *kinpira* holds up very well and is great for the following day's lunch or bento.

carrot slivers stir-fried with soy sauce SERVES 6

NINJIN NO KINPIRA

3 tablespoons best-quality rapeseed or light sesame oil

2 small dried red peppers, torn in half

4 cups (1000 cc) julienned carrots (1¾-inch/4-cm thin matchsticks)

2 tablespoons organic soy sauce

Heat the oil over medium-high heat in a large frying pan. Add the peppers and warm until fragrant. Turn the heat up to high and throw in the carrots. Toss several minutes over high heat until the carrots have softened but not wilted. Test for doneness by sampling a piece or two. Splash in the soy sauce and toss for a couple of seconds to draw the soy sauce flavor into the carrots.

RATIO: vegetable : oil : soy sauce—1 cup : 2 teaspoons : 1½ teaspoons

VARIATIONS: Mix julienned burdock with the carrots or substitute thin lotus root rounds, green pepper wedges, or whole okra.

PLANTING SEEDS

Planting seeds in planter boxes is one of those easy farming chores, quickly accomplished with a minimal amount of sweat. Also, when the seeds magically sprout, the gratification is immediate. But when it comes time to transfer the seedlings to the field, I start cursing their buoyant success and wish I could just throw a few over my shoulder and be done with it. But I can't, so I religiously plant each little sprout, then plunge headfirst into a summer of gorgeous vegetables along with a Sisyphean battle against the jungle of weeds. People say Japan's rainy season is in July, but don't be fooled. It rains all year long here.

At the end of August, when the late summer vegetables are finally kicking into high gear, we almost can't pick enough peppers, tomatoes, or eggplants every day. And sometimes we don't. But when we revel in our baskets piled high with green, red, and purple, devising yet another way to use the eggplants and peppers (we can freeze tomatoes), that is exactly the time we should be planning the winter vegetable planting.

And for this reason, I often miss the perfect time to plant. First, planting needs to be done right before it rains, since we don't irrigate in Japan. Judge that wrong and I end up carting water to the field in containers like one year (or two). Luckily my Sunny-Side Up! students thought this was great fun and helped. Second, I'm still getting a sense of the overall weather pattern and learning how to suss out the exact turn from summer to fall. Seeds won't like being in the hot dry summer soil, but they will thrive in the warm waning fall days, which are intermixed with rain.

And then there is that pesky thing called "daily life." Which day will allow enough time to prepare the field? Will Tadaaki be able to squeeze in an hour or so to plow that section of the field? Will the SSU! kids be around to help? Do I want them to?

I often wait until late September before I plant. Tadaaki (the real farmer) gets his fields done earlier, of course. Late summer/early fall is typically busy with Sunny-Side Up! curriculum planning and writing projects, so I'm often glued to my computer. Not looking forward to the physical effort, I tend to drag my heels, despite knowing that the window for planting our school garden field is narrowing. Every day in September, I feel that nudge at my back: "Go to the field, get it done." But somehow each day goes by without planting. The guilt mounts until Tadaaki breezes in to snatch up some egg orders from the fax machine. As he heads out the door, he ever so casually mentions, "It's gonna rain today." The truth is, I have already seen that and have already made the decision to plant. But sometimes I get derailed from my plans. Those four measured words, uttered so blandly, push me off of my chair and into the car with my hoe, line measuring device, and seeds.

I feel guilty for not including the kids, but sometimes it's easier just to do it myself.

And sometimes it's easier to buy vegetables from Suka-san's natural farming group. And I do. It's more than about giving up (or giving in), it's about realizing one's limitations and also about supporting a local community of natural farmers who are excited to try out new varieties and happy we use them for cooking events or the SSU! school lunch. Yellow and green zucchini, round green eggplants, black cherry tomatoes, oval cherry tomatoes in the summer; arugula, frisée or heirloom lettuce, celery, cauliflower, and cilantro in the late winter—these are just a few of the "unusual" varieties we can get now in our local area.

And I'm thankful to have them because sometimes it's just not possible to do it all ourselves.

Another classic *kinpira* is made from *udo*, a Japanese vegetable similar to celery. Celery is not part of the traditional Japanese diet, and many Japanese still do not care for the taste, but recently our local Japanese organic farmer friends are growing it (and when successful, we too have celery in our fields). Celery cut into fine matchsticks and cooked in the *kinpira* style is absolutely stunning. And also good the next day.

stir-fried celery and red pepper with soy sauce SERVES 6
SERORI NO KINPIRA

2½ tablespoons best-quality rapeseed or light sesame oil

3 small dried red peppers, torn in half

5 cups (1250 cc) 1¾-inch (4-cm) julienned celery (see Note)

2½ tablespoons organic soy sauce

Heat the oil over medium-high heat in a large frying pan. Add the peppers and cook until bright red. Turn the heat up to high and dump in the julienned celery. Toss several minutes over high heat, until the celery has lost its raw quality but still has a bit of crunch. Do not cook to the point where the celery is completely translucent. Throw in the soy sauce and toss for a couple of seconds to let the celery soak up the flavor. Serve in a medium-sized bowl as a before-dinner appetizer that stays on the table through the meal.

NOTE: Julienne tips: Cut the celery stalks into the general desired length, then slice down the middle curve to create a flat baton of celery. If the celery is thick, you might want to slice this baton horizontally before you cut into fine matchsticks.

RATIO: vegetable : oil : soy sauce—1 cup : 1½ teaspoons : 1½ teaspoons

VARIATION: Try julienned daikon instead of celery. The result will be a little more floppy and juicy but nonetheless quite tasty.

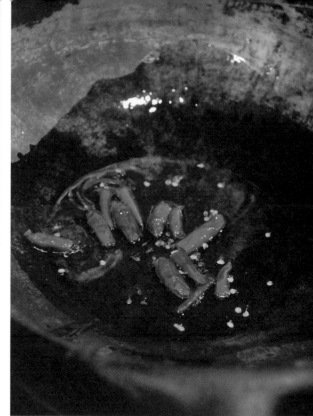

Sometimes I'm looking for the simple taste of salt, especially if I'm using miso or soy sauce already in other dishes. In this case, a quick stir-fry flavored with sea salt or even a few splashes of *shottsuru* (Japanese fish sauce) fills the bill.

stir-fried snow peas with salt SERVES 6
SAYAENDO NO ITAME

1¼ pounds (550 g) snow peas

2 tablespoons rapeseed oil

2 small whole dried red chile peppers, torn in half

¼ teaspoon salt

Pinch off the tops and pull down the side strings of the snow peas.

Heat the oil and chile pepper halves in a wok or large skillet over medium heat until the peppers turn bright red.

Dump in the snow peas and toss for several minutes over high heat until the peas turn a shiny, deep green and are still crisp. Add the salt about midway through the cooking process. Serve hot.

In our house, when we cook we just throw things into the pot (or pan) by feel. But that isn't really helpful for people learning how to understand Japanese farm food. When creating the recipes for this book, I was originally attracted to the one-size-fits-all theory that you could just plug different vegetables into the same method (e.g., stir-fries flavored with miso). But different vegetables react differently and adjustments need to be made. Eggplant and miso are a natural match, but there comes a time when I start craving salt or even *shottsuru*, a fish sauce produced in fishing ports on the Japan Sea. The basket of eggplants is still beckoning me from its perch on my kitchen counter, so I know some eggplant better be part of the meal that night. But instead of the flavors of the farm, I opt for the sea. Unlike other Asian fish sauces, *shottsuru* is remarkably not fishy, and when used in moderation is like a refreshing cool sea breeze in the hot, still countryside summers.

eggplant stir-fried with red pepper and shottsuru SERVES 6
NASU NO SHOTTSURU ITAME

1¾ pounds (800 g) Japanese eggplants (8 small)

8 tablespoons rapeseed or cold-pressed sesame oil

2 whole dried red peppers, torn in half

2 teaspoons *shottsuru* (page 5)

1 tablespoon finely sliced shiso leaves

Slice the eggplants down the middle lengthwise, then diagonally crosswise into slightly less than ½-inch (1-cm) pieces.

Heat the oil with the dried red peppers in a large wok or skillet over medium heat until the peppers turn bright red. Throw in the eggplant and toss gently for several minutes, until the eggplant slices are shiny and soft. Splash in the *shottsuru*, toss a couple more times, and turn into a medium-sized bowl. Fold in the shiso threads and serve hot.

VARIATION: Add a tablespoon of slivered fresh ginger when stir-frying the eggplant slices.

Tempura is one of the trickiest Japanese foods to prepare. I use an adaptation of Patricia Wells's recipe, and it's foolproof. Patricia's original recipe (inspired by Joël Robuchon) was for deep-fried zucchini blossoms and included a couple of teaspoons of curry powder, but I have adapted it here. Remember that the taste of the flour and its gluten content factor into making the perfect piece of tempura, as do oil flavor and temperature, so use the highest-quality ones you can find. And be prepared to serve from the stove.

In Japan, I usually choose one or two bright green mountain vegetables such as *seri* or *koshi abura*, but flowering tops of field greens work splendidly as well. Crunchy and bitter, dipped in sea salt, a few clusters are all you need.

mountain vegetable tempura SERVES 8
SANSAI TEMPURA

Best-quality rapeseed or peanut oil

1 cup (150 g) unbleached cake flour (page 10)

1 cup (250 cc) cold sparkling water

¼ teaspoon fine white sea salt

6 large ice cubes

10 (3- to 4-inch/7.5- to 10-cm) lengths of bitter budding flower tops, such as bok choy, mustard, turnip, or arugula

10 (3- to 4-inch/7.5- to 10-cm) clusters of curly watercress (a spicy variety is best)

Fine white sea salt or organic soy sauce, for dipping

Line a cookie sheet with a thick layer of newspaper and top with a layer of paper towels. Set next to the stove. Over low heat, warm 4 inches (10 cm) of oil in a medium-sized heavy, stainless steel saucepan. Whisk the flour with the sparkling water and salt in a medium-sized bowl. Take out two pairs of long cooking chopsticks or tongs. Use one pair to dip in the batter and one pair to remove the tempura from the oil. Increase the heat on the oil to about medium-high; the oil should not be smoking. Test the oil with a drop of batter before starting. It should sizzle and immediately form a small ball as it hits the oil but should not brown. Adjust the oil temperature as needed.

Drop the ice cubes in the batter and stir once or twice to chill the batter (depending on how long your tempura operation takes, you may want to remove the ice cubes occasionally to a small bowl, then put them back into the batter without the melted portion). Working with 3 or 4 pieces of one kind of greens at a time, dip them in the batter, give each a couple of brisk shakes to free any excess batter, and drop one by one into the hot oil. Turn gently as the batter becomes a light golden color (like summer wheat). When all sides are cooked, remove to the prepared cookie sheet. Serve immediately with fine white sea salt or soy sauce.

continued on next page

mountain vegetable tempura

VARIATIONS: Japanese farmers say you can cook almost any vegetable (or fish) in tempura batter, and I agree. At Soba Ra, Kanchan once served tomato tempura. Dipped in salt, it was startlingly delicious. The only caveat here is you must dredge the tomato wedges or cherry tomatoes in flour before dipping in the tempura batter. Also the flame should be lowered to medium before increasing to medium-high when you cook the tomatoes.

Freshly dug potatoes in the early summer make a fluffy, crispy tempura that even the adults fight over when it appears on our tempura plate at Soba Ro and Soba Ra. Made at home (with local seasonal potatoes), these fried potatoes are simple to execute and make a tasty side dish (or before-dinner snack) with salt.

new potato tempura SERVES 8
SHINJAGA TEMPURA

½ pound (225 g) medium-sized, local yellow-flesh potatoes

Best-quality rapeseed or peanut oil

½ cup (75 g) unbleached cake flour (page 10)

½ cup (125 cc) cold sparkling water

⅛ teaspoon fine white sea salt

3 large ice cubes

Fine white sea salt or organic soy sauce, for dipping

Wash and peel the potatoes if the skin is tough. Cut the potatoes into ½-inch (12-mm) wedges (measured on the thick side). Drop the potato pieces into a small pot of salted cold water. The potatoes should be covered by about 1 inch (2.5 cm). Bring to a boil over high heat and cook until the centers still have some give but the outsides are soft. Drain and cool.

Whisk the flour with the sparkling water and salt in a medium-sized bowl. Prepare a tempura station and pan of oil as described in the method for Mountain Vegetable Tempura (page 206).

When the oil is hot, drop the ice cubes into the batter and stir once. Add 5 or 6 pieces of potatoes at a time to the batter. Pick up one piece at a time, let the excess batter drip off, and slip into the hot oil. Roll the tempura pieces gently as the batter turns a pale (slightly) golden color. When all sides are cooked, remove to the prepared cookie sheet. Continue cooking until all the pieces have been fried, but (if possible) serve each batch immediately. Dip in fine white sea salt or soy sauce before eating.

Tadaaki hops the train every Thursday afternoon and travels an hour each way to practice the samurai arts of *iaijutsu*, *kenjutsu*, and *jujutsu*. On one of those nights I got into a cooking frenzy and made Salt-Broiled Herring (page 237), Salt-Massaged Cucumber with Miso and Sesame (page 175), and Eggplant Stir-Fried with Red Pepper and Shottsuru (page 205). Along with those dishes I served some local tofu with hand-grated fresh wasabi. I also made corn *kakiage*.

Baachan tends to fade as the hour gets late, so I was racing to put some food on the table before she lost interest in eating. Serving Tadaaki-style (one dish at a time), I called the boys and Baachan to the table to start eating without me. And in the kitchen, I munched on a crunchy-squishy corn *kakiage*, dipping the corner in sea salt before each burning hot bite. I ate two—they were that good.

corn kakiage fritters MAKES 8
TOMOROKOSHI NO KAKIAGE

6 young corncobs

2 scallions or 4 fat chives, chopped into fine rings

Best-quality rapeseed or peanut oil

1 cup (150 g) unbleached cake flour (page 10)

1 cup (250 cc) cold sparkling water

¼ teaspoon fine white sea salt

6 large ice cubes

Fine white sea salt or organic soy sauce, for dipping

Set the corncob in a large bowl and cut the kernels off of the cob with a sharp knife. After all the kernels are removed, go over the cob with the back of the knife to remove the last bit of corn from the cob. You should have about 3½ cups (850 cc). Add the scallions (about 4 to 5 tablespoons) and toss with your fingers to distribute and break up the kernel clumps.

Line a cookie sheet with a thick layer of newspaper, then put a layer of paper towels on top. Set next to the stove. Over low heat, warm 2 inches (5 cm) of oil in a 10-inch (25-cm) frying pan.

Whisk the flour with the sparkling water and salt in a medium-sized bowl. Dump the corn kernels and scallions into the batter, add the ice cubes, and stir. Remove the ice cubes.

Increase the heat on the oil to medium-high; the oil should not be smoking. Test the oil with a drop of batter before starting. It should sizzle and immediately form a small ball as it hits the oil but should not brown. Adjust the oil temperature as needed.

Ladle 4 individual scoops of batter with a soup ladle into the pan (like pancakes) and cook over medium-high heat until golden brown on the bottom, about 5 minutes per side depending on the heat adjustment. Carefully turn over using two heat-resistant curved rubber scrapers. Cook until the second side is golden brown and oil bubbles have largely subsided (indicating the water has cooked out).

Remove from the oil with a slotted skimmer to the prepared newspaper and paper towel–lined cookie sheet. Eat immediately with fine white sea salt or soy sauce.

I never really noticed that we ate *agedashi* vegetables every once in a while during the summer when the mood struck Tadaaki, since we don't talk much about the names of dishes. The food flows onto the table in a blur as the days go by. I'm just grateful to have a partner in putting together our meals. I started hearing about a mysterious dish called *agedashi dofu* a few years ago, but it was still off my radar. I finally asked Tadaaki what it was, and he explained that it was restaurant food and not made in his farm home. Most farm food uses up a lot of one vegetable because that's what we have. Nonetheless, I love the simple one-dish serving style of this method. This is best done on a day you are planning on making tempura afterward (to recycle the oil).

deep-fried okra and eggplant in broth SERVES 6
AGEDASHI OKURA TO NASU

2 cups (500 cc) organic rapeseed or cold-pressed sesame oil

6 small to medium okra

6 small Japanese eggplants

1⅔ cups (400 cc) Noodle Dipping Sauce (page 310)

1 tablespoon slivered ginger

Line a cookie sheet with several sheets of folded newspaper and top with a layer of paper towels. Set next to the stove.

Heat the oil in a deep, round frying pan (such as a wok) over medium-high heat until hot but not smoking.

Make a small lengthwise slit near the tip of each okra with a sharp knife so the steam can escape, or they may pop open in the hot oil. Cut ¼-inch (6-mm) deep lengthwise slices into the eggplant skin at ¼-inch (6-mm) intervals following the natural curve of the eggplant to create a wavy pattern from top to bottom. Fry the okra quickly until no longer raw but not wilted, then drain on the paper towel–lined cookie tray. Slip the eggplants into the oil and fry gently for several minutes, turning occasionally, until the eggplant has softened. Remove the eggplant and drain.

Arrange each eggplant in a small bowl so the bottom is fanned out and rest an okra pod attractively against the golden- and purple-ribboned flesh. Ladle in a scoop of noodle dipping sauce, sprinkle with the slivered ginger, and serve immediately.

VARIATION: Substitute green beans instead of okra if the season coincides with eggplant in your region.

Winter is the season for daikon, so it's no surprise it goes well in simmered dishes that warm your tummy. This is one of my favorite ways to eat daikon and it also happens to be a well-loved and oft-prepared dish from my husband's family. Because the daikon is only simmered with konbu and not the traditional *konbu-katsuobushi* dashi, the result is clear and completely infused with the natural taste of daikon with some gentle sea notes from the mild konbu. A dab of eye-watering hot mustard adds a nice kick.

simmered daikon with mustard SERVES 6
DAIKON NO NIMONO KARASHI-ZOE

1 medium daikon
(about 1½ pounds/700 g)

1 (6 by 4-inch/7.5 by 5-cm)
piece of konbu

2 tablespoons Japanese Mustard
(page 314)

3½ tablespoons soy sauce

Pour 3½ cups (850 cc) cold water into a small heavy pot. Float the piece of konbu in the water to soften.

Meanwhile, peel the daikon and cut it into ¾-inch (2-cm) thick rounds. Bevel the edges with a sharp knife if you like. This helps the daikon to absorb the liquid and cook evenly . . . and looks nifty.

Snip the softened konbu into ¼ by 1½-inch (6-mm by 4-cm) strips with sturdy kitchen scissors (or slice with a sharp knife).

Drop the daikon and konbu into the pot of cold water (there should be just enough water to cover the daikon). Bring almost to a boil over high heat, decrease the heat to medium-low, and simmer for 20-25 minutes until the daikon is soft in the center when poked with a bamboo skewer.

When the daikon pieces are soft but not starting to disintegrate, season with the soy sauce. Cool in the broth and serve at room temperature in small individual bowls with a dab of mustard on the side of the bowl. Eat by cutting off a manageable portion of daikon with your chopsticks, including a bit of konbu strand, and dipping a corner in the mustard.

Strangely, kabocha is in season throughout the winter, but also in the summer. In the summertime, Tadaaki's mother would add thick rounds of eggplant to the simmering kabocha. I tend to prefer not mixing two textures of vegetables when simmering because it's tricky to control the cooking process. Often one vegetable is done before the other—another reason why *nimono* (literally, "simmered things") is typically prepared by parboiling each vegetable separately, to the same point of doneness, before combining and simmering in soy sauce- and mirin-flavored dashi.

simmered kabocha and konbu SERVES 6
KABOCHA TO KONBU NO NIMONO

1 (6 by 4-inch/7.5 by 5-cm) piece of konbu

½ medium-sized kabocha squash, unpeeled (about 1⅓ pounds/ 600 g)

2 tablespoons Japanese Mustard (page 314)

3 tablespoons soy sauce

Pour 3 cups (750 cc) cold water into a small heavy pot. Soak the konbu in the water to soften.

Meanwhile, scoop out the seeds and pulp from the kabocha, peel roughly, and cut the kabocha in half crosswise. Slice into ¼-inch (6-mm) thick wedges (measured from the thick backside) with a sturdy-bladed kitchen knife.

Slice the softened konbu into ¼ by 1½-inch (6-mm by 4-cm) strips with a sharp knife or snip with kitchen shears.

Dump the kabocha and konbu into the pot of cold water (there should be just enough water to cover the kabocha). Bring almost to a boil over high heat, reduce the heat to low or medium-low, and simmer for about 15 minutes until the kabocha has softened through to the dark green skin.

When the kabocha is soft all the way through, season with soy sauce. Cool in the broth and serve at room temperature in small individual bowls with a dab of mustard on the side of the bowl. Cut off a bite-sized piece of kabocha with your chopsticks and try to catch up some konbu strands before dipping a corner of the kabocha into the mustard.

Several years ago, Tadaaki went a tad overboard on his shiitake mushroom use, and as a result Matthew took a firm disliking for all mushrooms, so we don't eat them much. But we do have local mushroom growers in the nearby foothills and a fairly year-round crop. Mushrooms are best in the fall, however, and we are fortunate that the foragers bring some interesting wild varieties to sell at our local Japan Agriculture (JA) farm stand down the road from us. Before marriage, Tadaaki went up to the mountains himself to gather mushrooms. He tried to keep up these fall forays and later often put one of the babies in a backpack to make the trek up into the local mountains. But like so many things in life, it just became too hard to continue. So now we buy mushrooms from the foragers and are duly thankful.

sake-braised
shimeji mushrooms SERVES 6
HON SHIMEJI NO SAKAMUSHI

½ pound (250 g) *hon shimeji* mushrooms (or any other mild-flavored, local mushrooms)

1 tablespoon (15 g) butter

¼ cup (60 cc) sake

¼ teaspoon fine sea salt

½ small red pepper, cut into fine rounds

1 small clove garlic, finely chopped (optional)

Wipe the mushrooms of any clinging dirt or debris. Slice off any discolored ends and separate into single stalks.

Heat a large skillet over medium heat until hot but not smoking. Decrease the heat to low and add the butter. When the butter is melted, add the mushrooms, sake, salt, red pepper, and garlic, if using. Toss to coat the mushrooms evenly with the butter-flavored sake. Cover and cook for 5 minutes over low heat. Stir once or twice while cooking. The mushrooms will have softened nicely but should not be too limp. Serve hot or at room temperature.

7

fish and seafood

Japan is an archipelago, so sea creatures and sea greens are fundamental components of the Japanese diet. Though generally farmers did not buy fresh fish except when guests came, they used several varieties of dried fish as soup bases, and air-dried fish occasionally appeared on the table.

Like my husband's farm family, I did not grow up eating much fish despite living close to the Monterey Bay. Fish was a special-occasion dinner bought only at the local fish market, Cook's in Menlo Park, California. Budget be damned, my Massachusetts-born mother bought thick swordfish or halibut steaks and broiled them up with butter and lemon for birthday dinners. Occasionally we had trout but not often, as my mother was paranoid we'd choke on the bones. And on the hottest summer days, my mother bought sweet little boiled shrimp packed in white butcher paper, again from the fishmonger. In contrast, the only fish my husband's family ate was dried—though very occasionally his aunt living at the Izu Peninsula seaside sent some butterflied fish partially dried by the salty air of the sea. Grilled over the kitchen hearth, the semidried fish always contributed to a memorable meal.

Perhaps because of the way I grew up or perhaps because of some deep natural inclination, I approach food through vegetables, but most Japanese probably do so through fish. I know my husband does, and so does Kanchan of Soba Ra—though Tadaaki and Kanchan both know instinctively how to integrate vegetables into their menus. At most restaurants (especially in Japan, but even abroad) I often wonder what happened to the vegetables since they are usually only a small garnish or an afterthought. This is the crucial difference between farm food and town (or restaurant food). Farmers are going to showcase the vegetable but allow the fish to complement and make the meal even more gorgeous than if it were only vegetables.

I have organized this chapter by preparation method (hand-chopped, seared, kelp-wicked, vinegar-marinated, hand-chopped patties, salt-broiled, miso-broiled, sake-steamed, deep-fried, and air-dried). I have also included a Fish and Seafood Methods chart (page 370) to show at a glance the different ways you can prepare the most common varieties of fish and seafood available in North America. More important than the method, however, is the fish itself, so ask your fishmonger to recommend a suitable (similar) variety. I cannot stress enough how essential it is to find a source for top-quality, fresh-from-the-sea (or river) local fish. If the fish has been flown a long distance—well, you do the math—it just won't be fresh. And I also encourage you to develop a relationship with your fishmonger, for the relationship with your seller is the foundation of safe buying practices and delicious fish. Besides, it's nice to know whom you are buying from because it adds to the overall enjoyment of cooking and eating. Better yet, get to know a fisherman, admittedly less practical, but how wonderful would that be?

THE FISHMONGER

We spent most of the first five years of our marriage searching our local area for the best sources for any food we did not grow. In those days, we bought our fish from a tiny shop on a corner of a back street in our five-shop town, kitty-corner from a small cow paddock. The fishmonger had no eyebrows and wore a slightly bizarre (and not particularly realistic) hair wig, topped with his billed cap, which every other worker (including my husband) wears in Japan. He was a sincere man who cared about his métier even though business did not seem brisk, and I wondered at the state of his health.

Our fishmonger only kept a few fish at any given time, so we often called ahead and asked him to pick up specific kinds of fish when he went to the market. He was more than happy to oblige. In Japan, the custom is to clean the fish and fillet it right before cooking, so whenever I came by to pick up my fish, I would lean against the steel sink that ran the length of the wall (avoiding the spray of his faucet) and chat with the fish guy as he cleaned my fish. If you buy fish at the supermarket, it won't be as fresh and you'll miss out on that conversation (and knowledge gleaned).

Over the course of the next couple of years, the fish shop's doors were closed more often than not, and eventually permanently so. But by that time, a fish market based in Niigata (a major fishing port) had opened up in the sprawling city next to ours. In those days, I would invariably see fellow foreigners at the fish market, mostly from other Asian countries such as Thailand or the Philippines whose foods also center on fish. But with the downward spiral in the Japanese economy, many foreign workers have long since returned to their native countries, and I don't often see faces other than Japanese in the market these days.

After some years as a dedicated fish market, the shop shuttered up to renovate and reopened as a grocery-cum-fish store. But they still had sparkling fish fresh from the sea—eyes clear and bright—all packed on ice, with many shellfish still alive and blowing bubbles. We buy a lot of fish, often in large amounts—especially for the

school lunch and preserving projects like salting anchovies or cod. I value the expertise of the fishmongers and rely on their advice to steer me toward the best fish for whatever preparation. They'll even take me in the back and show me a cutting technique—they're that willing to accommodate (and teach). One day when I was writing this book, I dropped by for some fish, and the senior fishmonger approached me with a smile. He asked about the book and if it was published yet—a bit premature but sweet that he was excited to see Japanese recipes in print, inspired by the pristine fish he had sold me.

As our world food supply becomes more and more disassociated from the producer, food safety issues increase at an alarming pace. We may not be able to choose our air or our water, but we can certainly choose our food. Buying fish from a fishmonger (and meat from a butcher) ensures that you will have safe food because an expert has vetted it. Several years ago I attended Slow Fish in Genoa, Italy. That event forced me to take a look at my own hypocrisy (of buying Alaskan cod or Chilean sea bass) and I immediately stopped buying anything but Japanese fish. Buying what is in front of us on the shelf (or chiller case) because it looks good on the surface isn't always enough; we need to try harder to find out where our food originates and to stay as local as we can. Do I know which fish is sustainably raised? No, maybe not all the time. But I do know the fish that is marked "wild" (as opposed to farmed), and I do follow my gut (and the advice of the fishmonger) when selecting what looks good. Just like vegetables, the fish will be screaming, "Buy me, buy me."

A lot of people don't like the family of fish that includes true mackerel and jack mackerel, something I could never understand until a recent conversation at a cooking class in Vietnam with Patricia Wells. People have a problem with these lean (but slightly oily), shiny varieties, which are sometimes fishy or dry if the cook isn't careful. But raw is seductively mild. The addition of miso in this simple preparation is brilliant, as are the chives. In Japan, I use wild green onions in the spring. If your jack mackerel filets have a slightly strong smell, the optional egg yolk will introduce a creamy note and make the fish milder.

hand-chopped jack mackerel with miso SERVES 6

NAMERO

3 sashimi-grade, very fresh jack mackerel (about 3½ ounces/ 100 g each)

2 tablespoons brown rice miso

1 tablespoon finely chopped chives or scallions

1 very fresh raw egg yolk, at room temperature (optional)

Lemon wedges (optional)

With a razor-sharp knife, remove the head from the fish by slicing the ventral gill diagonally up to the edge of the head near the dorsal fin. Then cut open and gut. Rinse off the blood and lingering insides under cold running water. Pat dry. Cut off the hard scale line that extends laterally up from the tail area on both sides of the fish. Remove the skin from the flesh by grasping the top corner of the skin and peeling it back away from the flesh. The ventral edge of the fish has a hard ridge and does not like to give up the skin, so take care. As this takes practice, don't lose heart if you are clumsy at first. If you have a nice fishmonger, he might perform this operation for you.

Slice the jack mackerel filets in ¼-inch (6-mm) strips, then again into a ¼-inch (6-mm) dice. With the fish still on the chopping board, drop the miso on top of the diced fish and sprinkle with the chives. Add a farm-fresh yolk if you like. Chop the ingredients into the mackerel with your razor-sharp knife until well distributed and the mackerel amalgamates together into a roughly chopped mass.

Serve as an appetizer, as is or with a lemon wedge, or even spooned on top of a mild water cracker. It's also lovely in hand-rolled sushi.

VARIATIONS: Substitute flying fish or sardine for jack mackerel. Excellent with tuna or bonito, but skip the miso. Add finely chopped garlic or grated ginger to the bonito.

In Japan, bonito (skipjack tuna) season starts in spring with lean, clear-flavored flesh and ends in fall with fatty, darkly flavored (and colored) meat. I love both seasons, but I particularly like to taste the change in flavor and fat as we move into the summer. I also like that the fish makes sense. In the spring you are looking for lighter and brighter food, whereas in the fall you are ready for stronger or heartier fare. Nature is funny that way. If we leave it be, it gives us what we want when we want. No need to eat out of season.

seared bonito
with ginger, garlic, and chives SERVES 6
KATSUO NO TATAKI

A side of sashimi-quality fresh bonito

Sea salt

DIPPING SAUCE

4 tablespoons soy sauce

4 tablespoons yuzu, *sudachi*, or Meyer lemon juice

GARNISH

3 tablespoons finely chopped chives

1 tablespoon coarsely chopped garlic

1 tablespoon finely julienned ginger

½ tablespoon yuzu, *sudachi*, or Meyer lemon zest (optional)

Cut out the dorsal bone to create 2 elongated triangular-shaped filets. Scrape off any hard spots on the flesh. Set the filets side by side on a cutting board or dinner plate and salt lightly on all sides from about a foot (30 cm) above the fish.

Poke the filets through the horizontal side, skin side up, with five 1½-foot (40-cm) long metal skewers, keeping the handles all at the same place and the tips radiating out like an open fan.

Heap straw in a barbecue and light (or prepare a high-flame charcoal grill). Carefully hold the skewered filets directly in the flames, rotating until the skin sizzles and all sides are seared. (Take heed: This operation is quite difficult if there is any breeze.) Plunge the filets into ice water to cool. Remove from the water, pat dry, and wrap in a clean kitchen towel before refrigerating. Alternatively, sear over a hot stove flame, wrap in a paper towel, and place in the fridge for 1 to 2 hours or 30 minutes in the freezer to cool.

When ready to eat, slice diagonally into ¼-inch (6-mm) thick pieces and fan out overlapping slices on a beautiful round dinner plate, working from the outside in like flower petals.

Make the dipping sauce by mixing the soy sauce and citrus juice. Sprinkle the sliced fish with the dipping sauce and garnishes. Serve immediately.

The konbu wicks out some of the moisture from the fish, leaving the flesh tighter and firmer in texture. In Japanese this is called *shimeru*, "closing up." That extra element of firmness renders this style of sashimi a good choice when putting together a fish shabu-shabu dinner (page 95). Sashimi treated by this method has a gentle flavor, and I often prefer *kobujime*-prepared fish to raw.

kelp-wicked red snapper SERVES 6
MADAI NO KOBUJIME

1 red snapper, skinned and filleted into 4 pieces (about 1 pound/ 500 g fish meat)

½ teaspoon fine sea salt

4 tablespoons sake

2 to 4 pieces konbu (enough to cover the surface of the fish)

Freshly grated wasabi (optional)

Organic soy sauce

Remove the pinbones from the fish with flat-bladed tweezers. Cut off any discolored parts. Sprinkle the salt lightly across the surface of the filets from a couple of feet above the fish. (This technique, called *tatejio*, ensures an even distribution of salt over any given surface.) Pour the sake onto a dinner plate and soak the konbu pieces in the sake to soften. Cover the belly side (as opposed to skin side) of the fish with one layer of konbu (you can place narrow pieces side by side if you do not have wide pieces).

Tear off two connected absorbent paper towels and place 2 snapper filets along the shorter edge, about 5 inches (12 cm) in. Fold that edge of the paper over the fish and gently roll up the fish to wrap. Repeat with the other 2 filets. Enclose in plastic wrap and refrigerate overnight (or at least 4 to 6 hours). This process wicks out the moisture and firms up the flesh of the fish, giving it a pleasantly tight texture.

Remove the fish from the fridge, peel off the konbu from each filet, and use the konbu to line a serving plate. Slice the fish into ¼-inch (6-mm) thick pieces at a diagonal, slide your knife under the sliced fish, and arrange it attractively on top of the konbu-lined platter, either in a single line of fish, or two or three. Serve with freshly grated wasabi (if possible) and a small dish of soy sauce.

SASHIMI

My teenage son Andrew loves sashimi but is not crazy about cooked fish. That makes sense, because raw fish is characteristically delicate in flavor with a faint taste of the sea. Admittedly, some of the oily, silver-skinned shiny fish can sometimes be off-putting for the uninitiated. Many shiny fish are served slightly vinegared, such as *shime saba* (wicked mackerel) or salt-wicked and citrus-marinated to "cook" the fish a little. Other sea creatures like sea urchin or squid may be a challenge because of their unusual texture, but lean white fish is sweet and easy to eat as long as it is ultra fresh.

Putting together a sashimi plate is easy if you have access to a good fish market with reliable fishmongers. The basic idea is to create a plate with a balance of texture, color, and taste. But in the end, there is no need to obsess. It may just come down to what's available to be eaten fresh that day, because not all fish can be eaten raw. Even in Japan, only fish sold as sashimi can be eaten raw—one more reason why you need a good fishmonger.

The fishmonger will slice the fish for you, but if you are a true sashimi (or sushi) aficionado, you may want to hone up your knife skills. Tadaaki is the master knifesman in our house, though I'm practicing. I always feel that patience and balance are innate Japanese attributes, though perhaps less so with the younger generations. Many of us Americans are impatient and not good with tools. Until I married Tadaaki, I had never handled a truly sharp knife and had never even considered that you must wash and dry your knife immediately after use, probably why many people in the U.S. use serrated knives on tomatoes—no sharp knife in the house. When

cutting fish, you need a very long thin blade and you stroke through the fish filet at a diagonal. The knife should go though the fish like butter—this is not a sawing or hacking effort! The action of a skilled master chef is poetry in motion, and I think a large part of why I love the theater of sushi.

The fishmonger will take care of the fish, but you are responsible for creating the bed on which your sashimi will lay once you get it home. In Japan, ¼-inch (6-mm) thick slices of precut sashimi is typically packed on hard plastic trays with a domed plastic lid so as not to smash the fish. The sashimi pieces are usually laying on machine-cut shredded daikon and a couple of (hothouse) shiso leaves. You might feel tempted to flop the whole thing on a plate and serve as is, but I wouldn't recommend that.

Possible garnishes are myriad, some easily available in the U.S., some not. Here are just a few of what I might use to garnish a plate as the *tsuma* (wife) that goes with sashimi: hand-cut shredded daikon, daikon sprouts, shiso leaves (whole or fine threads), lightly salt-massaged shiso chiffonade, finely chopped green onions or chives, finely julienned carrots, cress sprigs, finely sliced *myoga*, finely sliced radishes, or medium-thick rounds of thin Japanese cucumbers. The idea here is to create a gorgeous canvas against which your sashimi will lay. Each fish and each garnish will have its own area, so arrange them with color in mind.

If at all possible, track down some fresh wasabi (see Resources). Otherwise the tube variety will have to do—but try to get one that has a large percentage of real wasabi (not just colored horseradish). Squid and silver-skinned shiny fish such as anchovy, sardines, and mackerel go well with freshly grated ginger, not wasabi.

I have become more and more interested in the different methods of treating fish—a job I used to leave up to Tadaaki (division of labor in a busy farm life). And when we make it to the fish market, it's hard not to come home with too much because it all looks so good. I am usually fairly restrained, but Tadaaki (the expert sashimi slicer) goes a tad wild when let loose in the fish market. We end up with more than we can eat, and dinner tends to be late, but the fish is just too good to pass up.

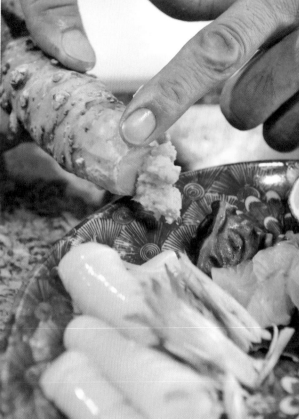

Shime Saba is the sashimi preparation that Tadaaki seems to crave most—and he makes it whenever he comes across some beautifully fresh mackerel. Mackerel is more of a winter fish, but it can also be delicious in the summer, depending on where it was caught. The vinegar "cooks" the mackerel a bit and takes away the fishiness that may accompany cooked mackerel. Like most other silvery fish, mackerel is eaten with grated ginger, not wasabi. Also, be sure not to skimp on the salt—it is necessary for the success (and safety) of this dish. The salt cures the fish and renders the mackerel able to be eaten raw.

vinegared mackerel SERVES 6
SHIME SABA

2 (5½-ounce/150-g) deboned mackerel filets, skin on

Fine sea salt

2 to 4 pieces of konbu (enough to cover the surface of the fish)

Rice vinegar

1 (¾-inch/2-cm) square piece of peeled fresh ginger, grated

Organic soy sauce

Set the mackerel filets on a dinner plate or in a shallow plastic container. Salt both sides heavily—the surface of the fish should be almost ⅛ inch (or at least 2 mm) thick with salt. Don't hold back! Cover with plastic wrap and refrigerate for 30 minutes.

Meanwhile, lay the konbu across a dinner plate and splash it with rice vinegar to soften.

After 30 minutes, remove the salt-covered mackerel from the fridge and rinse in cold water. Pat dry with a towel and set the filets on a chopping board. Remove any center bones with flat-headed tweezers and the skin with a razor-sharp knife (slide your knife blade in between the skin and the flesh, get some purchase and pull the skin out, keeping the blade angled down toward the skin and the board). This little operation takes practice, so keep at it. You will get better, I promise.

Piece together the vinegar-soaked konbu on top of the belly side of the skinned filets. Wrap each filet in one absorbent paper towel, and place both in a heavy-duty, large resealable plastic bag. Dump in the vinegar from the konbu soaking plate and add more vinegar until the paper is soaked. Squeeze out the air, roll, seal the bag, and let marinate in the refrigerator for 20 to 30 minutes while you finish preparing dinner. (If you are not ready to serve at the end of 30 minutes, unwrap as detailed below, pat dry, wrap in absorbent paper toweling, and refrigerate until ready to slice.)

Take the fish out of the fridge and remove from the bags. Peel off the paper towel and the konbu and discard both. Slice the mackerel into ⅓-inch (8-mm) thick pieces at a diagonal—but before cutting each new slice, cut a slit halfway through the middle of the slice of mackerel (at the exact same angle as you are cutting) to make the fish easier to eat. The cured fish meat should have a frosty cast and should not be rosy pink (thus indicating you did not salt the fish as heavily as needed). If not, repeat the salting process and vinegar bath for 15 minutes each to finish the cure.

Slide your knife under the sliced fish and arrange it attractively on a couple of small plates (or as part of a larger sashimi plate)—either in a single line of fish or two or three lines resting against each other. Serve with the freshly grated ginger and a small dish of soy sauce.

Kanchan prepared this for the Soba Dinner at Chez Panisse in 2008. A visit to the Monterey Fish Market on Pier 33 in San Francisco yielded a gorgeous halibut, so fresh that it hadn't yet gone into rigor mortis. Kanchan thought it might be a good fish for a miso treatment, but Tom Worthington from Monterey Fish advised against it. That particular kind of halibut was difficult to broil and could easily become chalky, so Kanchan opted to treat the halibut with citrus and vinegar instead. It was citrus season at the time (February), and after experimenting with different flavors, he decided to use a mixure of Meyer lemon with a bit of fresh orange juice and a hint of rice vinegar for his *sujime*. Kanchan was inspired to use Meyer lemons—a new flavor for him. In Japan, I like to use yuzu.

citrus and vinegar-marinated halibut SERVES 6

HIRAME NO YUZU-SUJIME

4 to 6 pieces of konbu (enough to wrap the whole piece of fish)

¼ cup (60 cc) rice vinegar

1-pound (450-g) piece of sashimi-grade halibut filet, deboned and skinned

½ teaspoon fine sea salt

4 tablespoons yuzu juice; or 3 tablespoons Meyer lemon juice plus 1 tablespoon orange juice

Freshly grated wasabi (or from a tube)

Organic soy sauce

Put the konbu on a dinner plate and splash it with the rice vinegar to soften.

Set the halibut on a board and sprinkle lightly but evenly with salt on both sides from a foot (30 cm) above the fish (*tatejio*).

Remove the konbu from the vinegar (save the konbu-flavored vinegar until the next day) and shake off the excess liquid—it should not be dripping. Lay the halibut filets, belly side up, on a board and cover each filet with the vinegar-soaked konbu, piecing together to make sure that the whole surface of each filet has been covered. Stretch out two 2-foot (60-cm) long pieces of plastic wrap and place a konbu-draped filet across the middle of each one. Cover the skin side of each of those 2 filets with the vinegar-soaked konbu and place 1 of the remaining 2 filets on top. Fold up the plastic wrap to enclose each pair of konbu-wrapped halibut filets and seal tightly. Place all of the filets in a resealable plastic bag and refrigerate overnight but no longer than 24 hours.

The next day (within an hour of serving, but preferably right before removing the fish from the refrigerator) combine the yuzu (or Meyer lemon and orange) juice with 1 tablespoon of the reserved konbu-flavored vinegar (if not enough, supplement from the vinegar bottle).

Thirty minutes before serving, take the halibut out of the fridge and remove from the plastic bag. Unwrap and peel off the konbu, but do not discard. Lay the halibut in a small nonreactive shallow pan (or plastic container) and pour the citrus juice-vinegar mixture over the fish. Refrigerate for 15 minutes, flip, return to the fridge for 15 more minutes, then remove from the juice and pat dry with a clean kitchen towel.

Slice the halibut at a diagonal into ¼-inch (6-mm) thick pieces. If the fish is wide, cut those slices in half again crosswise (the sashimi cut should not be much longer than 2 inches (5 cm), or shorter than 1 inch (2.5 cm).

Slide your knife under the sliced fish and arrange it attractively on a couple of small plates (or as part of a larger sashimi plate) in a few lines resting against each other. Slice the softened konbu into fine ribbons and mound next to the halibut slices. Serve with grated wasabi and a small dish of soy sauce.

In Berkeley, for the 2010 Soba Dinner preparations, one morning Kanchan, Christopher (my eldest), and Sylvan Brackett from Chez Panisse (and Peko-Peko Catering) all trouped across the Bay Bridge to check out the freshly caught fish at Monterey Fish. It was an early mission (very early), so Andrew and I chose to stay in bed. When we finally hooked up back at Sylvan's cooking studio in Oakland, Kanchan regaled us with his tale of grabbing out fish guts (liver and eggs, to be precise) and yellowtail collars from the refuse pile due to be jettisoned. He cackled with glee at his "finds" and shook his head over the American waste. While he did not serve those orphan parts at the Chez Panisse dinner, the cooks were the lucky recipients later that night. Kanchan simmered the eggs and livers in soy sauce- and mirin-flavored dashi. The texture was slightly crunchy on the tongue and mildly sweet in the mouth—lovely. And the boldly fatty yellowtail collars, broiled, were meaty and succulent. Good in the oven, these are even better on the barbecue.

charcoal-grilled yellowtail collar SERVES 4
BURI KAMA

1 yellowtail collar (9 ounces/260 g)

Sea salt

Grated daikon

Soy sauce

Prepare a barbecue using hardwood charcoal (the fire needs to burn down, so do this a good 45 minutes before cooking). The collar sputters a bit from its natural fish oils, so cook over low heat.

Lay the yellowtail collar on a small clean grate and set directly over the fire. Sprinkle lightly with salt from a foot (30 cm) above the fish (*tatejio*) and cook slowly for about 10 minutes. Flip carefully and salt the other side. Flip every 10 minutes or so and cook for a total of 20 to 30 minutes, depending on the thickness and the heat.

Alternatively, broil slowly on a rack set over a foil-lined broiler pan in the third position from the top of the oven. Check after 5 minutes to gauge the broiler heat. If the collar is browning too quickly, move the rack to a lower position. Turn several times for even cooking and browning. Depending on the broiler, this will take from 10 to 15 minutes.

Transfer the collar from the grill to an attractive plate. Squeeze a few spoonfuls of grated daikon in your fist to remove excess liquid, mound on the plate next to the collar, and drizzle the center of the mound with soy sauce. Let people dig in with chopsticks as a convivial first course or snack with drinks before dinner.

VARIATION: Substitute the collar for a similar fatty fish such as salmon.

Though I prefer the white-flesh varieties such as *tobiuo* or *tachiuo*, any of the oily-skinned, shiny fish do well as small chopped patties and are a nice change from the typical meat or chicken ones. If the patties seem to separate a bit during the cooking process, it means you should have added more egg yolk. Egg yolks differ dramatically in size, so they are always an approximation at best when listed in recipes. In general, a bit more yolk is better than too little because the yolk acts as a binder. The method here follows pretty closely the method for hand-chopped jack mackerel—another good choice for these patties—as are sardines or herring.

flying fish patties SERVES 4
TOBIUO NO HAMBAGU

About 1 pound (450 g) flying fish or cutlassfish filet, skinned

2 tablespoons brown rice miso

2 large raw egg yolks, at room temperature

2 teaspoons potato starch (*katakuriko*)

1½ tablespoons finely chopped scallions or chives

3 tablespoons good-quality rapeseed oil

1 lemon, cut into 6 wedges (or 2 *sudachi* cut in half)

Slice the filets into thin strips (¼ inch/6 mm), then crosswise into the same size dice (¼ inch/6 mm) with a razor-sharp knife. Leave the fish on your chopping board and spoon the miso directly on top of the diced fish along with the egg yolks. Sprinkle with the potato starch and strew with the chopped scallions. Chop the ingredients into the flying fish with your knife by lifting and fluffing until the mixture has come together into a well-distributed homogeneous mass.

Form into 4 patties by gently slapping between cupped hands.

Heat the oil in a large frying pan over medium-low heat. When nicely warm, drop the patties into the oil and fry 2 minutes on one side. Turn and fry 2 minutes on the opposite side. Cover and cook 2 more minutes on low. Uncover, turn the heat back up to medium-low, and cook 1 more minute before removing the pan from the heat. The patties should be golden brown and firm but not unforgivingly hard to the touch; if not, cook a tad more. Serve with a wedge of lemon or, better yet, half of a *sudachi* (page 367).

I love the slightly crusty grains of salt that meet your tongue on random bites of salt-broiled fish. The salt is a subtle flavoring but definitely present. This kind of preparation epitomizes the simplicity that draws me to Japanese country food. Supremely fresh fish and minimal work yield a beguilingly tasty dish that anyone will want to replicate—well, unless you're not a fish person.

salt-broiled herring SERVES 6
NISHIN NO SHIOYAKI

4 medium-sized fresh herring

Sea salt

Grated daikon

Soy sauce

Lay the fresh herring on a foil sheet set over a grate. Place the oven rack in the third slot from the top of the oven and preheat the broiler. Sprinkle the herring with salt and broil for 15 minutes. Flip carefully and salt the other side. Broil 10 more minutes. Share the fish or serve 1 fish per person for big eaters.

Squeeze a few spoonfuls of grated daikon in your fist to remove the excess liquid and mound on the plate next to the fish. Drizzle the center of the mound with soy sauce.

VARIATIONS: Use any other fish one normally eats whole such as trout, saury, sardine, *aji* (jack mackerel), or *sayori* (halfbeak). For the thinner or smaller fish, cut the cooking time down to 10 minutes on the first side and 5 on the second.

Cutting deep slits in the flesh of a slightly larger fish such as grunt will help circulate the heat and cook it more evenly. The salt leaves a dry frost around the slits when grilled, and thus makes for an impressive presentation. Grunts are fatty and mild, but not oily, so when cooked their meat is almost fluffy.

salt-broiled grunt SERVES 6
ISAKI NO SHIOYAKI

3 medium-sized fresh grunt, or any other whole thick, mild fish, gutted and scaled

Fine sea salt

Place the oven rack in the third slot from the top and preheat the broiler.

Cut ¼-inch (6-mm) deep diagonal slits in both sides of the fish. Check to make sure the hard fin on the dorsal side of the fish has been cut off. Lay the whole fish on a grate set over an oven pan. Sprinkle the fish lightly with salt and broil for 10 minutes. Flip carefully and salt the other side. Broil 5 more minutes. Serve family style, two people sharing 1 fish.

Miso tends to burn when broiling, so be very careful that the fish is not close to the heat source. Also do not forget to oil the grill with a mild oil such as rapeseed. The miso dries out on the skin, giving the fish a slight crust and a moist center.

miso-broiled cod SERVES 4
SUKESODARA NO MISO YAKI

3 tablespoons brown rice or barley miso

1 tablespoon sake

4 small (¾-inch/2-cm) thick cod or pollock filets (about 2½ ounces/70 g), skin on

Set the oven rack in the third slot from the top and preheat the broiler.

Measure the miso into a small bowl and whisk in the sake. Lay the cod filets on a cutting board or plate. Spread the miso mixture evenly over the surface of both sides of the fish.

Transfer the filets, skin side down, onto an oiled fish rack, and perch on a cookie sheet to catch any drips. Broil for 4 minutes, flip gingerly (the miso sticks), and broil the skin side for 3 minutes. Carefully remove the filets from the rack and serve immediately or at room temperature.

VARIATIONS: Salmon filets would also be a good choice. Barbecuing will result in a more flavorful fish but take care that the coals are at a very low ember.

CRAB "MISO"

I suggested live crabs from Cook's.

"I can get dead ones from Costco cheaper" was the return e-mail from my childhood friend Marcus. Oh, and he added that he didn't have a pot but could buy one. We weren't coming all the way from Japan just to eat dead crabs, so I told him to buy the pot and I'd buy the crab. I'd say he got off well.

Crab is one of those foods I crave when going to California—Dungeness crab and Tomales Bay oysters actually. Japanese fish is, hands-down, fresher and tastier than much of the fish I encounter elsewhere. It all starts with the fisherman. Japanese fishermen treat fish with the respect that comes from generations of working on the sea and a profound culinary culture of enjoying eating fish raw. Japanese fishermen cut behind the fins to bleed sashimi fish and ice it while still on the sea, while some American fishermen wait until they dock. But inexplicably, live crabs and delicate oysters are hard to come by in Japan.

A few years ago when I took the little Sunny-Side Up! kids on the yearly school trip to California, I bought some live crabs and boiled them up at my brother's house (where Christopher was staying). We invited three of Christopher's high school pals. None of them had ever seen a live crab. None. They picked a bit at the crabmeat and pushed it around the plate but ate a lot of Acme Bread Company baguette. In contrast, the SSU! kids couldn't get enough, and when the following year's trip was set, Kyo immediately piped up, "I want crab!"

Dump the pot of boiling water and crabs into your kitchen sink. Cool with cold water. Snag a crab and pull off its back, then scrape out the gills. But don't stop there. Pull out a spoon from a nearby drawer and spoon up the creamy rusty-orange substance adhering to the shell. It will be pleasantly salty from the water, wildly pungent, and incredibly delicious. So what is this orangey stuff? Crab guts. Try them. Please. If you're feeling timid, you could splash in a bit of cold sake to help wash it down. Heaven.

So crab it was, and the venue: Marcus's house. Marcus always generously offers his kitchen for my use (not without plenty of kibitzing) and graciously hosts the whole gaggle of us every year. He tends to stick the kids in the back room to watch videos, but there's no complaining. Adults are a boring lot anyway.

What's the big fuss about getting live crabs, when Cook's will happily boil them to order and perform the messy cleaning and cracking operation (imagine bits of shell and crab juice flying around). First, let's go back to the boiling and cleaning. What all is involved here? You must grasp the crabs firmly and confidently (gingerly doesn't cut it), while keeping your hand out of claw's way and then heartlessly throw the wriggling guy into a pot of boiling salt water. Quickly grab another and another until they're all in the pot. Slam on the lid and wait for the water to come back to a boil. Cook's recommends another 13 minutes after that, but you must factor in the water-to-crab ratio and adjust. If your crabs are crowded in the pot, it will take longer to reach a boil, so I cut the boiling time down. It's all about common sense.

We boil the crabs ourselves for those warmly glorious guts, though I like the Japanese word "miso" better. So much more thoughtful and reflective of the texture and taste itself. And though we can get wood fire–grilled crab these days at Camino in Oakland—pretty unforgettable, by the way—we'll still be looking around for a kitchen to boil the crabs from Cook's because it's the crab miso that haunts us.

I remember not liking sea urchin when I first started eating sushi. No more. Natto? At first those drippy, icky beans looked and smelled disgusting. Now I love it. But what fascinates me most about Japanese food is the range of tastes: from elegantly subtle to out-of-control funky fermented (*takuan* pickles, natto, and yes, crab miso). And in many ways, I see this elegant/funky combination reflected in the Japanese people and culture. I guess that's what attracts me to this country: the contrasts.

Although not my first taste of sushi, my first "regular" sushi bar was called Onna no Shiro near the gates of Grant Street in San Francisco around 1980. The sushi bar was connected to a karaoke hostess bar by a fake Japanese-style bridge. Best friend Cecily Dumas and I became pals with the young sushi master, Sachio Kojima, and the counter waitress, Mama-san. We followed him when he opened up his own place on Geary Street called Kabuto Sushi. At Kabuto, Sachio developed several signature dishes, including one of my favorites: salmon *mushiyaki*. At the time, I didn't think how ridiculously simple it would be to make at home. Of course the whole thing hinges on fresh local salmon, so do wait for salmon season. Also, at around 80 grams (3 ounces), Japanese fish filets are smaller than the ones in the U.S., so you might want to cut large filets in half.

foil-wrapped broiled salmon with butter SERVES 4
SAMON NO MUSHIYAKI

4 (¾-inch/2-cm) thick salmon filets, skin on (about 3 ounces/80 g each)

1 teaspoon sea salt

4 teaspoons sake

4 teaspoons butter

4 scallions or 8 to 12 chives

Set the oven rack on the third slot from the top. Preheat the broiler.

Season the salmon filets with sake and salt, then dab a teaspoon of butter on top of each filet before curling a scallion (or a few chives) on top of the fish. Wrap in foil (see opposite).

Broil for 10 minutes on a rack set over a pan to catch the drips.

Serve as is or remove from the foil packages.

VARIATIONS: Any fresh fish filets are moist and delicious prepared this way: red snapper, cod, yellowtail, swordfish, halibut . . . whatever. Just adjust the cooking time according to the thickness of the fish. Or omit the butter and scallion and increase the sake to 1½ teaspoons for a more pristinely austere version that will balance well with a meal containing tempura or other deep-fried food.

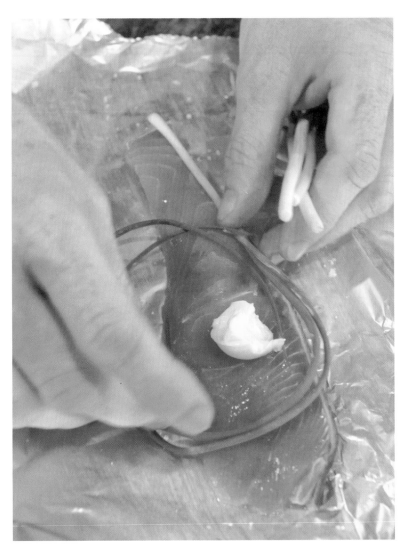

FOIL WRAPPING

Tear off four 8-inch (20-cm) long pieces of lightweight foil from a 12-inch (30-cm) wide roll and lay out side by side on your workplace. Set one filet on each piece of foil. Make sure the foil is big enough to enclose the filets well so the sake will not leak out. Sprinkle the filets lightly on both sides with about ¼ teaspoon salt from about a foot (30 cm) above the fish, then splash each with a teaspoon of sake.

Bring the two long edges of foil together and roll down, then squeeze the ends tightly to seal up the fish. Scrunch up the ends and bend them in toward the middle a bit to prevent the juices from running out.

Sea bass, with its lean, white flesh, benefits from a gentle cooking method. Rather than broiling, we prefer to foil-wrap sea bass, seasoned with a little salt and sake, and cook it in a bamboo steamer. This cooking method helps avoid the inevitable drying of lean fish like sea bass or halibut, making it an (almost) foolproof cooking technique. In the U.S. fish is often sold cut crosswise into steaks, whereas in Japan the fish is halved, then each filet is cut diagonally into thin filets. Try to get filets if possible—otherwise you could substitute thick half-steaks.

sake-steamed sea bass SERVES 4
SUZUKI NO SAKAMUSHI

4 (¾-inch/2-cm) thick sea bass filets, skin on (about 3 ounces/80 g each)

1 teaspoon (or more) sea salt

4 teaspoons sake

Fill a large wok or sauté pan with high sides and a curved bottom halfway with water and bring to a simmer over high heat. The pan should be large enough to be able to set a steamer over but not in the simmering water.

Season the fish with the sake and salt and wrap in foil (see page 243). Cook in the steamer over medium-high heat for 20 minutes. Set the steamer basket on a dinner plate to catch the drips. Place the hot foil packages of sea bass on individual plates or as part of a dinner plate with vegetables and rice.

VARIATIONS: Any lean fish filets can be substituted for the sea bass. You are looking for a mild, elegant taste.

The morning of one of our photo shoots, I zoomed over to the fish market while Miura-san was photographing flowers in the garden. I bought a slew of fish but ultimately ran out of time to prepare all of them. I don't quite remember what I had in mind for the snapper, but Tadaaki kindly took it over and put together this aromatic and subtly nuanced dish. The snapper wouldn't quite fit in the steamer, and before I could stop him he whacked off the tail, hence looked a little too bizarre to include a photo.

spring onion and ginger–stuffed steamed snapper SERVES 6
MADAI NO NEGI-SHOGA MUSHI

1 fresh snapper (about 2 pounds/ 1 kg)

1 *negi* or 2 thick spring onions, cut into julienne slivers

1 (1-inch/2.5-cm) square knob of ginger, peeled and slivered

Sea salt

¼ cup (60 cc) sake

Run the back side of a kitchen knife across the surface of the snapper to remove the scales. Take out the insides and cut off the hard dorsal fin. Wash the fish well in cold water to rinse out the blood and lingering guts. (Or have the fishmonger do this for you.)

Stuff the snapper with the slivered *negi* and ginger. Sprinkle salt lightly all over the fish inside and out. Place on top of a plate set inside a bamboo steaming basket set over simmering water. Pour the sake over the fish, cover, and steam for about 15 minutes, or until done. The fish should no longer be translucent but should not cook until dry.

VARIATION: Substitute any similar mild-flavored local medium-sized fish that will fit nicely (whole) in the steamer.

Freshly caught clams of all sizes and shapes are abundant in Japan and not expensive. Most of the smaller varieties are used in daily cooking, since they go well with miso soup. The important point is to get very fresh clams or even mussels. In this recipe, take care that the greens don't become muddy colored. I would sacrifice heat retention and leave the pot uncovered after they are cooked. These clams are also tasty for a cold snack the following day.

clams simmered in sake with scallions SERVES 6
ASARI NO SAKAMUSHI

8 cups *asari* or any small local clams

About 3 cups (750 cc) sake

1½ thin *negi* or 4 scallions (both white and green parts), cut into medium dice

1 teaspoon sea salt

2 dried japones or árbol hot chile peppers, crumbled (optional)

1 handful roughly chopped *mitsuba* leaves

Cooked Japanese rice, for serving

Scrub the clams in several changes of cold water to express some of the sand. Scoop the clams up with your hands or a wire sieve and drop into a large heavy pot with a lid.

Glug in enough sake to fill the pot about three-quarters the height of the clams. Sprinkle with the *negi*, salt, and chile peppers, if using. Replace the lid and cook on high heat until the clams have opened. Stir in the *mitsuba* and cook for about 30 seconds more. Serve in bowls as an appetizer or accompanied with a bowl of cooked Japanese rice. Discard any unopened clams.

VARIATIONS: Substitute flat-leaf parsley or cilantro for the *mitsuba*. For a heartier version, add 4 cups (1000 cc) spinach leaves, washed and chopped into 4-inch (10-cm) pieces, in place of the aromatic herbs. For another twist, swirl some of the hot clam liquid into 3 tablespoons of miso, whisk to emulsify, and stir back into the pot right before serving. Omit the salt.

My mother-in-law always puts eggs in her batter, as does Tadaaki, but I find egg makes the tempura spongy. Tempura requires a big pan full of oil, so of course the thrifty farmwife will fry up a variety of vegetables when she makes tempura—and the result will be a large draining tray heaped with batter-fried vegetables (and fish). The Hachisu family was numerous, so it took a bit of time to fry all the tempura. As a result, most of the fish or vegetables had cooled by the time they got to the table. And yes, they were a little spongy.

But now that I am older, I prefer to make tempura the way I like to eat it—crispy and burning hot. You will most likely end up with extra batter at the end—just toss it. If you are ready to go whole hog and fry up vegetables and fish in the same meal, I would use two smaller saucepans of oil so you can fry them at the same time (never fry vegetables after frying fish, despite what your farmer husband says about wasting oil). Serving this tempura hot from the oil means you may not be able to sit down right away and eat with the others. But then you might enjoy the occasional solitary meal.

cod tempura SERVES 4 TO 6
MADARA NO TEMPURA

Best-quality rapeseed or peanut oil

½ cup (75 g) good-tasting cake flour (page 10)

½ cup (125 cc) cold sparkling water

⅛ teaspoon fine white sea salt

3 or more large ice cubes

7 (¾-inch/18-mm) thick cod filets (2 to 2½ ounces/60 to 70 g each)

Fine white sea salt, organic soy sauce, or warm Tempura Dipping Sauce (page 311) for serving

Line a cookie sheet with paper towels on top of one whole newspaper (folded in half) to absorb the oil from the tempura. Set the sheet next to the stove. Over low heat, warm 4 inches (10 cm) of oil in a medium-sized, heavy, stainless steel saucepan.

Meanwhile, whisk the flour with the sparkling water and salt in a medium-sized bowl. Take out two pairs of long cooking chopsticks or tongs. Use one pair to dip the fish in the batter and one pair to remove the tempura from the hot oil. (Or just use your bare fingers to dip the fish in the batter if your sink is handy for a quick washup.) A flat slotted or mesh skimmer also works well to scoop the cooked tempura from the sizzling oil. Increase the heat on the oil to medium—be careful that the oil does not smoke. Test the readiness of the oil by dripping a little batter into the oil before you begin to fry. The batter should form a small ball as it hits the oil but should not brown immediately.

Toss the ice cubes into the tempura batter with chopsticks. Dip 3 or 4 cod filets in the batter, lift up each filet (one by one), and slip into the side of the pot of hot oil. (Remove the ice cubes to a small bowl and add more if necessary for subsequent batches. The point is to chill the batter but not dilute it.) The oil will bubble furiously, then slowly subside. Make sure the filets are not sticking to each other. Gently pry them apart with your chopsticks if they are. Turn the filets as they cook to promote even cooking and adjust the oil temperature as you go. The fish should be cooked at a moderate rate in the actively bubbling oil, but the batter crust should not take on color too fast. When the bubbles start to subside and the fish is golden brown, remove to the paper-lined cookie sheet. Serve hot with fine white sea salt, soy sauce, or warm dipping sauce.

VARIATIONS: Most any fish filets will substitute well for the cod as long as the fish is very fresh. Watch the bubbles and the oil temperature. The cooking time will depend on the thickness of the filets.

There is something intriguing about the slightly dry sheen that forms on the surface of the fish as it dangles out in the fresh air. *Himono* (dried or semidried fish) are perhaps most commonly made from the more oily, silver-skinned fish varieties such as jack mackerel (*aji*), but butterfish (*ebodai*), with its pink flesh, is a beautifully mild alternative. We don't air-dry fish as much as we should for the simple reason that it takes a bit of foresight. You must visit the fish market in the morning because the fish has to hang outside for at least half a day. Air-dried fish is a common breakfast food, perhaps because it needs only a simple pass under the broiler, so is quickly prepared—and because the dry, slightly salty flesh goes well with a morning bowl of rice.

air-dried butterfish SERVES 4 TO 6
EBODAI NO HIMONO

4 butterfish, gutted, degilled, and butterflied (heads intact)

Salt

Grated daikon (optional)

Soy sauce (optional)

Lay the fish on a wide pan or board and salt lightly on both sides from about a foot (30 cm) above the fish. This method is called *tatejio*—the distance from the fish ensures even coverage of salt.

Hang the fish outside in a cool shady spot to air-dry for half a day or so but not longer than 1 day. Either poke the fish directly on a hook twisted into a shaded board or thread string through the heads and hang from a tree. In Japan, we also use tiered fish-drying baskets made of blue nylon (usually sold only in the winter when most of the fish drying is done). I have seen these nets sold online from China in lots of 500 though not elsewhere. The net baskets are useful but not crucial to the process.

Grill the fish lightly over a low-ember charcoal fire (or on a rack set in the third level from the top under a broiler flame)—about 4 minutes, skin side up, then 6 minutes, stomach side up (this is opposite if broiling in the oven). The saying goes: *Umi hara, kawa sei*—"Cook the flesh side of sea fish first, but the skin side of river fish first."

Serve 1 fish per person hot or at room temperature. Delicious as is or with (squeezed) grated daikon drizzled with soy sauce.

MIRINBOSHI

Tadaaki mostly goes about his egg business and farming without paying much attention to my various endeavors. Sometimes he stops by Sunny-Side Up! to play with the kids or jumps into the book photo shoots, but other times he keeps his distance, giving me space to make my own mistakes.

One night after dinner, I plopped down on the sofa next to where he was reading his book and asked him to run by a few of his methods so I could write up the recipes. Dipping his head a little, he peered over his glasses at me and laughed. "So my recipes really are going to be in your book?"

"Yes, dear, they are. Haven't I been telling you that for the last year?"

Fired up by the book (though not letting on), Tadaaki keeps coming up with new cooking methods or reviving old ones. One night we were hashing out reshooting the chopped jack mackerel, and Tadaaki remembered a well-loved but forgotten dish from childhood called *mirinboshi*.

When fish are butterflied, head and all, the result is a beautiful, almost circular splayed fish. After hanging for a short period to air-dry, the semidried fish is grilled over low embers or in the fish-broiling drawer of the ubiquitous Japanese two-burner gas stovetop.

For *mirinboshi* (mirin-dried) fish, marinate 4 butterflied jack mackerel (*aji*) in 2 tablespoons each mirin and soy sauce overnight. Hang to dry in a shady place for at least half a day and up to 8 hours. Broil on a piece of foil set over a wire grate on the third from the top rack slot of the oven 6 minutes, stomach side up, and 4 minutes, skin side up, or grill over low-ember coals.

This is one of those Japanese foods that I had never eaten but see is readily available prepackaged in Japanese grocery stores in the U.S. Soy sauce and mirin are all you need to make these tantalizingly sweet-salty dried fish—and a little planning.

8

meat

As newlyweds, Tadaaki and I would stop by his parents' house for dinner occasionally, and Tadaaki would most likely be in the kitchen with his mother while I ended up chatting with Tadaaki's gruff but essentially kindly father, "*otosan*." (Once our children were born, *otosan* and *okaasan,* "mother" and "father," became *ojiichan* and *obaachan*, "grandpa" and "grandma.") We would sit dangling our legs at the *horigotatsu*, a low, quilt-covered table set over a pit in the floor that, although originally heated by charcoal, now had an electrical unit to keep our toes warm. The shoji doors of the six-mat room were kept closed to trap the heat given off by the lone kerosene heater. The rest of the house was so cold you could see your breath. That is how the traditional Japanese farm family lived during the winter. (Summers are blissfully cool inside the house, since the houses are built to breathe and to allow farmers a bit of respite from the sultry heat of our Japanese summers.)

Tadaaki had been living with his parents since graduating from college and by then had taken over most of the cooking, so it was my job to keep Otosan entertained. I'm not sure how well I performed that task, but I know he thought it unmanly of Tadaaki to continue cooking when he had a perfectly able bride to take over the work.

Every conversation Otosan initiated began with the same question (in the form of a statement): "Americans eat a lot of meat, don't they?" And each time, I gave the same answer: "No not really. Not anymore." But my words never really sank into Otosan's consciousness. I suppose deep-seated ideas believed for decades are the most difficult to shift. On the other hand, questions (or statements) like these are part of the pro forma conversation dance so often performed by older Japanese.

I never did grow up eating big joints of meat like some of my friends because there were six of us kids and beef was expensive. We ate *Sunset* magazine-inspired menus my mother seasoned using a cupboard full of Spice Island dried herbs and spices. At sixteen, a junior in high school, with my mother in graduate school (and sick of Stouffer's beef stew, or soup and sandwiches for dinner), I took over planning, shopping for, and cooking the family dinners. That was the year beef prices dropped, but we never did acquire a "big meat" style of eating. By the time I got to Japan, it was already the late eighties, and the typical meat-and-potatoes diet of American lore had evolved into a more eclectic combination of foods.

But my husband's family truly did not eat meat at all. Perhaps as a result, Tadaaki isn't attracted much by chops or burgers but seems to love meat as part of a stir-fry—just a little for flavoring. As for me, I'd rather avoid throwing in some meat but Tadaaki is a wiry-framed, broad-shouldered farmer who craves protein, rice, and salt after a day of physical toil. In the last forty years, meat has become a larger part of the farmer's diet. Dishes that used to be reserved for guests or special occasions have become part of the daily fare. I have included some of those honest home-style dishes that serve as tummy warmers but also "company" dishes such as sukiyaki, shabu-shabu, and beef *tataki*, whose success hinge on high-grade cuts of sirloin. And I have chosen food that is not only authentic day-to-day Japanese food but also has flavor combinations attractive to the Western palate.

CLEANING A CHICKEN

Plucking feathers off a bird is more tedious than disgusting, but the first time you thrust your whole hand into a chicken's body cavity to pull out a mass of bloody organs does involve a certain mind-set. Twenty years ago, when we were first married, I wanted to eat our chicken and knew I couldn't palm the cleaning job off on Tadaaki. After all, he did the killing. Probably more than the pile of slimy guts, it was the smell that bothered me, so I learned to remove myself from the process and focus on the metamorphosis from bird to familiar "chicken" shape unfolding at my hand.

As Western holidays, Thanksgiving and Christmas preparations usually fall to me. A few years ago I decided it was time to involve the little Sunny-Side Up! kids again in the bird cleaning—as education. We had done turkey and chicken cleaning events (despite the mothers being worried we'd freak out the kids or turn them off of chicken meat), but with the bird flu scare, I had put a stop to chicken coop visits or any activities involving touching chickens. The epidemic hysteria had died down and the flu had passed us by, so I announced my intentions to the staff. Our vegetarian teacher hung out in the backyard doing day care duties, but the other teachers (reluctantly) pitched in with the chore. Most important, they were not to show distaste or hesitation and were to approach the job as normal. And none of the kids could manhandle or treat the chickens with disrespect.

After wrangling for hours with slippery, slick duck feathers the Christmas before, I wanted to try plucking the chickens without the obligatory boiling water dunk. My theory proved true: no need for the wetting to dislodge the feathers. And as a result, the feathers were less difficult to pull. The bonus: no smell.

As with most kids, it was fun at the outset but got to be a drudge, so their interest waned. At first, a few little ones were scared of the dead birds, but a matter-of-fact attitude helped them overcome those fears. Not surprisingly, the best eaters were the best workers—as if they understood the implicit contract between themselves and the getting of their food to the plate. They were all fascinated with the assembly line Tadaaki eventually set up to eviscerate the eight birds we were cleaning for Thanksgiving dinner that year.

And it was one of the best ever, with an unforgettable combination of friends. The conversations, in both Japanese and English, were animated. Our kids are all getting older, so we squeezed thirty-two people around two dining room tables. Nobody complained the chicken was tough. More to the point, our friends appreciated every part of their meal and sent their plates back clean. The SSU! preschoolers weren't invited for Thanksgiving but got to taste their handiwork in the form of country soup a couple of days later. And they, too, were properly thankful.

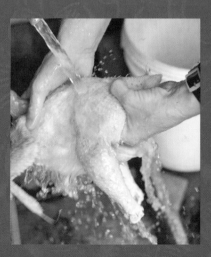

Restaurants in Japan often specialize in one kind of cooking, such as yakitori, soba, or tempura. Yakitori literally means "grilled chicken," but essentially a yakitori shop or stand will slow grill all sorts of skewered meats. These meats are flavored with salt, soy sauce-based brushing marinade, or even miso thinned with sake. I prefer the salt because it does not overpower the natural flavor of the chicken and leeks.

chicken and leeks grilled on a stick SERVES 4
NEGIMA

2 boneless chicken thighs with skin (about 1¼ pounds/550 g)

¾ teaspoon sea salt

4 thin *negi* or thin leeks

Cooked rice (optional)

Cut the thighs into 1½ by ¾-inch (4 by 2-cm) pieces and drop into a heavy, resealable plastic bag. Sprinkle with salt and massage in gently to distribute. Squeeze out any air and seal the bag well. Let sit in the refrigerator overnight or at least several hours.

If using bamboo skewers, soak in cold water for an hour. Meanwhile, prepare a barbecue using hardwood charcoal. (The fire needs to burn down, so do this a good 45 minutes before cooking.)

Cut the whites of the *negi* or thin leeks into 1½-inch (4-cm) lengths and thread them crosswise on the soaked bamboo or metal skewers, alternating with the salted chicken pieces. Make sure there will be enough area of burning charcoal to cook the skewered food. Cook slowly over a low ember fire, turning frequently. The chicken skin and leeks have a tendency to burn, so keep the skewers away from the direct heat of the charcoal. Be patient and pour yourself a drink, since they will take at least 30 minutes to cook.

Alternatively, broil slowly on a rack set over a broiler pan in the third slot from the top of the oven. Turn for even cooking and browning. Cook for about 10 to 15 minutes, flip, and cook less than 10 minutes—just until the meat has firmed up but is not rock hard.

Serve hot as appetizers or with cooked rice.

VARIATION: Marinate in soy sauce instead of salt. Brush on a little more soy sauce as you broil the skewers.

When Tadaaki asked me, "How would you like to be a Japanese farmer's wife?" I told him I'd have to think about it. I didn't know if I could stay in Japan forever, and having grown up in the San Francisco Bay Area, I wasn't sure I could become as "organic" as this guy was. Tadaaki's ideal life was a life without electricity. I couldn't live without a washer and dryer. I wondered what kind of life we would have together. Though I did decide to make the plunge, I experienced periodic bouts of uncertainty at the irrevocable path upon which I had embarked. So my older sister Pam came to Japan to help give me some perspective.

Tadaaki invited us for lunch at his parents' to introduce them to Pam. We took the train and Tadaaki met us at the station wearing geeky dress-up clothes with sleeves too short. Where were the jeans? But for lunch he made a Chinese chicken salad from his own chickens with a sesame-miso vinaigrette. Who was this guy? Pam immediately saw through the clothes and gave her seal of approval. And over the next few years, she often admonished me to "be nice to Tadaaki," as if she thought I might lose such a paragon. And that's how I became a Japanese farmer's wife.

chicken salad with
sesame-miso vinaigrette SERVES 6
TORINIKU SARADA GOMA-MISO VINEGURETTO

2 skinless, boneless chicken breasts (about 9 ounces/250 g each)

2 tablespoons sake

2 teaspoons grated ginger

1 teaspoon sea salt

2 small heads of butter lettuce

Sesame-Miso Vinaigrette (page 304)

Fill a deep frying pan or wok halfway with water and bring to a simmer over high heat. The pan should be large enough to be able to set a steamer over but not in the simmering water.

Sprinkle each chicken breast with 1 tablespoon sake, then smear each piece with 1 teaspoon grated ginger and ½ teaspoon salt. Wrap in foil (see page 243). Set the foil-wrapped chicken in the steamer and cook for 20 minutes over medium-high heat. Remove the steamer from the heat and allow the chicken pieces to cool in their juices.

Tear off any outer discolored leaves of the lettuce and cut off the stem end with a sharp knife about 1 inch (2.5 cm) from the bottom (this helps remove unwanted dirt). If possible, don't wash the lettuce—just wipe any clinging dirt with a damp towel (see page 170). Leave the lettuce leaves whole if they are not too big, otherwise cut crosswise into 3-inch (7.5-cm) wide pieces.

Make the sesame-miso vinaigrette—but reserve a teaspoon or so of the ground sesame seeds to sprinkle on the salad after dressing. Whisk again right before serving.

When the chicken is cool, remove it from the foil packets but do not discard the liquid. Shred the chicken by hand into ¼-inch (6-mm) thick pieces and moisten with a tiny bit of the steaming liquid if the meat seems slightly dry.

When ready to serve, remove the lettuce from the fridge and mound attractively on a large platter or individual plates. Strew the chicken pieces over the top, drizzle sparingly with some sesame-miso vinaigrette, and sprinkle with reserved roughly ground sesame seeds.

RATIO: sesame : miso : rice vinegar : rapeseed oil—2 : 1 : 2 : 4

This version of country teriyaki is not at all syrupy and uses no sugar. A simple soy sauce–mirin marinade is all you need to infuse the chicken thighs with that hauntingly dark and completely addicting teriyaki flavor. Although easily cooked on the stove, these are something special when barbecued.

teriyaki chicken SERVES 6
TORI NO TERIYAKI

4 boneless chicken thighs with skin (about 2⅔ pounds/ 1200 g)

½ cup (125 cc) mirin

½ cup (125 cc) soy sauce

1 (2 by 1-inch/5 by 2.5-cm) piece of ginger, peeled and grated

Put the chicken thighs in a heavy, resealable plastic bag. Mix the mirin, soy sauce, and grated ginger in a small bowl or measuring cup. Pour over the chicken thighs and massage in gently to distribute the marinade. Squeeze out the excess air and seal the bag well. Let sit in the refrigerator overnight or at least several hours.

Heat a heavy cast-iron pan over high heat and sear the chicken thighs, skin side down, 2 at a time. (You don't want to crowd them or create a soupy mess in the pan from excess marinade; it will just steam the meat.) After a minute or two, some oil from the skin should have rendered and any excess marinade should have bubbled out. Turn the thighs, sear for a minute, then lower the heat, cover, and cook 6 more minutes on low heat. Uncover, flip the chicken back onto the skin side, wipe the accumulated condensation from the inside of the lid, re-cover, and cook 6 more minutes. At this point you can let the meat rest for a short time to finish cooking over a low-ember barbecue or uncovered over medium heat in the cast-iron pan. It should take about 3 or so more minutes on each side in the pan or about 6 on the barbecue, depending on the heat. The skin has a tendency to burn, so be careful.

(Bone-in chicken thighs can be used as well but will need an extra 10 minutes of cooking time.)

Let rest for 5 minutes before cutting.

RATIO: mirin:soy sauce—1:1

VARIATION: Make a sandwich the next day with sliced teriyaki chicken meat, good bakery pain de mie bread, Japanese Mayonnaise (page 312), sliced onion, and lettuce leaves.

When Tadaaki started making these several years ago, they immediately became one of my favorite things he made and were especially nice to come back to after a trip abroad. Soft miso-flavored meatballs in a steaming bowl of stock hits the spot after fifteen hours of transit. These meatballs keep well for several days in the fridge, though I would poach them halfway before chilling and reheat the next day (or the next) in fresh, simmering liquid. You can also strain and chill the original simmering liquid to use for reheating the meatballs or finishing ones that are partially cooked.

simmered chicken-and-miso meatballs SERVES 4
CHIKIN MITO BORU

STOCK

1 (3 by 6-inch/7.5 by 15-cm) piece of konbu

6 tablespoons brown rice miso

¼ small head of napa cabbage, quartered lengthwise (about ⅔ pound/300 g)

3 thin *negi* or 6 fat scallions

MEATBALLS

1 pound (500 g) coarse-ground or hand-chopped chicken thigh

2 tablespoons chopped scallions or *negi* (whites and green tops)

2 tablespoons brown rice miso

1 tablespoon finely grated ginger

1 tablespoon potato starch

Cooked rice, for serving

Fill a medium-sized, heavy pot with 2 quarts (2 liters) of cold water. Drop the konbu and *negi* into the water and bring to a simmer. Measure the miso into a large soup ladle and dip the ladle slightly into the simmering water to wet the miso. Whisk enough hot water into the miso so that the miso will not leave lumps when fully submerged into the simmering konbu stock.

(Prepare the meatballs while you are waiting for the water with konbu and *negi* to come to a simmer.)

Dump the chicken meat into a large mixing bowl and add the scallions, miso, grated ginger, and potato starch. Mix well with your hands to distribute all the aromatics.

Form ten 2-inch (5-cm) diameter meatballs by tossing the meat between your two palms. The shape does not need to be perfectly round but it is important for the outer surface to seal. The surface should be slick and glossy.

Lay the lengthwise-cut napa cabbage quarter wedge on a cutting board, remove the core with a V cut, and slice crosswise into thick strips (about ¾ inch/2 cm). Add to the simmering stock and bring back to a simmer.

As soon as the stock begins to simmer again, drop as many meatballs as can comfortably cook in your pot (they should not be crowded when they rise to the surface) and cook at a lively simmer until the meatballs pop up, about 6 minutes or so. Check for doneness by catching up one with a wooden spoon and pressing gently on the meatball. It should not have a lot of give but also should not be rock hard.

Spoon up 2 or 3 meatballs into a small bowl along with some of the napa cabbage and a little broth. Serve with a bowl of rice.

VARIATIONS: Use a combination of breast and thigh meat instead of all thigh meat. Cut the *negi* into ¾-inch (2-cm) lengths or the scallions into 2-inch (5-cm) lengths, and add to the soup with the napa cabbage. Serve the cooked *negi* pieces with the cabbage and meatballs.

My mother never made deep-fried foods, so for many years I was scared to attempt them. Living in Japan changed that because much of the fried food here is so light and tasty—probably because of the attention to detail in using excellent frying oil. I couldn't not make them. My husband's aunt, Katchan, is the master *kara age*–maker in our house. She brings trays of these bite-sized, crispy chicken pieces for family dinners during the summer obon period or the New Year (*oshogatsu*). Recently Katchan was unable to make it for one of our family dinners, so I offered to prepare *kara age* in her stead. And with great gusto, Tadaaki's brother Noriaki pronounced it *"Umai!"* ("Delicious!") Phew. Some cooks use a combination of flour and potato starch; I prefer just starch. Also, I make bigger pieces than normal because that cuts down on the fried surface and gives you more juicy chicken in each bite. Leftover chicken pieces can be heated up the next day in a dry frying pan, covered, over low heat. Shake the pan occasionally to recrisp all sides.

deep-fried ginger chicken SERVES 6 TO 8
TORI NO KARA AGE

6 boneless chicken thighs, skin on
   (4 pounds/1800 g)

½ cup (125 cc) organic soy sauce

¼ cup (60 cc) sake

2 tablespoons grated ginger

Best-quality rapeseed oil
   for deep fat frying

1 cup or more (150 to 200 g)
   potato starch

Cut the thighs into eighths or twelfths, depending on the size. The pieces should be about 2-inch (5-cm) rough squares. Drop the chicken pieces into a freezer-style resealable bag. Add the soy sauce, sake, and ginger, and massage in with your fingers to distribute the marinade among the chicken pieces. Squeeze out any air from the bag, roll, and seal. Refrigerate overnight or at least several hours if possible.

Remove the chicken from the refrigerator. Line a cookie sheet with a thick piece of newspaper topped with a layer of paper towels. Set next to the stove. Warm 4 inches (10 cm) of oil in a medium-sized, heavy stainless steel saucepan over low heat.

Measure the potato starch into a small to medium-sized bowl. Take out a pair of long cooking chopsticks or tongs for checking the chicken and removing it from the oil.

Increase the temperature on the oil to about medium. The oil should not be smoking. Test the oil with a drop of the potato starch before starting. It should sizzle and immediately form a small ball as it hits the oil but should not brown. Adjust the oil temperature as needed.

continued on next page

deep-fried ginger chicken

Massage the chicken quickly with your left hand to distribute the marinade and then, working with 6 or 8 pieces at a time, drop the chicken in the bowl of potato starch. Dredge the chicken in the starch with your right hand, shake off any excess with a couple of brisk shakes, and slip into the hot oil. While your hands are still covered with marinade and potato starch, drop the next 6 to 8 pieces into the starch and dredge before washing your hands.

Nudge the bobbing chicken pieces gently with your chopsticks or tongs to turn and separate, if need be. The skins will become a deep golden color but should not be browning too quickly. Carefully observe the bubbles that shoot out from the chicken pieces, and when they start to subside (or "quiet down," as Tadaaki says), they should be ready. It will take 6 minutes or so per batch.

Remove from the oil and drain on the paper-lined cookie sheet. Then transfer them to a dinner plate lined with a piece of attractive absorbent paper folded in two, asymmetrically on the diagonal. (We use calligraphy practicing paper. It doubles as cooking paper in Japanese farm kitchens.) Serve immediately and eat as is. This is another one of those dishes that requires "mama at the stove." That's life as a Japanese farmwife (though until recently it was my husband who tended to perform these selfless tasks).

RATIO: soy sauce : sake : grated ginger—4 : 2 : 1

WAGYU

Horikoshi-san handed me the 4-kg bag of wagyu I had ordered for the school lunch and shot me a look. His eyes lit up for a second as he breathed the following words with uncharacteristic reverence: *"Nama de taberareru."* ("You can eat this raw!") I only buy wagyu and I only get it from our local butcher shop, Marukyu. Wagyu means nothing more than "Japanese beef," though abroad wagyu often refers to the heavily marbled beef typical of Kobe or Matsuzaka. If the meat doesn't look good, Horikoshi-san won't buy it from the supplier. He has a small shop with loyal customers that trust him, so his standards are high. But when Horikoshi-san gave me "that look," I knew the beef that day was something extraspecial. My oldest son, Christopher, and I had been going through a rough spot, so on the drive home, the idea to make *gyu tataki* (seared tenderloin) for him jumped into my mind.

Touching food makes me feel alive, so back in my kitchen I didn't waste any time and tore open the package. I salted the wagyu lightly on all sides, poked it with long metal skewers, grabbed a lighter, and carried the meat outside. Rummaging around the storage house, I found some rice straw and plopped it into a big heap in the barbecue. Oops, forgot the ice water bath. Back in the house for that. The breeze had picked up a tad by the time I had set everything up, but nonetheless I forged ahead. Working quickly, I lit the straw and poked the skewered meat straight into the flames, rotating to sear all sides before plunging the filet into the ice water bath.

My gentle hands tossed Suka-san's butter lettuce leaves with a few tendrils of shiso chiffonade as I drizzled in a bit of my Japanese organic rapeseed oil, local Yamaki soy sauce, and organic rice vinegar. I mounded the glistening leaves alongside the thinly sliced, seared wagyu and splashed some ponzu into a celadon green soy sauce plate. I called Baachan and we sat down for our Thursday evening "coze."

In those days, the boys still tagged along with Tadaaki to practice the ancient samurai art of sword on Thursday afternoons, a four-hour round-trip by train. On the way home, they usually called to find out what the dinner plan was, because in our house that's always the question of the day. So when Christopher called from the train to ask what was for dinner that night, I told him.

His immediate and deeply satisfied "Yesssss" erased the recent tension-filled days. Food never fails to soothe what ails us.

Not only fish, but many foods can be eaten as sashimi: Beef, chicken *sasami* (tenderloin strip of breast), and even fresh sliced vegetables such as daikon or turnip are lovely raw, thinly sliced, and dipped in soy sauce or ponzu. I crave raw foods, so am naturally drawn to sashimi-style foods. Searing beef tenderloins over a straw fire renders the meat pleasantly cinched up on the surface but virtually raw inside, thus it is imperative to ask the butcher if the meat can be eaten as beef sashimi (*gyu sashi*). In Japan the concept of eating raw fish or meat is deeply embedded in how the producers or fisherman treat their meat and fish, therefore many varieties are safe to eat raw. And fishmongers or butchers know their stuff, so you can rely on their expertise.

seared beef tenderloin SERVES 4 TO 6
GYU TATAKI

1 pound (500 g) top-quality, grass-fed sirloin tenderloin

Sea salt

Country-Style Ponzu (page 309)

GARNISH

1 tablespoon wasabi, preferably freshly grated

Zest from half a yuzu, *sudachi*, or Meyer lemon

1 small fresh chile, sliced into fine rings (optional)

Half a yuzu, *sudachi*, or Meyer lemon

Set the tenderloin on a cutting board or dinner plate and salt lightly on all sides from about a foot (30 cm) above the meat (*tatejio*).

Run five 1½-foot (40-cm) metal skewers through each filet laterally, keeping the handles all at the same place with the tips radiating out like an open fan.

Heap straw in a barbecue and light it; or build a roaring fire. Carefully hold the skewered filet directly in the flames, rotating until the surface sizzles and all sides are seared. (This operation becomes quite difficult if there is any breeze.) Plunge the filet into ice water to cool. Remove from the water, pat dry, and wrap in a clean kitchen towel before refrigerating. Alternatively, sear directly in a hot stove flame or red-hot barbecue, wrap in paper towels, and place in the fridge for 1 to 2 hours (or 30 minutes in the freezer) to cool.

When ready to eat, slice crosswise into ⅛-inch (3-mm) pieces and fan out overlapping slices on an attractive plate.

Dab wasabi on the side of the plate and garnish with a scattering of citrus zest and chile, if using. Set the half piece of citrus in the middle of the "sashimi flower." Splash a little ponzu into individual small soy sauce plates for each person. To eat: Catch a speck of wasabi with your chopsticks and scrape onto a single piece of meat, dip in the sauce, and pop in your mouth.

Very similar in spirit to *Nikujaga* (Pork and Onions Simmered with Potatoes, page 281), and another well-loved dish of my sons. *Gyudon*, served in a large, deep bowl called a *donburi*, means "beef on top of rice in a *donburi* bowl." There is something elementally appealing about *gyudon* for the Japanese. It is at once warming and simple. Also who can argue with a one-dish meal? Though I always ask, "Where's the vegetable?"

beef and onions simmered with ginger SERVES 6 TO 8
GYUDON

1 (5 by 3-inch/13 by 8-cm) piece of dried konbu

2 (9-ounce/250-g) packages *ito konnyaku* or *shirataki* noodles, drained (page 11)

2 medium-small onions, (about ⅔ pound/300 g)

1 (2-inch/5-cm) square piece of ginger, peeled

½ pound (225 g) thinly sliced beef shoulder meat

⅓ cup (80 cc) sake

½ cup (120 cc) soy sauce

1 tablespoon mirin

Plain Rice (page 143), for serving

7-spice powder (*shichimi togarashi*, page 7)

Measure 4 cups (1000 cc) of cold water into a medium-sized, heavy pot or casserole and drop in the piece of konbu.

Prepare a small pot of boiling water for the *ito konnyaku*. Take the *ito konnyaku* out of its bag and snip the rubber band off. Cut the ball of noodles in half through its center, drop into the boiling water, and parboil for 5 minutes. Drain in a colander.

Cut the ends off the onions, then again in half vertically. Peel and slice crosswise into thin (⅛-inch/3-mm) rounds. Slice the ginger crosswise into paper-thin pieces. Add the onions, ginger, and *ito konnyaku* to the pot with the soaking konbu. Bring to a boil, turn down to a lively simmer, and cook for several minutes until the onions have almost softened.

When the onions are almost done, cut the meat slices in half horizontally a couple of times (about the size that you can eat in one bite when cooked), roughly separate the pieces with your fingers, and drop into the simmering onions and *ito konnyaku*.

Stir to promote even cooking and to break up any meat clumps. Cook until the meat has almost lost its pink before adding the sake, soy sauce, and mirin. Taste for sweetness (the onions have natural sweetness, so depending on the onions, the sake and the small amount of mirin should provide the added "sweetness" necessary). Add a splash more mirin if you prefer it sweeter or soy sauce if you prefer it saltier, and simmer a minute or so more before serving.

Mound the cooked rice in deep soup bowls, preferably *donburi* style, and ladle the soy sauce–flavored meat, noodle, onion, and ginger on top. Sprinkle with *shichimi togarashi*, and serve. Or you can serve the *gyudon* and rice in two small separate bowls (my preference).

ARTISANAL CHARCOAL

Not much surprises me after living in Japan for more than twenty years, but the Noto Peninsula took my breath away. Here was the Japan of my dreams: verdant hills unmarred by unsightly telephone wires, with the local architectural-style still being honored. And it had the sea crashing against the rocks along the coast, host to myriad varieties of fish and sea greens.

I was there to meet up with Miura-san (my photographer) and Kim (my editor in Japan) to visit Sakamoto, a *ryokan* (traditional Japanese inn) of legendary repute. I was not disappointed. On day two of our visit, Sakamoto-san recommended we visit the charcoal guy. Winding through the coastal roads, I had no idea what awaited us at the charcoal kilns.

After forty years of cooking since my early teens, it's not often I have a food-related revelation, but when I do, it rocks my world. I suppose you must remember that moment when you discovered artisanal salt years ago, or when you finally embraced small-producer olive oil instead of the gallon can of Bertolli. The excitement at finding something so fabulous that it changes the way you look at food is a seminal moment in any cook's life.

Our navigation system said we were there, but the kilns weren't discernible from the unassuming office and side buildings. Nonetheless we drove down into the parking area and stepped out of the car. The thirty-something owner approached us, hand outstretched—decidedly not the usual style in rural Japan but perhaps in deference to the foreigners (Kim and me). This also told me that the young owner was not your typical guy; he followed his own rules.

Choichiro Ohno began apprenticing with his father while still in his early twenties and took over the business when his father died several years later. He runs the family kilns on his own and is mad passionate about charcoal. It only took about two sentences into his explanation for me to catch the enthusiasm and to start "jonesing" for that charcoal. I had to have it. Not to let the opportunity slip by, I prepared a business card with my address and a ¥10,000 bill.

I had always assumed (erroneously) that the charcoal I bought at the local home center was produced in Japan, but I had unwittingly been using charcoal mass-produced in China all these years. I thought back to the countless barbecued meals I had unwittingly infused with that soulless smoke. And so I bought four 10-kg bags of that beautiful small-batch charcoal produced in hand-crafted kilns at only ¥2,000 ($26) a bag. Ohno-san offered to strap two bags together to halve the delivery charge, so I got ¥1,000 back from my ¥10,000 bill.

This summer we are madly barbecuing (both Western and Japanese style) because I am desperate to use my new artisanal charcoal. We've already gone through 1½ bags, but I've got Ohno-san's card and he promised to send more.

When summer rolls around, our boys often ask to have a *yakiniku* party. Sometimes they invite friends, but sometimes it's just the family. My mother-in-law always finds these dinners to be great fun—a break in the routine. The smoke element makes this really more of an outside dinner. But that's part of the excitement, being outside on a warm summer night, perhaps catching a hint of a breeze (if we're lucky), with the aroma of smoldering artisanal charcoal wafting across the yard and the sizzling meat perfuming the air. That is summer.

charcoal-barbecued sirloin and vegetables SERVES 6
YAKINIKU

VEGETABLE OPTIONS

Japanese eggplants, sliced in half
  vertically

Japanese green peppers (or poblano
  chiles), cored, seeded, and cut in
  quarters

Okra, whole

Summer squash, cut into ½-inch
  (12-mm) rounds

Squash, cut into ¼-inch (6-mm) slices

Onion, cut into ½-inch (12-mm) rings

Scallions, white part and a couple of
  inches of green

1 pound (500 g) marbled sirloin, cut
  by the butcher into 1 by 3 by ⅛-inch
  (2.5-cm by 7.5-cm by 3-mm) strips

Sea salt

Lemon wedges

Kochujang (Korean hot pepper paste)
  (optional, page 7)

Soy sauce (optional)

Plain Rice (page 143) or Brown Rice
  (page 144), for serving

Heat a small *shichirin* or "hibachi"-style barbecue until the coals are hot and no longer have flames. (Use two if you have an extra one.)

In the meantime, attractively arrange a selection of vegetables on one or two dinner-sized plates. Place the meat on a couple of plates as well and sprinkle lightly with salt. Each person will need a small plate for the barbecued meat and vegetable pieces as they are cooked.

Using metal chopsticks (if you have them, otherwise disposable chopsticks), each person should cook his or her own meat to their liking, but the vegetables are a bit of a free-for-all. Whoever has an empty hand or spare moment should pop some vegetables on the grill with chopsticks and everyone should take turns flipping them. This is a cooperative and fun kind of eating experience. I like to eat my sizzling *yakiniku* with a sprinkle of sea salt and a squeeze of lemon (and occasionally with a dab of *kochujang*). Vegetables can be eaten as is, sprinkled with salt or dipped in soy sauce. Serve with a bowl of cooked Japanese rice.

VARIATIONS: Substitute thinly sliced beef tongue, lean beef slices marinated in half soy sauce and half marmalade, or thin slices of pork cheek (*tontoro*) for the sirloin.

Sukiyaki is not particularly farm food. Sukiyaki beef is typically an expensive, marbled cut, so it's more of a meal for company and perhaps most often served at restaurants. But we do eat it in our home because I find the preparation effortless and, with our own local ingredients, could not imagine encountering a better version in a restaurant. Dipping the just cooked (but not overcooked) beef and vegetables into the creamy beaten egg is not to be missed, so don't skip the egg. The hot broth heats up and infuses the egg with a sweet soy essence as you slurp the whole combination into your mouth. Also the egg mitigates the sweetness. I prefer mirin to sugar, but the boys are the opposite. Either way, the liquid part should neither be too salty nor cloyingly sweet. The liquid part should just cover the bottom of the pan, not even ¼ inch (6 mm) deep.

You will need a portable tabletop gas burner to make this dish at the table.

sukiyaki SERVES 8

2 (9-ounce/250-g) packages *ito konnyaku* or *shirataki* noodles, drained (page 11)

16 shiitake mushrooms, woody stems removed

2 bunches bitter greens (chrysanthemum, *komatsuna*, or mustard), cut into 2-inch (5-cm) lengths

4 thin *negi* or spring onions, cut into 2-inch (5-cm) lengths

1 (10.5-ounce/300-g) block Japanese-style "cotton" tofu, cut into 8 pieces

8 very fresh farm eggs, at room temperature

Mirin, soy sauce, organic granulated sugar, and sake

1½ pounds (675 g) sirloin (marbled or not), sliced crosswise into 3/32-inch (2.5-mm) thin sheets by a butcher (see Note)

Cooked Japanese rice, for serving

Slice open the plastic bag, remove the *ito konnyaku*, and snip the rubber band off the ball of noodles. Cut the *ito konnyaku* in half crosswise and drop in a small pot of boiling water to parboil for 5 minutes. Drain in a colander before sliding the noodles into a soup-sized serving bowl for the table.

Arrange the vegetables attractively on a platter or basket. Invert the tofu onto a small plate before cutting and serving. Place 1 whole unshelled egg in each of eight small rice bowls. Set a bowl in front of each guest and don't forget an empty bowl for the shells. The guests should break the egg into their bowls and beat it briefly with chopsticks.

Place a tabletop burner in the middle of the table and set a cast-iron sukiyaki pan or frying pan on the burner. Pour in ½ cup (125 cc) water, 2 tablespoons mirin, and 3 tablespoons soy sauce to start. Have containers of extra water, mirin, soy sauce, sugar, and sake available on the table to adjust the taste as the sauce reduces. The ratio here is 4:2:3 (water:mirin; or sugar + sake:soy sauce).

Add some of each kind of vegetable and several pieces of tofu to the seasoned water, making sure each vegetable stays in its own area. Once the vegetables are almost cooked (greens should still remain brightly colored), push away some of the vegetables for a clear space and lay several pieces of meat completely flat in that space. Cook until almost all the pink is gone but not quite.

Use a serving spoon to scoop the pieces of meat and vegetables and tofu into the bowls with beaten egg or have the guests serve themselves with chopsticks. Do not replenish the vegetables or tofu until the guests finish all of the first batch (otherwise you'll end up mixing bright green vegetables with the well-simmered remnants). Serve with a small bowl of Japanese rice.

NOTE: If you are able, prepare a platter for the butcher to lay the meat slices in an overlapping pattern. This will make serving much easier and prettier.

The first time I had Japanese steak was at a small but exclusive steak restaurant. My friend Kinuyo had brought me there, and I realized at the time that steak was a special meal, probably not home food. Beef was quite expensive then, and I had to buy it at a fancy department store basement meat shop if I wanted top-quality steak or tenderloin. The muslin-wrapped hunk of beef from which steaks were cut was always brought out with a certain reverence. At most steak restaurants the meat is cooked on a flat metal griddle—a *teppan*. *Teppanyaki*-style cooking was made famous in America by Benihana, of the flashing knives show—a bit comical, choreographed food entertainment. Basically Japanese chefs in sushi bars, steak shops, or even ramen shops work extremely fast. I'm fast, too, but not flashy (and don't flip things in the air). The restaurant steak was excellent, but I could have done without the vegetables on the griddle. Japanese steak is usually well marbled, so quite succulent, though some meat is marbled to the point of being almost pink. A thin steak cut is better cooked on the pan, so don't be tempted to break out the barbecue.

japanese-style steak SERVES 6
STEIKI

A couple of pieces of best-quality beef suet

2 (¾-inch/2-cm) thick, well-marbled grass-fed sirloin steaks (about 1 pound/500 g)

Sea salt or organic soy sauce, for serving

Heat a heavy cast-iron pan or griddle over high heat and rub with one of the pieces of suet until some of the fat has rendered and filmed the pan.

Slap one of the steaks (straight from the fridge, not room temperature) on the pan and cook for 30 seconds. Flip and cook the other side for 30 seconds. Lower the heat, cover, and cook 2 minutes more on each side over low heat for rare or 3 minutes for medium-rare. Add 1 more minute for each degree of doneness. Water will bead up on the inside of the lid, so be sure to wipe the condensation a few times during the cooking process, otherwise the liquid will fall back onto the pan and cause the steaks to steam rather than sear.

Wipe out the pan and repeat the process with the second steak. Do not cook 2 steaks at once, as they will end up steaming rather than searing.

Let the steaks rest 5 minutes before cutting crosswise into ¼-inch (6-mm) strips. If the strips are too long, cut in half, though the presentation is prettier left whole. Eat dipped in a little salt or soy sauce. Makes tasty leftovers for the next day's lunch or a chilled summer dinner.

VARIATION: Marinate the beef for a half day in soy sauce and a splash of sake. Be sure to shake off the marinade well before searing. Eat as is (no salt or additional soy sauce needed). I made this variation at Andrew's request and it was almost better than the original. I liked that the soy sauce flavor infused the steak yet stayed in the background.

This is one of those plain country dishes that really needs to be made with the best ingredients you can find. The key to keeping the freshness alive is not to overcook the meat—or potatoes, for that matter. You will be surprised at how the flavors click together to make a quick supper that is light yet warming.

pork and onions simmered with potatoes SERVES 6 TO 8

NIKUJAGA

1 (2-inch/5-cm) square piece of ginger, peeled

4 to 5 small onions, peeled (about 1 pound/450 g)

10 to 12 medium-sized creamy-style potatoes, peeled (about 2 pounds/900 g)

1 (5 by 3-inch/13 by 8-cm) piece of dried konbu

3 dried red peppers (japones or árbol)

2 (9-ounce/250-g) packages *ito konnyaku* or *shirataki* noodles, drained (page 11)

½ pound (225 g) thinly sliced pork belly

¾ cup (175 cc) sake

⅔ cup (150 cc) soy sauce

Cooked rice, for serving

7-spice powder (*shichimi togarashi*, page 7)

Slice the ginger crosswise into paper-thin pieces. Cut the ends off the onions, then again in half vertically. Set the onions, cut side down, on the chopping board, and slice crosswise into thin rounds (⅛ inch/3 mm). Cut the potatoes into 2- to 3-inch (5- to 7-cm) chunks. Pour 6 cups (1500 cc) water into a medium-sized heavy pot or casserole and slip in the konbu, ginger, onions, and potatoes. Break the dried red peppers in half and drop in the pot with the other ingredients. Bring to a boil, turn down to a rolling simmer, and cook until the potatoes are almost done.

In the meantime, snip the rubber band off the *ito konnyaku* and cut the ball of noodles in half. Drop in a small pot of boiling water and parboil for 5 minutes. Drain in a colander before sliding the noodles in with the simmering potatoes.

Cut the meat crosswise into 3-inch (7.5-cm) pieces and stir into the pot when the potatoes are starting to soften but the centers still have resistance when poked with a thin bamboo skewer. Cook until the meat has almost lost its pink before swirling in the sake and soy sauce. Continue simmering until the potato centers are soft.

Serve in small individual bowls with a bowl of rice on the side. Sprinkle *nikujaga* with 7-spice powder, if desired.

Katsudon was a big favorite of my kids when they were growing up, though I never loved this dish until I fried the cutlets with homemade panko. Taking these extra steps is well worth the effort. The result is exceptional and I am craving *katsudon* as I write this. Tadaaki is a busy farmer, so his version uses cutlets precooked by our butcher. Store-bought panko works fine and is all the rage in the States, but making your own is a snap and yields a much more flavorful result. Homemade panko is essentially grated bread crumbs dried in the oven.

pork cutlets with soy sauce–flavored egg SERVES 8
KATSUDON

2 medium yellow onions, sliced into fine half-rings

1 tablespoon julienned ginger

1⅓ cups (300 cc) Dashi (page 307)

2 tablespoons plus 2 teaspoons soy sauce

1 tablespoon plus 1 teaspoon mirin

5 fried pork cutlets, sliced into 1-inch (2.5-cm) strips (recipe follows)

5 eggs, at room temperature, beaten with a fork

Cooked Plain Rice (page 143) or Brown Rice (page 144), for serving

Simmer the onions and ginger with the dashi in a 9-inch (23-cm) frying pan until the onions have softened but retain a slight crunch. Add the soy sauce and mirin and taste—the broth gets natural sweetness from the onions, so mirin is added sparingly. Ideally the broth will have a gentle salty-sweet overtone without being overpowering. Bring the broth to a simmer over low heat.

Slide a wide kitchen knife under each of the sliced fried cutlets, and gently rest the whole cutlet, in one piece, on top of the simmering broth and onions. Choose your placement carefully because the cutlets should not overlap.

Swirl the beaten eggs over the cutlets in a circular fashion, starting from the outside and working into the center of the pan. The eggs love to slurp into the cracks between the cutlets, so take care to pour them on top of the meat. Cover and cook at a gentle simmer for a few more minutes, until the eggs are almost set but still a tad runny in places. Carefully place several side-by-side slices of cutlet on top of individual bowls of rice and spoon some of the egg and onion broth over the meat. Serve immediately.

FRIED PORK CUTLETS

5 (½-inch/1-cm) thick boneless pork
  chops (3.5 ounces/100 g each)

⅛ teaspoon sea salt

Unbleached all-purpose flour

3 eggs, at room temperature, beaten

Panko (page 10)

3 tablespoons mild-flavored oil,
  such as rapeseed or peanut

Tear off two pieces of cooking parchment or wax paper approximately 24 inches (60 cm) long and shake a small amount of water on one side of each. Lay one piece, water-drop-side up, on your countertop. Place the cutlets on the parchment paper, leaving several inches between each one. Season the exposed meat surfaces lightly with the salt. Cover the meat with the other piece of parchment, damp side down. Pound lightly but evenly with a meat mallet or rolling pin. Remove the top parchment paper and discard. Sprinkle generously with flour, working one piece at a time. Flop the cutlets back and forth in the sprinkled flour so that the entire surface of the cutlets are covered with flour, then shake off any excess.

PREPARE A STATION: floured cutlets on parchment paper to the left, beaten eggs in a shallow bowl next, panko to the right on a small plate, and finally a clean cookie sheet for the finished breaded cutlets. Also keep a bowl of backup panko directly behind the panko plate with a large spoon for ease of replenishing. One by one, dip each floured cutlet into the beaten eggs with one hand. Let the excess egg drip off for a second, then drop onto the plate with the panko. With your other (dry) hand, dredge the cutlet in the panko.

You can prepare up to this part in advance. Place the cutlets on a dinner plate, cover with plastic wrap, and store in the fridge. The cutlets will keep overnight but take longer to cook since the meat will be cold, so cook an additional 2 minutes on each side, covered, over low heat.

Heat the oil in a large frying pan over medium-high heat. Throw in a few crumbs of panko to check the oil temperature. If they sizzle and jump, the oil is hot enough. If they immediately turn dark brown, lower the heat and wait a minute for the oil to cool down. Fry the cutlets until golden brown on each side, about 2 minutes per side. At this point the cutlets should still be slightly pink inside.

These cutlets are delicious as is with a wedge of lemon, but you will need to cook them for a couple of minutes more on each side, covered, over low heat.

Tadaaki made this one night when we had fields of flowering mustard and *komatsuna*. The flowering tops of brassicas, particularly rape (*natane*), are called *nanohana* in Japanese and are similar to rapini. Tadaaki tends to throw some meat into his stir-fries because he feels it gives the dish more depth. I'm more of a purist, so prefer my vegetables without meat. But this dish really won me over, and I quickly became a convert (almost). Japanese stir-fries can be flavored with soy sauce, miso mixed with sake, or even salt. In this dish, I like the clarity of the salt.

pork and flowering mustard stir-fry SERVES 4
BUTA TO NANOHANA ITAME

½ tablespoon organic rapeseed oil

Scant ½ pound (200 g) thinly sliced pork belly, cut crosswise into 3-inch (7.5-cm) pieces

1 tablespoon finely slivered ginger

1 (10 ½-ounce/300-g) bunch flowering mustard or rapini, cut into 2-inch (5-cm) lengths

½ teaspoon sea salt

Fill a pot with water and bring to a boil.

Heat a wide frying pan or wok over high heat. Add the oil quickly followed by the pork belly slices and ginger slivers. Sauté until the fat sizzles and there is some minimal browning, but don't overdo it.

Place the flowering mustard in a mesh strainer with a handle and lower into the pot of boiling water. Cook for about 30 seconds, or until no longer raw. Keep the strainer at the top of the water surface in order to scoop the mustard greens out in one brisk pass. Shake off the hot water and toss into the cooked pork belly. Toss a few minutes more over high heat and season with the salt. Cook for about 30 seconds more, then serve.

VARIATIONS: Substitute soy sauce for the salt or chopped ginger for the slivered ginger.

Done right (slowly), this is a meltingly tender dish. If you hurry it up, then you will not be able to reduce enough of the fat. The result will still be tasty, but you will not be able to eat as much. We often make this as a side dish for our traditional family dinner on New Year's Eve. *Buta no Kaku-ni* not only keeps well but also improves with age, so you can enjoy this over the course of several days.

pork belly simmered in okara SERVES 6
BUTA NO KAKU-NI

2-pound (1-kg) slab pork belly

1 bag *okara* (soybean pulp), about ⅔ pound (310 g)

1½ cups (375 cc) sake

½ cup (125 cc) soy sauce

¼ cup (60 cc) mirin

1 (1-inch/2.5-cm) piece of ginger

2 tablespoons Japanese Mustard (page 314), for serving

Cut the pork belly in thirds lengthwise and fourths crosswise, making about twelve 2¼ by 1-inch (6 by 4-cm) pieces. Drop the pork into a medium-sized heavy pot, add cold water to cover by about 1 inch (2.5 cm), and stir in the *okara*. Cover and bring to a simmer over medium-high heat. Lower the heat and simmer slowly for about 2 hours or more (up to 3 or 4 hours).

Put the pot outside the back door (if wintertime) and let cool (and chill) naturally. Alternatively, cool to room temperature and place in the refrigerator until the fat has solidified.

Gently remove the tender meat pieces from the *okara* and solid fats. Place the meat in a strainer and rinse with warm water.

Discard the *okara*, fat, and simmering juices. Nestle the pork pieces into the smallest pot that will hold them. Add the sake, soy sauce, and mirin. Peel the knob of ginger, slice into thin sheets, and drop in with the pork. Bring to a simmer, uncovered, over medium-high heat. Lower the heat and cook at a gentle simmer for 30 minutes.

Cool the meat in its simmering broth (very important for allowing the meat to suck up the flavorings). Spoon the meat pieces into a serving bowl with some of the simmering broth. Pass the mustard on the side.

Years ago, we got a call from our friend Matsuda-san, the mayonnaise man. A well-known prime-time show called *Dochi No Ryori Show* was coming out to film a crew making teriyaki burgers slathered with Matsuda-san's mayonnaise, which is made from Tadaaki's eggs. I don't watch Japanese TV, but friend Sylvan Mishima Brackett was much impressed when he heard. Apparently he was a big fan of the show and had his aunt in Japan tape episodes and send them to him in California (in the days when we still used VHS tapes). In each episode of *Dochi No Ryori Show* two dishes are pitted against each other in a contest to determine which one is more delicious. Once the menu is decided, the production teams go out on location and film each of the ingredients in situ. My perfect hamburger is 100 percent wagyu, cooked rare over a charcoal fire, but those burgers that day were pretty darn good. The teriyaki burgers lost to whatever the other dish was but perhaps wouldn't have with a bit more care put into sourcing the ingredients. Every component counts when you are building a great burger. I also like these as little patties served alongside vegetables.

teriyaki burgers SERVES 6
TERIYAKI HAMBAGU

2 tablespoons rapeseed oil

1 small to medium yellow onion, finely chopped

Pinch of salt

2 pounds (1 kg) coarsely ground pork shoulder (30 percent fat content)

½ cup (125 cc) cooled Teriyaki Sauce (page 318)

1 cup loosely packed fresh bread crumbs

1 large egg, at room temperature, beaten with a fork

Heat 1 tablespoon of the oil in a medium-sized frying pan over medium-high heat until hot but not smoking. Scrape in the onion and stir to distribute the oil. Turn the heat to low, add the salt, and cook until soft and translucent but not completely wilted. Remove from the heat and cool.

Dump the meat into a large mixing bowl and distribute the fat particles roughly with a pair of long chopsticks (do not overwork). Add the teriyaki sauce, cooled onion, bread crumbs, and egg. Mix quickly but well by cutting through the meat with your flat hand and by folding up the meat from the bottom of the bowl.

Form six 1½-inch (4-cm) thick patties by tossing the meat in cupped hands until the surface has sealed.

Heat the remaining tablespoon of oil in a large, heavy frying pan over medium-high heat. Working quickly, gently slide the hamburgers one by one into the pan. Cook 2 minutes, flip, and cook 2 more on the other side. Cover, decrease the heat to low, and cook 3 more minutes. Uncover (wipe the water condensation from the inner lid), flip the hamburgers one more time, cover, and cook 3 more minutes on low. Remove the pan from the heat, uncover, and let rest 3 minutes in the pan before serving with rice and a salt-flavored vegetable dish or salad such as Stir-Fried Snow Peas with Salt (page 204), Carrot and Mitsuba Salad with Citrus (page 187), or Napa Cabbage Salad with Sesame Seeds (page 188).

continued on next page

TO BARBECUE: Precook as on page 262, but only cook 1 minute on each side, uncovered, over medium-high heat, and then only 2 minutes per side over low heat, covered. Let cool and finish on a low-ember barbecue, turning several times for about 10 minutes to heat up and finish the last bit of cooking.

VARIATIONS: Use beef or chicken instead of pork. Eat as is or on hamburger buns with sliced onion, tomato, lettuce, and Japanese Mayonnaise (page 312). Also good when made into smaller patties and served as part of an outdoor party spread with drinks.

Mention curry rice to any Japanese and they're likely to swoon. But my youngest son, Matthew, takes curry loving to a whole other dimension. He could eat it at least once a week for breakfast, lunch, and dinner (and often does).

I periodically have a vegetarian teacher at my little school, so I have found it makes sense to prepare vegetable and herb stocks rather than chicken. My method for making curry rice easily produces a vegetarian dish—just omit the meat.

curry rice SERVES 4 TO 6
KARE RAISU

5 medium yellow onions
(about 1½ pounds/675 g)

1 (1-inch/2.5-cm) square piece of ginger

4 medium-large carrots
(1½ pounds/675 g)

Large handful of herbs such as parsley, thyme, or oregano, with stems (optional)

2 tablespoons mild oil, such as rapeseed or peanut

1 teaspoon sea salt

1 tablespoon dark sesame oil

8 medium potatoes
(2¼ pounds/1000 g)

3 tablespoons soy sauce

2 teaspoons garam masala

1 pound (500 g) thinly sliced pork belly (optional)

Cut the ends off the onions, then cut them in half from end to end and peel. Drop the peels into a medium-sized stockpot or large saucepan. Slice the onions crosswise into thin (⅛-inch/3-mm) half-rounds.

Peel the ginger and drop the peelings in with the onion peels; finely chop the ginger and set aside.

Cut the ends off the carrots and peel. Add the ends and peelings to the stockpot. Cut the carrots into 2-inch (5-cm) lengths. Slice in half vertically if the pieces are too thick.

Cover the ends of the vegetables and the peelings generously with cold water—throw in some herbs if you have them—and make a light vegetable stock by bringing the covered pot of water to a boil, uncovering, and boiling for as long as it takes you to get through the next steps. (Most people just use water, but I like the idea of grabbing all the flavor you can from the carrots and onions to infuse the water used in the curry.)

Heat the oil in a large, heavy pot over high heat. Add the sliced onions and stir to coat all the strands. Add the salt, stir, and continue cooking over high or medium-high heat, stirring occasionally, until the onions have completely caramelized. Be patient as this will take a while—at least 20 minutes or more (depending on the pot). Toward the end of the caramelization process, stir in the chopped ginger and sesame oil. Remove from the heat when done.

continued on next page

curry rice

CURRY ROUX

6 tablespoons (72 g) mild oil

9 tablespoons (72 g) flour

2 tablespoons best-quality hot curry powder (or homemade)

1 tablespoon best-quality mild curry powder (or homemade)

2 cups (500 cc) hot vegetable stock

Cooked Plain Rice (page 143) or Brown Rice (page 144), for serving

Meanwhile, peel the potatoes and cut into 1½-inch (3.75-cm) chunks.

When the onions are fully caramelized, strain the stock into a clean pot. Add the potatoes and carrots to the onions, then add enough strained vegetable stock to cover (about 4½ cups/1500 cc). Bring to a boil over high heat, lower the heat to medium, and cook at a lively simmer, uncovered, until the vegetables are cooked. (If you are cooking for a crowd, it may be safer to simmer each vegetable separately in stock or water to just cover so you can control the cooking time of each vegetable. Save the cooking juices and add to the curry pot with the vegetables, but don't flood the pot.)

Make the curry roux by heating the oil over medium heat in a medium-sized saucepan or frying pan. Dump the flour into the oil and mix together to form a paste. Scrape the paste across the bottom of the pan with a flat wooden spoon to cook the flour for at least 3 minutes. The flour should bubble up and whiten a bit at the edges. Add the curry powders and scrape-fry for a minute or so more.

Spoon the hot stock over the roux, one soup ladleful at a time. The roux will bubble madly. Stir with a flat wooden spoon until smooth, or use a whisk should you have any lumps. Add more stock gradually until you have a creamy sauce and simmer over low heat for about 10 minutes. Remove from the heat and set aside.

When the potatoes and carrots are about half done, whisk the curry roux sauce into the simmering vegetables. Continue cooking until the vegetables are soft in the center but not disintegrating. Monitor the overall sauce consistency as the vegetables are cooking. You want to end up with a creamy and loose, not gloopy sauce. But this is a matter of taste and preference. It's not an exact science. Add more stock if needed, or increase the heat to high and boil more furiously if the curry is too runny.

When done, swirl in the soy sauce and sprinkle with garam masala. At this point you have vegetarian curry. Serve with cooked rice.

continued on next page

curry rice

FOR TRADITIONAL CURRY: Roughly chop the pork belly and sauté in a large frying pan until the liquid has cooked out and the fat sizzles and browns. Deglaze the pan with a little of the simmering curry soup, scraping up any clinging meat particles from the bottom of the pan. Stir the meat into the curry and serve on top of rice. (I prefer my curry on the side of the rice, topped with plenty of plain yogurt and shiso chiffonade or chopped cilantro.) Eat with a large soupspoon.

VARIATIONS: Though not traditional, cauliflower is also a nice addition. Any green vegetables (like broccoli or green beans) should be parboiled separately and added at the end to keep their color. In the summer I like to add some chunks of Japanese eggplant in the last few minutes of cooking—they add a juicy element to the curry that is particularly appealing.

THE BOY GOAT

I got there a little after six, but Tadaaki had already killed the boy goat and strung him up by his hooves to drip the blood out. The morning air was still and cool, though it would turn hot by noon. I had come because it was I who had wanted to eat the goat and I needed to be part of his transition from live animal to meat. I needed an image of his kill and his blood to really feel the impact of what it was so capriciously easy to say, "I want to eat the goat." I came because I had to, and won't soon forget the power of that still early morning.

When goats have kids, they usually have two. The first year we had two girl babies, and Christopher sold them with no trouble. Girl goats are desirable because they give milk. Boy goats are kept for making babies or meat. Our mommy goat had a boy and girl the next year, though the girl died right away. The boy goat was cute, but I steeled myself not to get close. It was less complicated for me because I wasn't the one feeding him and his mother; still, I knew we wouldn't keep this goat, and I knew he was going to be eaten.

We couldn't mate the boy goat with his mother, so Tadaaki, Christopher (sixteen at the time), and I discussed what we would do with him. Even if we took him back to the goat farm, he would most likely end up killed for his meat. Here was the moral issue: Should we kill him ourselves and eat him, or should we turn away and have someone else do it out of our line of sight? We debated this at length. Tadaaki was reluctant but willing.

When you witness the kill (or participate in the cleaning process) you are really reverential when you later treat the meat. This is very powerful stuff. The image of the goat stayed with me firmly, viscerally, as I prepared a rub for the legs and ribs. We considered spit roasting, but in the end it just seemed too involved. Tadaaki likes the pit barbecue, so pit barbecue it was.

We invited friends to share the boy goat, and before we ate, Tadaaki talked of killing the goat. At the moment before the kill, he had told the goat, "Okay, this is it, this is your chance to fight. It's either you or me." Of course he was the one with the knife. That is his way. Tadaaki is deeply respectful and gently in tune with the natural world. He's more at home loping through the mountains than crunching numbers in Tokyo. But that's what captivated me, and that's why I married him.

On Monday some of my preschoolers asked me where the boy goat was. I told them we ate him. "Why?" they wondered. "Because he couldn't make baby goats with the mommy," I returned matter-of-factly (getting down to their level and looking them straight in the eye). "Oh," they answered. And they were satisfied. It was a fact of life, and they got it. That's what we teach our kids and the SSU! kids: respect and accountability. The truth is I was sad about the goat, but they needed me to be strong and give it to them without all the baggage.

I don't think everyone has to witness or be involved in killing an animal to appreciate meat, nor do we have to imagine the blood or the killing act each time we sit down to a steak dinner. Nonetheless it really does intensify your enjoyment of that steak (or chicken, or fish, or whatever) if you've raised it, caught it, or killed it. Food that has that history for you, those "legs," so to speak, is unforgettable. And it becomes hard to eat food with no history because that food is often lifeless and plain.

9

dressings and
dipping sauces

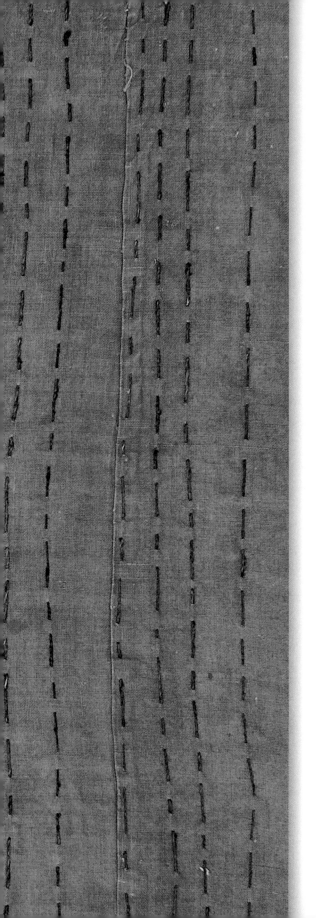

Japanese vegetables are most often parboiled, refreshed, squeezed, and dressed. Though some vegetables are left raw, especially when very thinly sliced, salt-massaged, or made into a salad. There are very few sauces in Japanese farm cooking because few are needed. Farm food is created from field vegetables exploding with their own flavors. The dressings are added not only to complement the vegetables but also to allow a variety in flavor even when there may not be a variety in available vegetables. The methods in this chapter have been mentioned elsewhere in the book, so the explanations and preparation techniques presented here are fairly straightforward. However, it is useful to read this chapter in its entirety to really get a sense of how easy it is to pick up a certain "dressing" and use it with vegetables from your garden or local farmers' market to create a Japanese dish. All of the dressings are extremely versatile.

I never understood the rationale behind store-bought dressings or sauces, especially since you're most likely getting a lot more than you bargained for. Homemade takes only seconds to put together and is so, so much better. And like many recipes in this book, these dressings are even better when you put some effort into finding the best ingredients possible to make them.

Of all the Japanese vegetable dressings, this one is the most well known and can be found on the menus of Japanese restaurants all over the world. Though I find it is often oversweetened to the point of being almost cloying. Also a common mistake is not grinding the seeds enough.

sesame-miso dressing

MAKES ENOUGH FOR 2 CUPS (225 G) OF VEGETABLES

GOMA-AE

4 tablespoons unhulled
   sesame seeds

3 tablespoons brown rice miso

2 tablespoons rice vinegar

Toast the sesame seeds over medium-high heat in a dry frying pan for a minute or so until they are fragrant and start to pop. Grind the seeds in a *suribachi* (Japanese grinding bowl) or mortar until most of the seeds have broken down and are almost pastelike. Smash in the miso and blend in the rice vinegar until creamy.

RATIO: sesame : miso : vinegar—4 : 3 : 2

VARIATIONS: A few slivers of yuzu or Meyer lemon peel are also a nice addition.

This creamy, subtly nutty treatment goes well with strong-flavored boiled, refreshed, and squeezed greens or boiled and refreshed vegetables. Many cooks add sugar to *shira-ae*, but that seems like a crazy idea because the sesame and tofu are naturally sweet—as are most of the vegetables you would pair with this. Good on mustard greens, rapini, *komatsuna*, mizuna, broccoli, or cauliflower.

tofu-miso dressing
MAKES ENOUGH FOR A LARGE BUNCH OF GREENS

SHIRA-AE

1 (10.5-oz/300-g) block Japanese-style "cotton" tofu

2 tablespoons unhulled sesame seeds

2 tablespoons brown rice or barley miso

2 tablespoons rice vinegar or *Warisu* (page 307)

¼ teaspoon sea salt

Zest of 1 small yuzu or ½ Meyer lemon, slivered (optional)

Place the tofu on a cutting board propped up on one end, angled into the kitchen sink for draining. Lay another chopping board or plate on top of the tofu to press out excess water for 1 hour.

Toast the sesame seeds over medium-high heat in a dry frying pan until they are fragrant and just starting to pop. Grind the sesame seeds in a *suribachi* (Japanese grinding bowl) or mortar until most of the seeds have broken down. Add the miso and vinegar to the mortar and blend.

Squeeze handfuls of tofu to express any lingering moisture and add to the dressing with the salt. Continue grinding to emulsify all the ingredients until creamy. Gently fold in the cooked greens or vegetables. Garnish with slivered yuzu peel, if you like.

RATIO: sesame : miso : vinegar—1:1:1

Walnuts (or pecans) substitute well for the traditional sesame in *goma-ae* (page 298), and they give the dressing a softer, perhaps fuller taste—sometimes a welcome change from the sesame-miso. This is exceptional made from black walnuts (*onigurumi*) if you can find them. Good with spinach or any other strong-flavored greens. Also nice with broccoli or cauliflower.

walnut-miso dressing

MAKES ENOUGH FOR A LARGE BUNCH OF GREENS

KURUMI-AE

5 heaping tablespoons whole walnuts

2 tablespoons brown rice miso

1½ tablespoons rice vinegar

Grind 2 heaping tablespoons of walnuts in a *suribachi* (Japanese grinding bowl) or mortar until the nuts have been smashed a bit and resemble finely chopped nuts. Scrape into a bowl and reserve. Drop the remaining 3 tablespoons of walnuts into the grinding bowl and smash well until the oil has exuded from the walnuts and a rough paste has formed. Mash in the miso and rice vinegar and blend until creamy. Toss boiled, refreshed, squeezed greens or parboiled vegetables into the walnut-miso dressing with the reserved roughly crushed walnuts.

RATIO: walnuts : miso : vinegar—10 : 4 : 3 (about)

VARIATION: Substitute pecans for the walnuts.

Somewhere along the way a few years ago, I fell completely in love with miso. Miso became a taste I craved. While this vinaigrette may never replace artisanal olive oil and homemade red wine vinegar, this miso-based dressing is good on just about anything. I particularly like it on peppery greens such as mizuna and mountain *mitsuba*; julienned vegetables such as celery, carrots, daikon, or turnips; blanched and refreshed green beans or pea pods (snow or snap); or even sliced new onions (though you may want to soak the onion threads a few minutes in cold water to remove some of their raw hotness). It is also good on chicken or crab salads.

miso vinaigrette
MAKES ENOUGH FOR A MEDIUM-SIZED SALAD
MISO VINEGURETTO

1 tablespoon organic miso

1 tablespoon organic rice vinegar

2 tablespoons organic rapeseed oil

Muddle the miso with the vinegar and whisk in the oil. Keeps for several weeks or more, jarred, in the refrigerator.

RATIO: miso : rice vinegar : rapeseed oil—1 : 1 : 2

One of the first Japanese salad dressings I made, and for years it was the go-to substitute in our house for the classic olive oil and red wine vinegar dressing. In those days I used dark sesame oil and hot pepper oil (*rayu*), but am less inclined toward such heavy flavors these days because of my new love, the oh, so elegant organic rapeseed oil I buy from my pal at Matsuda Mayonnaise. Good on leafy greens such as lettuce, mizuna, or *mibuna* (page 365).

soy sauce vinaigrette
MAKES ENOUGH FOR A MEDIUM-SIZED SALAD
SHOYU VINEGURETTO

1 tablespoon soy sauce

1 tablespoon rice vinegar

2 tablespoons rapeseed oil

Whisk the soy sauce and vinegar together in a small bowl before drizzle-whisking in the rapeseed oil to emulsify. Take care to rewhisk if you do not dress the salad immediately after making the vinaigrette.

Spoon enough well-emulsified vinaigrette on the salad to film the leaves and gently toss with light hands. The leaves should not be drippy, nor should there be any dressing pooled up in the bottom of the bowl after serving (if so, you have overdressed the salad). Save any extra dressing in a jar in the refrigerator. Keeps for several weeks or more.

RATIO: soy sauce : rice vinegar : rapeseed oil—1:1:2

VARIATION: Also excellent with a tablespoon of roughly ground toasted sesame seeds.

Miso and sesame are sort of a match made in heaven, especially if you add a little vinegar to cut their richness. Good on poached chicken salad (page 260).

sesame-miso vinaigrette
MAKES ENOUGH FOR 1 MAIN-DISH SALAD
GOMA MISO VINEGURETTO

2 tablespoons unhulled
  sesame seeds

1 tablespoon brown rice miso

2 tablespoons rice vinegar

4 tablespoons rapeseed oil

Measure the sesame seeds into a small frying pan and roast over medium-high heat while lifting and shaking the pan to avoid burning the seeds. (They burn easily!) When the seeds start to pop, remove from the heat.

Slide the seeds into a Japanese grinding bowl (*suribachi*) or mortar and grind roughly (reserve a teaspoon or so of the smashed seeds to sprinkle on the salad after dressing). Mash in the miso to form a thick paste and add the vinegar to lighten (and brighten) the miso-sesame mixture. Whisk in the rapeseed oil slowly until emulsified. (Be sure to whisk again right before dressing your salad.)

Strew the dressed salad with the reserved roughly ground seeds.

RATIO: sesame:miso:rice vinegar:rapeseed oil—2:1:2:4

citrus vinaigrette

MAKES ENOUGH FOR 1 MEDIUM-SIZED SALAD

KANKITSU VINEGURETTO

We have access to incredible citrus—one of the few organic fruits readily available in Japan. I use this citrus vinaigrette when I'm looking for an ultrafresh taste on my salad, and it is especially good with lettuce salads tossed with fresh crabmeat or small boiled and chilled Gulf shrimp. In that case, I would not presalt the lettuce leaves, just add some sea salt to taste when you dress the salad. Good with raw carrots, turnips, daikon, or napa cabbage and a bit of aromatics such as slivered green onion or tops from the salad vegetable to liven up the delicate dressing.

½ teaspoon fine sea salt

2 tablespoons mild citrus juice (yuzu, Seville orange, Meyer lemon)

2 tablespoons rapeseed oil

Sprinkle the sea salt onto julienned vegetables such as carrot, daikon, cabbage, or turnip (but don't mix the varieties) and gently distribute with your hands.

Measure the citrus juice into a small bowl and whisk in the oil. Pour over the julienned vegetables and toss once or twice. Add a small amount of slivered green onion, vegetable tops, or whole aromatic herb leaves such as *mitsuba* to give a slight bite for balance. Toss quickly but lightly and serve.

RATIO: mild citrus (yuzu, Meyer lemon, grapefruit) : rapeseed oil—1 : 1

miso-mustard vinaigrette

MAKES ENOUGH FOR A MEDIUM-SIZED SALAD

KARASHI-MISO

I love leeks vinaigrette and often make it at Christmastime. Japanese negi are exceptionally tender, so one night I thought of making this miso-mustard dressing instead of the classic mustard vinaigrette. It reminded me a bit of *negi nuta*, a vinegary miso dish we have occasionally at our friend Kanchan's restaurant, Soba Ro. Good on winter lettuce salads or julienned carrot, turnip, or daikon salads.

3 tablespoons brown rice miso

3 tablespoons rice vinegar

1 tablespoon hot Dijon mustard (preferably Edmond Fallot)

Muddle the miso, rice vinegar, and Dijon mustard in a mortar or whisk in a small bowl. Keeps for a couple of weeks chilled in the fridge.

RATIO: miso : vinegar : mustard—3 : 3 : 1

dashi MAKES ABOUT 1⅓ CUPS (300 CC)

Dashi is probably the most important building block in Japanese cooking. Many chefs (especially those from Kyoto) wax poetic about the special methods they employ to draw out the natural umami of the konbu and *katsuobushi* when making dashi. Even the water must come from the Kyoto area. Our dashi is a bit more straightforward and quite tasty, despite our more laissez-faire attitude and lack of Kyoto water. We use well water from our family well, and it works just fine. I'm sure the water wherever you live will work just as well. The important thing to remember here is that dashi—or for that matter any food—should not become an obsessive chore. If you start with great ingredients, your food will taste good.

1 (6-inch/15-cm) length of konbu

Handful of dried bonito shavings (*katsuobushi*)

Place the konbu in a medium saucepan containing 2 cups (500 cc) of cold water. Bring almost to a boil (you will see minute bubbles form on the edges of the konbu) and remove the konbu. Throw in the dried bonito shavings and simmer friskily, but not crazily, for 8 minutes. Remove from the heat and let stand 8 minutes. Set a small fine-mesh strainer over a 1-quart (1-liter) measuring cup and pour the dashi through the strainer to remove the dried bonito shavings. You should have 1⅓ cups (300 cc) dashi. If you do not, add water (pouring through the strainer holding the strained *katsuobushi*) to make the amount of liquid needed. Use within a day or so, if kept chilled in the fridge.

dashi vinegar MAKES 1⅓ CUP (300 CC)
WARISU

Warisu is a good alternative to straight rice vinegar when you want a softer vinegar flavor, such as when you are making Sesame-Miso Dressing (page 298). It is also nice on mild salads since there is a hint of *katsubushi* and konbu that gives the dressing a certain element of complexity. Make *warisu* when you have leftover dashi from making another recipe such as miso soup (page 80) or *ohitashi* (page 171).

⅔ cup (150 cc) Dashi (above)

⅔ cup (150 cc) rice vinegar

Mix the dashi and rice vinegar together and pour into a well-labeled bottle or jar. Keeps for a couple of months refrigerated.

I first tasted *tosajoyu* at Kozushi, a phenomenal sushi shop that I came upon by sheer chance (or was it fate?) in the first few weeks after I had arrived in Japan. The master would always serve his sashimi with *tosajoyu*, then change out the small saucers for a lighter soy sauce when I moved on to the sushi. Tadaaki's *tosajoyu* contains nothing more than excellent local soy sauce and *katsuobushi*, though other cooks may add sake, mirin, or even konbu. Use for dipping sashimi or drizzling on tofu.

katsuobushi-infused soy sauce
MAKES ABOUT 1⅔ CUPS (400 CC)

TOSAJOYU

2 cups (500 cc) soy sauce

1 large handful of *katsuobushi* (*hanakatsuo*, page 6)

Bring the soy sauce and *katsuobushi* to a simmer over medium-low heat and cook at a gentle simmer for 10 minutes. Remove from the heat and let cool for about 8 to 10 minutes, or until you can comfortably insert your finger into the liquid. Strain and store for up to a year in the fridge.

Ponzu is one sauce I see completely bastardized all over the Internet and in Japanese cookbooks. Traditionally it was made from the juice of *daidai* (a bitter orange similar to Seville orange), not yuzu or vinegar (as many recipes say). Ponzu also usually has some dashi splashed in, but farmers most likely skip that unless they happen to have some handy. Farmers also like a strong salty flavor, since they work hard in the fields before sitting down to dinner. Good with most *nabe* such as Kelp-Wicked Red Snapper Shabu-Shabu (page 95), Monkfish Nabe with Mizuna (page 90), and (beef) Shabu-Shabu (page 97).

country-style ponzu
MAKES 1 CUP (250 CC)

INAKA PONZU

½ cup (125 cc) soy sauce

½ cup (125 cc) bitter orange juice, yuzu juice, or ½ lemon–½ tangerine juice

Chopped chives (optional)

Mix the soy sauce and bitter orange juice (*daidai*) in a small bowl. Sprinkle in some chopped chives, if you like. Use within a day or so, but store in the fridge.

RATIO: soy sauce : citrus juice—1:1

kaeshi MAKES ABOUT 2⅔ CUPS (600 CC)

Kaeshi is an ingenious concoction that flavors dashi when making dipping sauces for noodles and tempura, or a hot broth for a noodle soup. While not the farm kitchen method, I was beguiled with how *kaeshi* relates to the dashi as a building block and could not leave it out of the book. Andrew, who works at our friend's soba restaurants, was kind enough to walk me through the process (and approve of the results).

½ cup (125 cc) *hon mirin* (page 8)

1⅛ cup (125 g) organic sugar

2 cups (500 cc) organic soy sauce

Bring *hon mirin* to a simmer over high heat and cook, stirring constantly, until you no longer smell alcohol (3 to 5 minutes). Stir in the sugar and continue cooking (and stirring) until the sugar granules have dissolved. Add the soy sauce and watch as the *kaeshi* heats up and comes almost to a boil. You will see tiny bubbles form on the perimeter—remove the pan from the heat as soon as the entire surface of the *kaeshi* becomes a creamy tan from minute bubbles. Store for up to a year in the fridge.

RATIO: soy sauce : mirin : sugar—4 cc : 1 cc : 1 g

noodle dipping sauce
MAKES ABOUT 1⅔ CUPS (400 CC)

MORI TSUYU

This "sauce" (which is more like a soup) can be served hot or cold, depending on the season. Good for dunking udon, soba, and *somen* noodles.

1⅓ cups (300 cc) Dashi (page 307)

6 tablespoons *Kaeshi* (above)

Flavor the dashi with the *kaeshi* and use at room temperature, cold, or slightly warm, depending on your mood or the season.

RATIO: dashi : *kaeshi*—3.3 : 1

hot noodle broth MAKES ABOUT 1¼ CUPS (300 CC)
KAKE TSUYU

Kake tsuyu is a light, slightly sweet broth in which you serve a bowl of steaming noodles. Simmer some slivered *negi* and thinly sliced root vegetables such as turnips and carrots with roughly chopped chicken or duck meat, if desired. Plunk just-cooked (refreshed) noodles in the broth for a warm, comforting meal.

1⅓ cups (300 cc) Dashi (page 307)

1 tablespoon *Kaeshi* (page 310)

Mix dashi with *kaeshi* and use as is in *tamago dofu* (page 117); or bring to a gentle simmer in a small saucepan before serving as a noodle soup.

RATIO: dashi:*kaeshi*—10:1

tempura dipping sauce
MAKES ABOUT 2 CUPS (500 CC)
TEN TSUYU

In farming families you will more likely see tempura served with soy sauce, but for those who like a lighter, soupier dipping sauce, *ten tsuyu* is the traditional sauce that accompanies tempura in restaurants.

1⅓ cups (300 cc) Dashi (page 307)

2½ tablespoons *Kaeshi* (page 310)

Combine the dashi and *kaeshi* in a small saucepan. Warm gently over low heat and ladle into small dipping bowls for each diner.

RATIO: dashi:*kaeshi*—4:1

Making mayonnaise successfully depends on fresh eggs, initial patience, and confidence in the process (experience doesn't hurt). Use only the freshest farm eggs, otherwise it will be very difficult to emulsify (and risky for salmonella). You make Japanese-style mayonnaise by using rice vinegar instead of lemon and adding a little sugar or honey, though we usually do not sweeten ours. For Western-style mayonnaise, I use about 75 percent rapeseed oil and 25 percent good-quality extra-virgin olive oil (or more), depending on what I am making.

I buy organic Japanese rapeseed oil from Matsuda-san in 16-kg drums (big), but luckily my school assistants pour it into more conveniently sized jars for me.

japanese mayonnaise MAKES ABOUT 1 CUP (225 CC)
MAYONEIZU

1 very fresh raw egg yolk,
   at room temperature

1 teaspoon Dijon mustard
   (or ¼ teaspoon dried mustard)

1 teaspoon rice vinegar

About ¾ cup (180 to 200 cc)
   rapeseed oil, at room temperature

Fine sea salt

½ to 1 teaspoon sugar or honey
   (optional)

Put the egg yolk, mustard, and ½ teaspoon vinegar in a small, deep-sided bowl.

Whisk lightly to combine, then whisk in a fine stream of oil until the mayonnaise "takes." If it does not emulsify soon, it never will. In this case, you will have to start over, whisking the broken egg yolk and oil mixture into a new egg yolk. Increase the total amount of oil as well.

Once the mayonnaise becomes a creamy sauce (not oily looking), you can add the oil a bit faster. At this point, I usually add a big glurp of oil, then whisk powerfully. Continue adding oil until the mixture is thick and holds its shape. Add sea salt to taste and the sugar or honey, if using. Taste for tartness and oil balance; add more oil or some of the remaining ½ teaspoon vinegar, if needed. The mayonnaise keeps for a few days in the refrigerator.

Mustard made from straight mustard powder by nature is going to be fiery hot and won't have the creamy complexity of a good Dijon mustard, such as Edmond Fallot. You make the choice, however. Either way, you get the hotness needed for some of the rich Japanese dishes such as Simmered Kabocha and Konbu (page 214) or Pork Belly Simmered in Okara (page 286).

japanese mustard MAKES 2 TABLESPOONS
KARASHI

2 tablespoons Oriental mustard powder

Measure the mustard powder into a small bowl and muddle in 1 teaspoon water until the paste is pliable but not runny. Let sit for 15 minutes, turned upside down on the counter, to mature and develop flavor. Use the same day or possibly the next if you fold it tightly into a small piece of plastic wrap and refrigerate.

In the fall of 2011 about twenty or so friends from Berkeley converged on Japan over the course of several weeks for a food and art installation project called OPENharvest. And during their visit here, they probably ate hundreds of bowls of ramen between them—sometimes more than once in one day. They were crazy for ramen. That ramen-fever rubbed off on me, so while I worked through book edits that fall, I too began to crave ramen and often snuck off for a solitary bowl at lunchtime. With ramen on the brain, I realized this book would not be complete without a recipe for *rayu* (red pepper oil) or *yuzu kosho*. Who did I turn to? Sylvan Mishima Brackett, my pal who runs Peko-Peko Japanese Catering, also one of the main organizers of the OPENharvest event, and a master of *gyoza* (page 128). Sylvan shot me an e-mail back right away with a list of ingredients he uses and the admonishment to "heat the chile and garlic slowly" since "heating kills their flavor." I was on my own for proportions, but managed to hit it right on the first try. Making homemade *rayu* is so fundamentally simple, I am baffled why I have never made it before now.

chile-infused sesame oil
MAKES ABOUT 1 CUP (240 CC)

RAYU

¾ cup (180 cc) best-quality dark sesame oil

¼ cup (60 cc) rapeseed or safflower oil

3 large cloves of strong-flavored winter garlic, cut into thick slivers

12 small dried red Japanese chile peppers, roughly crumbled

1 tablespoon unhulled sesame seeds

3 large pinches of *katsuobushi* flakes (*hanakatsuo*, page 6)

2 teaspoons sea salt

2 teaspoons best-quality hot paprika powder

Pour the oil into a small saucepan along with the garlic slivers and crumbled chile peppers. Heat slowly over low heat on a flame tamer, if you have one. Roast the sesame seeds over medium-high heat in a small dry skillet until the seeds start to pop.

Shake the pan and lift off of the heat a little to avoid burning the seeds. Reserve in a small bowl. Watch the oil closely as it warms.

As soon as teeny bubbles start to form around the garlic slivers and dried peppers, add the rest of the ingredients, and swirl the pan to distribute. Continue heating, but pick up the pan and swirl it anytime more bubbles appear. Do not let the oil simmer, as this will cause the *rayu* to become bitter. After about 5 minutes, turn off the heat, but let the *rayu* cool naturally on the flame tamer (or heat source). Continue to be vigilant about keeping the bubbles at bay by lifting up and swirling until they subside completely. Once the *rayu* has cooled sufficiently, with no danger of bubbles, cover and continue to cool naturally until it returns to room temperature.

Strain into a large glass measuring cup and divide between two small, dry jars. Scoop some of the strained aromatics into one of the jars to keep on extracting intensity—this style is used spooned over rice, or whatever, and is all the rage. It is called *taberu rayu* ("eating" *rayu*). Both keep for a year or more, refrigerated.

I have seen many *yuzu kosho* methods floating around the Internet, but, in my mind, this recipe (from Sylvan Mishima Brackett) is the most authentic. We are lucky to have a local person selling top-quality *yuzu kosho* at our local farm stands (¥350/$4.50 for a teensy jar holding 2 tablespoons), but homemade *yuzu kosho* will yield a brighter paste. You can use a mini-prep processor, but I recommend grinding by hand in a *suribachi*. It's a little time consuming, but so much more satisfying. The fragrant yuzu skin can be replicated successfully, though not duplicated by Meyer lemon peel or another floral-skinned local lemon. Small Indian or Thai chiles can substitute for the Japanese chile peppers. *Yuzu kosho* is unforgettable in salt-flavored ramen (page 131) and also gives a lively zip to Citrus Vinaigrette (page 306).

yuzu kosho
MAKES ABOUT 5 TABLESPOONS

10 medium-sized yuzu or other fragrant lemon-like citrus

4 small or 2 medium-sized, fresh green Japanese chiles

2 tablespoons white sea salt

Pare off the outer zest of the yuzu with a very sharp knife. As the winter season wears on, the inside yuzu fruit tends to separate from the peel, so it may be difficult to avoid some of the white pith. Try your best, as the pith is bitter and will affect the taste of your *yuzu kosho*—keep the pith to the minimum possible. Lay the zest on a cutting board and chop briefly: once in each direction (you do not want to leave essential oils on the cutting board). Slide the zest into a *suribachi* (Japanese grinding bowl) or mini-prep food processor.

Slice off the tops of the chiles and roughly chop. Add to the zest along with the salt. Grind until the zest and chiles have broken down and a chartreuse green paste has formed. Scrape into a small jar. Cover the surface with plastic wrap and screw the cover on tightly. Keeps for several months or more stored in the refrigerator.

VARIATIONS: To lower the heat factor, seed the chiles. You can also substitute fresh red chiles for the green.

This sauce is typically used on eggplant *shigiyaki* (page 53). I am less than enamored with sweet sauces, but do like this one on the fried eggplant with some hot threads of ginger scattered on top. Some shredded shiso will also contribute an additional note of complexity. Tadaaki absolutely adores *amamiso-dare*, perhaps because it was one of the few sweet foods he ate growing up and it satisfied that deep craving for sugar that many children (and adults) have. Good with fried eggplant or zucchini halves.

sweet miso sauce

MAKES ENOUGH FOR 1 POUND (500 G) OF VEGETABLES

AMAMISO-DARE

4 tablespoons best-quality miso

2 tablespoons mirin

6 tablespoons sake

1 tablespoon finely sliced shiso leaves

1 tablespoon slivered ginger, for garnish

Whisk the miso, mirin, and sake in a small frying pan. Bring to a simmer over medium heat and let bubble gently for 5 to 10 minutes until slightly thickened. Stir in the shiso threads and pour over succulent fried vegetables. Sprinkle with the slivered ginger and serve immediately.

RATIO: miso : mirin : sake—2 : 1 : 3

teriyaki sauce MAKES 1 CUP (250 CC)
TERIYAKI SOSU

I had not eaten teriyaki anything since the Tiki Room at Disneyland until we had teriyaki burgers at a television shoot staged at our friend Matsuda-san's place. We don't add much sugar to our food, so for me it made sense to make teriyaki sauce by reducing Tadaaki's country version of teriyaki marinade. It worked. This sauce keeps indefinitely but will intensify in the fridge, so be careful not to use too much and overflavor when adding to ground meat.

1 cup (250 cc) mirin

1 cup (250 cc) soy sauce

1 (1-inch/2.5-cm) square piece of ginger, peeled and grated

Simmer the mirin, soy sauce, and ginger in a small saucepan over medium heat and reduce by about half. Cool. Add to ground meats to give teriyaki flavor. (Dry meats such as chicken or pork will benefit from equal parts fresh bread crumbs and eggs to help keep them moist.)

teriyaki marinade MAKES 1 CUP (250 CC)
TERIYAKI MARINEI

Inspired by the teriyaki burger photo shoot for *Dochi no Ryori Show* up at Matsuda-san's place, Tadaaki marinated some chicken one day and served it teriyaki style that night. I was pleasantly surprised by the gentle teriyaki flavor that was neither too sweet nor too overpoweringly seasoned.

½ cup (125 cc) mirin

½ cup (125 cc) soy sauce

1 (2 by 1-inch/5 by 2.5-cm) piece of ginger, peeled and grated

Mix the mirin, soy sauce, and grated ginger in a small bowl or measuring cup. Use as a marinade for chicken or pork chops. There should be enough marinade so that it covers all the surfaces of the meat but the meat does not need to be swimming in it. Massage the teriyaki marinade gently into the meat to distribute. Refrigerate the marinating meat for half a day or overnight (up to 2 days—though be aware that the flavor will intensify as each day passes). Discard any extra marinade after you remove the meat.

sweet soy-flavored sauce
MAKES ⅔ CUP (150CC)

MITARASHI SOSU

Mitarashi sauce is almost like a glaze, though a bit thicker. I prefer my *dango* (page 358) a tad more austere, with just the taste of charcoal-caramelized soy sauce. But if you like a sweeter flavor, by all means dunk the *dango* balls in *mitarashi* sauce after cooking.

8 tablespoons soy sauce

1 tablespoon potato starch (*katakuriko*)

4 tablespoons organic sugar

In a small bowl, whisk the soy sauce into the potato starch and pour into a small saucepan with the sugar. Stir to blend and bring to a simmer over medium-low heat, stirring occasionally to keep the sugar from sticking on the bottom. Simmer gently for 10 to 15 minutes until the bubbles are thick and the sauce is glossy. Remove from the heat. Keeps for several weeks in the refrigerator; warm before using.

RATIO: soy sauce : sugar : potato starch—8 : 4 : 1

black sugar syrup MAKES 5 TABLESPOONS

KUROMITSU

Along with *kinako* (soybean powder), *kuromitsu* is one of the most commonly used components in Japanese sweets. One of the first sweets I encountered in Japan were single servings of *kuzu mochi* (page 355) smothered in *kinako* powder set into little plastic trays with a tiny plastic squeeze bottle of *kuromitsu* for each *mochi*. I remember licking that tray clean each time I ate one. *Kuromitsu* reminds me of blackstrap molasses, so feel free to substitute. *Kuromitsu* is also good drizzled on vanilla ice cream or vanilla-flavored custard.

8 tablespoons Japanese black sugar, lumps smashed

In a small saucepan, heat the black sugar with 4 tablespoons water over medium heat until large bubbles form. Decrease the heat to low, and simmer for about 1 or 2 minutes until slightly thickened. You should have 5 tablespoons, if you have more, cook a bit longer; if you have less, stir in a bit of water. Remove from the heat to cool. Keeps indefinitely in the fridge stored in a jar, but warm slightly to take the chill off before using.

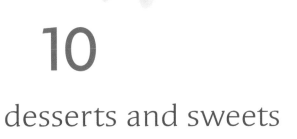

10

desserts and sweets

DESSERTS FOR JAPANESE MEALS

TRADITIONAL JAPANESE SWEETS FOR TEA BREAK

A traditional Japanese meal does not end with dessert, but most Western meals do, so many restaurants in Japan have adopted the Western model. Some serve fruit at the end of the meal and some serve an actual dessert, though usually something small and simple, more often than not ice cream.

Japanese love their tea breaks at ten and three, and this is when they eat sweets. That custom is deeply ingrained in the cultural fabric of Japan and originates from the farmer's need to rest, regain energy, and connect with family members or neighbors. Another custom that persists today is the custom of presenting tea and sweets (or fruit) to guests as soon as they sit down.

Rather than go the conventional *macha*, *kinako*, or azuki ice cream route, I felt fruit ice creams with a high milk-to-cream ratio would be more in keeping with the fruit-at-the-end-of-the-meal concept. I chose fruits that are grown commonly in Japan, many of which are also grown on our farm. It is difficult to find organic fruit in Japan, but we do have local growers producing berries, apricots, plums, kiwis, peaches, loquats, and melons. And we are most fortunate to have access to a stunning array of gorgeous citrus from our eighty-five-year-old friend Mochizuki-san, a character in her own right. We grow (or have grown) several kinds of fruit—apples, persimmons, Meyer lemons, *daidai* (sour oranges), yuzu, *sudachi*, *natsumikan*, kumquat, loquat, *ume* (sour plums), peaches, apricots, raspberries, blueberries—but caterpillars, unpredictable weather, and disease affect the success rate of our variable harvests. And some of the trees have died, not to be planted again. Desire is often more than our energy level (or hours in the day).

But a book on Japanese farm food would not be complete without some traditional Japanese sweets. When guests arrive, the hosts and guests drop to their knees and exchange bows of greeting (traditional farm people, that is; modern urbanites or the younger generations do not adhere strictly to this cultural norm). Everyone takes a seat on square cushions (*zabuton*) set around a low table on the tatami-matted floor. The hostess immediately brings out fresh fruit cut up into wedges that one spears up with toothpicks to eat. Some sort of packaged sweet, or store-bought confection, or perhaps rice crackers (*senbei*) are also de rigueur, though on cultural celebration days such as New Year (*oshogatsu*), Children's Day (*kodomo no hi*), Day of the Dead (*obon*), and Full Moon Festival (*jugoya*), traditional sweets are prepared in farm households. In our house *ohagi* and *manju* were the main sweets, depending on the holiday.

I have included desserts that are in keeping with the spirit of and are complementary with a Japanese meal as well as a few traditional sweets that should be served with tea midmorning or midafternoon.

OUR CITRUS GROWER

We "met" over the phone (she's a bit of a phone queen).

"Mama!" she would boom at the other end of the receiver . . . not my favorite name, but I gave up correcting her.

When the boys were still small but no longer babies, I began to seek out the life I had had in mind when I married. First, I took the boys to France (that was a start), and second I began making more and more preserves (from confit to marmalade). In those days, I still left the Japanese pickles to my mother-in-law.

At the outset we ordered the organic citrus fruit through a natural farming group, but as the years went on, we began calling the grower directly. And she would call us back to check how we liked it. Her name is Mochizuki-san and she was seventy-two at the time.

In the fall of 2000 we moved into my parents-in-law's farmhouse, which we had recently renovated. And I remember fielding calls from Mochizuki-san during Christmas dinners. I stood in the fax closet so I could hear better and didn't have the heart to tell her we had guests. Her husband was in the end stages of a battle with cancer, and she needed to talk.

So we talked. And talked. And thus the relationship grew. Eventually her family and our family met up halfway in Atami for the day. Later she came to visit us by train. We returned the visit by plane and boat, bringing along my father and stepmother. Mochizuki-san lives on an island near Hiroshima in the Seto Inland Sea. Her son and daughter-in-law live on the same property but do not help with the citrus growing and there are only a few other organic growers on the island, none of whom are young. I am in awe of Mochizuki-san's drive to keep growing, despite her increasing years, and consequently am energized and that much more thankful for the fruit she sends. And her Herculean efforts give me that much more desire to create citrus desserts or preserves.

I rarely use chocolate; no need with that gorgeous citrus. It beckons me and beguiles me. I want to use it. No, I am compelled to use it. The fruit tastes so good, even if you flub the dessert, it will still be wonderful. But each year I wonder if this will be the last year for Mochizuki-san to send us citrus.

I adapted this recipe (slightly) from Lindsey Shere's *Chez Panisse Desserts*, just about the only dessert book I ever use these days. Her recipes transform fruit into desserts that still taste like the fruit itself. Fruit of any kind is really the most orthodox of desserts in Japan, but fruit ice cream is always welcome. (Japanese are big consumers of ice cream.) Try to use unwaxed or organic fruit, since you will be using the peel to infuse the custard.

tangerine ice cream MAKES ABOUT 1 QUART (1 LITER)
MIKAN AISU

4 organic tangerines

⅔ cup (135 g) organic
granulated sugar

½ cup (125 cc) milk

4 large egg yolks,
at room temperature

2 cups (500 cc) heavy cream

A few drops of vanilla extract

Slice off the outside peel layer of 2 tangerines with a sharp knife or vegetable peeler, working in a circular fashion. Be careful not to remove any of the bitter white pith.

Measure the sugar and milk into a heavy-bottomed nonaluminum saucepan, drop in the tangerine peels, and heat over medium-high heat until just before the mixture reaches a boil. Remove from the heat and let sit, covered, for 10 minutes to extract the flavor from the peel.

Whisk a few ladles of warm milk mixture into the yolks and return to the saucepan. Heat over low heat, stirring, until the custard has thickened slightly (see page 328).

Strain directly into a plastic container. With a Microplane, finely grate the peel of the 2 remaining tangerines directly onto the warm custard. While you are waiting for the custard to suck up the flavor of the zest (about 5 minutes), juice the tangerines. Stir the cream, 6 tablespoons tangerine juice, and vanilla into the warm custard.

Cool to room temperature, then chill overnight in a plastic container. Freeze according to the directions of your ice-cream maker.

VARIATION: Substitute any kind of orange-like citrus for the tangerines.

ICE CREAM

Ice cream can be made with all cream or a combination of cream and milk. Ice milk is made from cow or soy milk. Ice cream or ice milk may or may not contain eggs. Some part of the cream or milk is usually heated, though American backyard hand-cranked ice cream allows you to dump all the ingredients into the ice cream hopper (no eggs) and just crank away. Other than the creamless soy milk "ice cream" on one end of the spectrum and the full-cream fig and blackberry ice creams on the other, almost all of the ice cream recipes here are adjusted from the original 2:1 ratio of cream and milk to 1:1. In general, a lighter ice cream works best at the end of a Japanese meal. Also pairing a scoop of ice cream with a scoop of sorbet is a brilliant flavor presentation. The sorbet and ice cream could be of the same fruit or perhaps complementary ones. Keep it simple.

There are some basic rules of thumb to follow for all ice cream or ice milk recipes presented in this book, so please heed the following advice:

For Egg Yolks: Crack the eggs into a small bowl, gently lift out the yolks with your fingers, and slide into a medium-sized bowl. Discard the whites and shells or use the whites to make a meringue or any other fluffy confection. Whisk a soup ladle or so of the warm milk mixture into the yolks (otherwise the yolks will curdle when you introduce them cold turkey into the warm cream mixture) and return to the heavy-bottomed saucepan.

Cooking Custard: Heat over low heat, stirring constantly with a flat wooden spoon, until the custard has thickened and coats the back of the spoon when you drag a finger through the lingering "batter" clinging to the spoon. Timing here depends on several variables: the amount of custard you are making, the thickness of the pan (thicker enameled cast iron pans will cook the custard quickly), and your heat source. It is important to watch carefully as the custard changes.

Straining and Cooling Custard: Remove from the heat and continue stirring for a couple of minutes, then pour through a fine-mesh strainer directly into a plastic container. Drape a clean kitchen towel over the warm custard and let cool (this avoids condensation on the inside top of the container that may introduce unwanted water into the mixture). When cool, remove the towel, cover with the container lid, and refrigerate overnight.

Freezing: "Follow the directions that come with your ice-cream maker" is sort of a given, but what really useful advice do those directions impart? One good rule of thumb is not to fill your ice-cream maker container more than halfway. If you are making ice cream on a hot day and do not have a freezer unit built into the machine, churn the custard in the early morning or cool evening. In general, the ice cream is done when it starts to mound up around the churning blades and the surface breaks slightly. If you need to freeze in batches, be sure to mix each batch into the previous batches so the ice cream is evenly emulsified and not layered by batch. An ice-cream maker with a built-in freezing unit is highly recommended for producing ice cream effortlessly.

Serving: High-milk-content "ice creams" tend to be difficult to serve when frozen rock solid, so soften them a little before serving.

Storing: As a general rule of thumb, ice creams and sorbets keep well for several weeks or more.

I love the idea of serving a scoop of sorbet kissing a scoop of ice cream made from the same fruit. Simple, but so logical, this kind of dessert satisfies the longing for a bit of fruit at the end of the meal and also successfully combines creamy with icy textures, two dessert textures to which I am particularly drawn (along with crunch). Stick a piece of Sesame Brittle (page 344) in the ice cream and you'll have all three.

tangerine sorbet MAKES ABOUT 1 QUART (1 LITER)
MIKAN SHABETTO

4½ pounds (2 kg) organic sour-tasting tangerines

1 cup (200 g) organic granulated sugar

Wipe the tangerines and grate the peel of one with a lemon zester that creates thin shreds, or use a wide-bladed Microplane for a finer texture. Grate the peel directly into a small bowl in order to catch the precious citrus oil as well as the zest. Do not grate as far as the bitter white pith.

Juice all of the tangerines and strain out the seeds through a wide-mesh strainer set over a medium-sized bowl. Push against the sides of the strainer with the back of a wooden spoon to force as much of the pulp as possible into the juice.

Heat the sugar and 1 cup (250 cc) of the juice into a heavy-bottomed, nonreactive saucepan. Heat over medium-high heat, stirring, until the sugar has dissolved. Mix the sweetened hot juice into the unheated tangerine juice, scrape in the tangerine zest, and chill. Freeze according to the directions of your ice-cream maker.

VARIATION: Substitute any kind of orange-like citrus for the tangerines.

Sometimes we take field trips with the little SSU! preschoolers up to Yamaki, our local organic soy sauce, miso, and tofu place. Tsunokake-san conducts a tour in English (we're an English-only immersion program). After the tour, the kids get to taste some tofu and also make some of their own. After the tasting and tofu making, we troop downstairs and make fresh rice balls from the rice steamer full of hot rice that we've brought. Wrapped with crispy nori, they are delicious. And after lunch we troop back in for the last treat of the day: soy milk "ice cream." My version has a large milk percentage so it marries well with the bright flavor of poached kumquats. The black sesame seeds complete the eye-catching color palette.

soy milk "ice cream" with poached kumquats and black sesame MAKES ABOUT 1 QUART (1 LITER)
TONYU AISU TO KINKAN

2 cups (500 cc) milk

1 cup (250 cc) best-quality unflavored soy milk

¾ cup (150 g) sugar

3 large egg yolks, at room temperature

2 tablespoons black sesame seeds, for garnish

Poached Kumquats (recipe follows)

Measure the milk, soy milk, and sugar into a heavy-bottomed saucepan, and heat, stirring, over medium-high heat until the sugar has melted. Turn the heat down to low.

Whisk a soup ladle or so of warm milk mixture into the yolks and return to the saucepan. Heat over low heat, stirring, until the custard has thickened slightly (see page 328). Strain, cool to room temperature, and chill overnight in the fridge.

Freeze according to the directions of your ice-cream maker.

Toast the black sesame seeds in a small dry frying pan over medium-high heat until the seeds start to pop. Be sure to shake the pan constantly and occasionally lift it off the heat to keep the seeds from burning. When done, pour into a small bowl to cool, otherwise the seeds will continue cooking in the hot pan (and most likely burn). Toasted sesame seeds will keep in a sealed container for a week or so.

Scoop 2 small mounds of soy milk "ice cream" onto a pretty saucer for each person. Top with a spoonful of poached kumquats (with some of the syrup) and sprinkle with toasted black sesame seeds. Serve immediately.

POACHED KUMQUATS

½ pound (225 g) kumquats

½ cup (100 g) organic
granulated sugar

Wipe the kumquats and slice into ⅛- to ¼-inch (3- to 6- cm) rounds. Discard the ends.

Measure the sugar into a small heavy saucepan and add 1 cup (250 cc) water. Bring to a boil over medium heat, stirring to help dissolve the sugar. Add the sliced kumquats and lower the heat to a gentle simmer. Cook for about 10 minutes, until translucent. Scrape into a plastic container or jar and let cool to room temperature before storing in the fridge. Keeps for a few weeks.

VARIATIONS: Reverse the proportions of soy milk and milk, or use only soy milk for a nondairy version. Omit the eggs if you like, but the result will be much icier.

During the summer of 2011 I got a call from a Japanese acquaintance who asked if I would be willing to do a photo shoot with Todd Selby at our farm and school in early August. Up to my eyeballs writing recipes, nonetheless I couldn't say no. Our potatoes were exceptionally good that year (and we still hadn't finished digging them up), so I thought it would be fun to haul the SSU! Saturday kids over to the potato field to do a little digging.

Japanese-style potato salad with thinly sliced raw red okra, chopped green peppers, and Tadaaki's homegrown onions would pair well with some barbecued chicken teriyaki and cherry tomato halves dressed with a miso vinaigrette and shiso threads. And what better than a purply-red ice cream made from local blackberries for dessert?

blackberry ice cream MAKES ABOUT 1 QUART (1 LITER)
KIICHIGO AISU

3 cups (600 g) blackberries

2 cups (500 cc) heavy cream

¾ cup (150 g) granulated sugar

A few drops of kirsch (optional)

Pulse the blackberries in a blender or food processor. After the berries are emulsified, whirl for a few seconds to produce a smooth purée. Pass the berry purée through a fine-mesh strainer or food mill, pressing the berries against the sides of the strainer to extract every ounce of the precious purée concentrate and to leave the seeds behind.

Heat the cream with the sugar in a medium-sized saucepan over low heat, stirring occasionally, until the sugar has dissolved. Stir the warm sweetened cream into the seedless berry purée and add a few drops of kirsch, if using. Gently mix until incorporated and chill.

Freeze according to the directions of your ice-cream maker.

VARIATIONS: Substitute any other similar berries such as raspberries or boysenberries.

LINDSEY REMOLIF SHERE'S
CHEZ PANISSE DESSERTS

Our eighty-five-year-old organic grower friend, Mochizuki-san, sends us boxes and boxes of Japanese citrus such as *otachibana*, a native "grapefruit" that yields hauntingly tantalizing zest, and *natsumikan*, a sour yet bright lemony-flavored orange varietal, as well as small pale lemons with flowery-smelling skin. So I make a lot of citrus desserts.

And the best book for inspiration is *Chez Panisse Desserts*, a celebration of all things fruit and much, much more. Lindsey grew up on a fruit orchard and her recipes are simple, elegant, and compellingly delicious.

My own copy is quite bedraggled, but I can still find new desserts or pieces of advice, previously overlooked, even after almost three decades. Lindsey's advice is firm, yet never heavy-handed and often humorous. I love it when she writes: "It is important to buy good quality spirits. You need very little and they keep forever (if you can keep from drinking them)."

I met Lindsey by chance several years ago in Italy at a Slow Food dinner. We chatted for an hour before remembering to introduce ourselves. Warm, approachable, self-possessed, with a throaty chuckle that betrayed her gentle sense of humor: This is how I saw Lindsey Shere that evening. Like so many things, friendships are built over time. Nowadays I enjoy the occasional visit with Lindsey and her erudite husband, Charles, in Healdsburg. I'm also pals with their daughter Giovanna, a fellow writer in Portland, and love that she combines both her parents' personalities in one person. I cherish that connection forged from Japan to Italy and then back to California and now Portland. For Portland is where my eldest son, Christopher, is in school. And I love the layers of knowing (and enjoying) the person who wrote the recipes I have been using so faithfully for all these years.

So when it came time to put trustworthy delicious fruit ice cream and sorbet recipes in this book, I turned to Lindsey Remolif Shere, the founding dessert chef at Chez Panisse and the person who put her indelible mark on four decades of deliciously simple, honest (never trendy but always relevant) desserts.

While Fig Ice Cream is not Japanese, we do grow figs here and we do eat ice cream, so it works for me. I served this ice cream, adapted from Lindsey Shere's *Chez Panisse Desserts*, with Plum Sorbet (page 335) and Shiso Granita (page 336). The trio was spectacularly balanced in taste and color.

fig ice cream MAKES 1 QUART (1 LITER)
ICHIJIKU AISU

1 pound (500 g) ripe figs

1½ cups (400 cc) heavy cream

8 tablespoons (115 g) organic granulated sugar

3 large egg yolks, at room temperature

A few drops of Cognac (optional)

Remove the stems and cut the figs into quarters. Cook the figs with 3 tablespoons water, stirring frequently, over low heat in a heavy-bottomed nonaluminum saucepan until very soft, about 20 minutes. Pulse the cooked figs in a food processor to chop coarsely or smash with a potato masher. Measure out 1½ cups (400 cc) of purée and reserve.

Measure 1 cup (250 cc) of the cream with the sugar into a medium-sized nonaluminum saucepan and heat over low heat, stirring occasionally, until the sugar has dissolved.

Whisk about half of the warm cream mixture into the yolks, then scrape back into the heavy-bottomed saucepan with the remaining warm cream.

Heat, stirring, over low heat, until slightly thickened (see page 328). Strain and stir the remaining ½ cup (125 cc) cream, reserved fig purée, and Cognac, if using, into the custard. Cool to room temperature, then refrigerate overnight.

Freeze according to the directions of your ice-cream maker.

VARIATION: Substitute ripe persimmon purée for the fig purée.

I made sorbet for the first time when developing recipes for the book. Why? I suppose until then I was too busy making ice cream. But this plum sorbet (adapted from Lindsey Shere's *Chez Panisse Desserts*) made me regret all those years of plum seasons that passed us by. A jewel-bright ruby red, this tart sorbet is a great foil for the subtly creamy Fig Ice Cream (page 334).

plum sorbet MAKES ABOUT 1 QUART (1 LITER)
PURAMU SHABETTO

1 ⅓ pounds (600 g) ripe plums

¾ cup plus 2 tablespoons (175 g) organic granulated sugar

A splash of kirsch

Cut the plums in half and remove the pits. Put 5 pits on a chopping board and rap each one smartly with a rubber hammer or meat tenderizer. Be sure to pull up right on impact so you don't smash the inside kernel to smithereens (this operation takes a little skill, but the almondy kernels add a lovely hint of noisette to the plum).

Cut the plums into ½-inch (12-mm) slices with a razor-sharp knife (otherwise you'll just be smashing the skin as you saw through). Place the fruit in a heavy, medium-sized nonaluminum saucepan, and add ¼ cup (60 cc) water and the inner kernels. Cook over low to medium heat until soft, about 15 minutes. Stir often from the bottom to discourage the plums from sticking.

Remove from the heat and purée in a food processor or blender. Measure out 2⅓ cups (320 cc) plum purée into a plastic container. Boil the sugar with ½ cup plus 2 tablespoons (150 cc) water in a small saucepan. Stir the sugar syrup and kirsch into the purée and chill the mixture in the refrigerator overnight. Freeze according to the directions of your ice-cream maker.

On one of my trips to Portland to see Christopher, in college there, I stopped by Powell's to check out the Japanese cookbook section. I discovered an attractive book written by Victoria Wise. This recipe is adapted from a recipe for Green Tea and Shiso Granita in that book, *The Vegetarian Table: Japan.*

shiso granita MAKES ABOUT 3 CUPS (750 CC)
SHISO GURANITA

15 green (or red) shiso leaves

¼ cup (150 g) organic granulated
 sugar

Place the shiso leaves in a medium-sized bowl or 4-cup Pyrex measuring cup. Heat the sugar and 3 cups (750 cc) water to boiling in a medium saucepan, stirring the sugar to dissolve. Pour the boiling sugar water over the leaves and steep until cool.

Set a strainer over a plastic container large enough to hold 3 cups and strain out the leaves. Cover and transfer the shiso-flavored sugar water to a freezer shelf. Let sit, undisturbed, in the freezer for 1 hour. Remove to the countertop, open the lid, and gently stir in the crystals that have formed on the perimeter. Repeat this operation every 30 minutes, breaking up any larger crystals as you go. The finished granita should be flaky.

Serve alone in a beautiful glass bowl or goblet. This is also wonderful alongside Fig Ice Cream (page 334) and Plum Sorbet (page 335). Keeps frozen for several weeks.

SORBET

Guests at our house have usually included a lot of kids, so, with the exception of Matthew (who is not terribly fond of cream), ice cream was always one of their most favored desserts. I didn't make many sorbets until recently, but now that the boys are older (and our friends are too), I'm looking for a more fruit forward light taste at the end of company dinners. Sorbet fits that bill admirably and, paired with ice cream, satisfies the sweet cravings of anyone, even kids.

Sorbets are made from fruit and sugar. Done. How easy is that? A blender or food processor makes short work of the puréeing process, and a strainer or food mill is essential for removing unwanted seeds. (Cheesecloth could pinch-hit here, though it's a bit messy.)

Sorbet is easiest served straight out of the ice-cream maker, slightly slushy and brightly flavored from the just-churned fruit purée. Once frozen, serving becomes a challenge, depending on the fruit and sugar content (cooked fruits with extra sugar, such as plums, seem to require less effort). Remove the sorbet from the freezer and let it soften a little at room temperature before attempting to construct your plates.

In the midst of my ice cream- and sorbet-making frenzy, two small pale green melons sitting in a basket in my kitchen caught my eye. They had been grown by our friend Toshiharu Suka, so I knew they would be full of flavor and juxtapose nicely with subtly nuanced white peaches. I was not disappointed. Upon cutting them open, I found they were at their absolute perfect peak of ripeness, with peachy centers and pistachio green flesh.

melon sorbet MAKES ABOUT 1 QUART (1 LITER)
MERON SHABETTO

3 pounds (1350 g) nicely flavored ripe melons (such as Charantais, Crenshaw, or cantaloupe)

1 cup (200 g) organic granulated sugar

A few drops of kirsch

Cut the melons in half and scoop out the center pulp and seeds with a soupspoon. Discard or save the seeds to dry and plant later. Scoop the melon flesh into a medium-sized bowl, but don't scrape too close to the bitter rind.

Purée in a food processor or blender. You should have about 4 cups (1000 cc). Heat 1 cup (250 cc) of melon purée with the sugar in a heavy-bottomed, nonreactive saucepan, stirring over low heat until the sugar is dissolved.

Pour the warm sweetened melon into the rest of the purée and flavor with the kirsch.

Freeze according to the directions of your ice-cream maker.

As I was in the thick of writing the dessert chapter, my editor friend Kim sent me a link to a mango farm on the Ogasawara Islands (Japan). The ordering window is short: from August 1 to August 8. It was July 31, so I phoned the next day. Too late—they had had a bad crop and were already sold out. Miura-san found me another grower, this time in Okinawa. I called her and chatted for a while, reminiscent of the early days talking with Mochizuki-san. It took a few more weeks for her mangos to be ripe, but they were worth the wait. Mangoes are dear wherever you are, so this sorbet should be reserved for special occasions (or special guests). I used Rhum du Père Labat, an artisanal white rum crafted from rainwater by an old guy at a small distillery on L'île de Marie-Galante, an island in the Caribbean. Apparently the guy follows instinct more than a formula, and Tadaaki imagines him dipping his cigarette smoke–stained finger into the vat of rum to taste (and further enhance) his liquor—a bit of fantasy that adds to the wild overtones of this unique rum.

mango sorbet MAKES ABOUT 1 QUART (1 LITER)
MANGO SHABETTO

3 pounds (1500 g) perfectly ripe mangoes

2 teaspoons artisanal white rum (preferably with a "wild" taste)

Juice of 2 limes

¾ cup (150 g) organic granulated sugar

Slice the mango flesh off the pits over a medium-sized bowl to catch all the essential juices. Working one by one (to avoid losing any drops of juice as it runs off onto the counter from the cutting board), lay a piece of mango, peel side down, onto a cutting board. Scrape off the flesh as close to the peel as you can with the back of a knife. Also remove as much pulp as you can from the pits and drop into the mango bowl. After each piece is peeled, be sure to scrape the accumulated mango juices into the bowl along with the fruit.

Purée the mango pieces with their juices in a food processor or blender. There should be about 3½ cups (850 cc). Add the rum and lime juice.

Heat the sugar with ½ cup (125 cc) water in a small saucepan, stirring over medium-high heat to dissolve. Simmer for 5 minutes. Pour into a small bowl or measuring cup to cool.

When the syrup has cooled to almost room temperature, mix in the seasoned mango purée and chill.

Freeze according to the directions of your ice-cream maker.

In the early years of our marriage, Tadaaki's father would be out in the early summer, wrapping each piece of fruit on his white peach tree with newspaper to keep the birds away. Those were my formative years in Japan. I fought against much and often did not appreciate the subtle flavors around me. Why couldn't we have a yellow peach tree, I wondered? Why does he wrap the peaches in newspaper instead of the "special fruit paper" used by the local apple pear growers? I found the peaches fairly tasteless and blamed it on the newspaper for not letting the sun's rays hit the fruit directly during the ripening process. This may or may not have been the case, but more likely I overlooked the essential point of a white peach. For white peaches are juicy, delicate, and refreshing when served chilled in the sultry summer. But in the intervening years, the white peach tree fell prey to disease and was cut down. I never mourned it until now.

It was midsummer when I was writing this book. Fruit was all over the place—on our trees and at the farm stands. We were also the recipients of various kinds of fruit, including a box of unblemished white peaches, so white peach ice cream just made sense. Refreshing, light on the cream, elegant.

white peach ice cream MAKES ABOUT 1 QUART (1 LITER)
HAKUTO AISU

¾ cup (180 cc) heavy cream

¾ cup (180 cc) milk

¾ cup (150 g) organic granulated sugar

3 egg yolks, at room temperature

1 pound (500 g) ripe white peaches

A few drops of kirsch (optional)

Pour the cream and milk into a small nonreactive saucepan with ½ cup (100 g) of the sugar and heat over low heat, stirring occasionally, until the sugar has dissolved.

Warm the egg yolks with a couple of ladles of the warm cream mixture and pour back into the saucepan with the remaining warm cream and milk.

Heat, stirring, over low heat until the custard has slightly thickened (see page 328). Strain, cool to room temperature, then chill overnight.

Prepare the peach purée the next day about an hour before freezing the ice cream. Cut the peaches in half and peel over a medium-sized bowl to catch all the precious juices (white peaches have a very delicate flavor, so you do not want to lose any speck of them running onto the counter or cutting board). Once peeled, slice into ½-inch (1-cm) segments with a sharp knife, dropping the pieces into the drip-catching bowl. Mix with the remaining ¼ cup (50 g) sugar and let macerate for 30 minutes.

Smash the peach pulp with a potato masher until the pulp retains some small chunky bits (but no large lumps). You should have about 1½ cups (375 cc) of purée.

Fold the peach purée into the chilled ice cream custard and splash in a few drops of kirsch, if using. Freeze according to the directions of your ice-cream maker.

Once I had embraced white peaches as an ice cream, I was all in, so thought white peach sorbet would make a light palate cleanser, particularly good after fried foods such as tempura. I try to avoid using out-of-season lemons in the summer but it couldn't be helped. I sampled the "batter" before adding lemon and found it a tad flat. A few drops of lemon added that bright note to bring all the flavors up to the front, so don't leave it out.

white peach sorbet MAKES ABOUT 1 QUART (1 LITER)
HAKUTO SHABETTO

1 ¾ pounds (800 g) ripe white peaches

¾ cup (150 g) organic granulated sugar

A squeeze of lemon juice

A few drops of kirsch

Cut the peaches in half and peel over a medium-sized saucepan to catch the juices. Once peeled, slice with a sharp knife, dropping the pieces into the drip-catching saucepan as you go.

Add 2 tablespoons water and cook over low heat, stirring, for about 10 minutes, or until the peach pieces are hot to their centers. Remove from the heat.

Purée in a food processor or blender but do not wash the warm saucepan. You should have about 3 cups (750 cc). Return the peach purée to the saucepan and stir in the sugar. Continue stirring off heat until the sugar is dissolved. Squeeze in a few drops of lemon juice and kirsch. Chill.

Freeze according to the directions of your ice-cream maker.

Years ago, Tadaaki got a line on some small, intensely flavored pineapples grown organically in Okinawa. We waited (im)patiently for them each year. But since they were only available during a one-week period in August, sometimes we missed it. The tricky thing is that the harvest time follows nature, so each year it is slightly different. But then one year we heard devastating news. The pineapple grower had drowned the winter before, and his wife had not been able to continue on in his place. We ordered pineapples from another organic grower, but they just were not the same—until this year. Growing things takes more than planting seeds or tending trees. It takes a person who really cares. And it takes a person who understands intuitively what the vegetables or fruits need to thrive. We still did order periodically, but did not feel as compelled to as before. Nonetheless, I did not give up hope for that perfect pineapple to come my way again. And it did. The pineapple ice cream (and sorbet) I made from the pineapple was the best of the summer—and maybe the best ice cream and sorbet I have ever tasted.

pineapple ice cream MAKES ABOUT 1 QUART (1 LITER)
PAINAPPURU AISU

1 small ripe organic pineapple (about 1 pound/500 g)

¾ cup (180 cc) heavy cream

6 tablespoons (90 cc) milk

¾ cup (150 g) organic granulated sugar

3 egg yolks, at room temperature

A few drops of vanilla extract

Lop the top off the pineapple and remove the peel with a sharp knife. Cut out the eyes with the tip of the knife. Stand the pineapple upright on a cutting board and quarter vertically. Lay each quarter wedge down on the board and slice off the hard center core section. Cut the pineapple into large chunks and slide into a medium-sized nonreactive saucepan. Heat almost to boiling. Remove from the heat and pulse in a food processor or blender until chunky but not puréed. There should be about 1¼ cups (550 cc) or so of purée.

Pour the cream and milk into a small nonreactive saucepan with the sugar and heat over low heat, stirring occasionally, until the sugar has dissolved.

Warm the yolks with a couple of ladles of warm cream mixture and pour back into the saucepan with the remaining warm cream and milk.

Heat over low heat until slightly thickened (see page 328). Strain into the pineapple purée. Add a few drops of vanilla, stir gently to mix, and chill overnight.

Freeze according to the directions of your ice-cream maker.

On its own or paired with Pineapple Ice Cream, this sorbet will surprise you. (Reserve the core, peel, and top to make homemade pineapple vinegar. Steep with a handful of organic sugar and a few gallons of water for three months in a clear glass jar covered with cheesecloth under the hot summer sun.)

pineapple sorbet MAKES ABOUT 1 QUART (1 LITER)
PAINAPPURU SHABETTO

2 small ripe organic pineapples (about 2½ pounds/1 kg or so)

½ cup (100 g) organic granulated sugar

Kirsch (optional)

Cut the tops off the pineapples and slice off the peel with a sharp knife. Pare out the eyes with the tip of the knife. Stand the pineapples upright on a cutting board and quarter vertically. Lay each quarter wedge down on the board and slice off the hard center core. Cut the pineapples into large chunks and purée in a food processor or blender. There should be about 3 cups (750 cc); if not, adjust the sugar (1 cup/250 cc pineapple purée : 3 tablespoons/45 g sugar).

Heat the sugar with ¾ cup of the pineapple purée in a heavy-bottomed nonreactive saucepan, stirring over low heat to dissolve. Fold into the unheated pineapple purée and stir in a couple of drops of kirsch, if using.

Freeze according to the directions of your ice-cream maker.

I came across a recipe for peanut brittle in David Lebovitz's *The Perfect Scoop*, and especially loved that he had gotten it originally from Mary Jo Thoresen. I had intended to use that method for my sesame brittle, but not in love with corn syrup (or using thermometers), I opted for adapting David's "croquant" method on the adjacent page. I met David at Food Blog Camp and am hooked on his quirky blog posts. He also puts out some damn good dessert cookbooks (and a laugh-out-loud memoir with recipes). Mary Jo and her husband, Curt, cooked with the Chez Panisse crew at the second Soba Dinner we staged there in 2010. I find comfort in the interconnectedness of the world of food, especially since I live on a farm in rural Japan. Through food, I am part of a larger, supportive community.

sesame brittle SERVES 12
GOMA BURITORU

1 cup (150 g) unhulled sesame seeds

1 cup (200 g) organic granulated sugar

Line a baking sheet with a piece of heavy-duty aluminum foil.

Toast the sesame seeds over medium-high heat in a slope-sided wide frying pan until fragrant and just starting to pop. Sesame seeds burn easily, so you must be attentive. Shake the pan, lifting it off the heat once in a while. Spread out the sesame seeds (up the sides of the pan) to even the heat distribution. When the seeds start to pop, immediately remove from the heat and pour them into a small bowl to cool.

Measure the sugar into a light-colored medium-sized, medium-weight saucepan. If you use organic sugar, the caramelization process is somewhat difficult to gauge and the sugar can easily burn. A light-colored pan is useful; also a medium-weight pan (as opposed to heavyweight) will slow the heating process a bit, so it works in your favor.

Heat over medium heat and roll the pan a bit as the sugar starts to bubble and brown on the edges. A heatproof spatula is helpful to gently nudge the sugar "islands" into the melting caramel if you are careful and don't overwork.

As soon as all the sugar granules are completely melted, dump in the sesame seeds, mix quickly but thoroughly, and scrape onto the foil-lined baking sheet. Smooth the hot sugar and seed mixture as thinly as you can—it cools immediately on contact with the foil, so move smart!

Cool completely, peel away from the foil, break into pieces, and serve as a garnish to complementary desserts such as ice cream. Use part of the foil to line a plastic container or tin box. Store pieces of sesame brittle, set side by side (not stacked or overlapping), using the rest of the foil (torn into pieces) to separate the layers. Keeps for several week at room temperature, depending on the humidity.

VARIATIONS: Replace the sesame seeds with 1½ cups (150 g) roasted chopped peanuts, pecans, or walnuts.

In the sixteenth century, Portuguese merchants and missionaries became the first Westerners to enter what was then feudal Japan. The Portuguese eventually were given the boot by Shogun Iemitsu Tokugawa in the middle 1600s, when Japan closed her gates to the world. The shogunate did not take kindly to Christian proselytizing; however, the Portuguese did manage to introduce a number of foods that were adapted and assimilated into what is now traditional Japanese cuisine. Tempura and *castella* are just a couple of those foods. *Castella* is similar to pound cake but has a syrup component and is more dense in texture. Also *castella* is not often made at home.

Kanchan serves pound cake at the end of most meals at his restaurants, so for me it works as a Japanese dessert. In my early years in Japan, I had a little pound cake business going. I learned to hate those temperamental, though tasty cakes. My younger sister Lisa is the cake queen in our family and she swears by (and gave me) Rose Levy Beranbaum's *The Cake Bible*. When I make cakes, I use that book because I trust my cake-savvy sister (and Rose Levy Beranbaum). But this recipe (adapted from Lindsey Shere's Rose Geranium Pound Cake method) won't disappoint you.

pound cake MAKES 4 SMALL LOAVES OR 1 LARGE BUNDT CAKE
PAUNDO KEIKI

2½ sticks (170 g) unsalted butter, at room temperature, plus more for the pan(s)

2⅔ cups (400 g) unsifted cake flour, plus more for the pan(s)

1⅓ cups (265 g) organic granulated sugar

¾ teaspoon fine sea salt

6 eggs, at room temperature

1½ teaspoons vanilla extract

Preheat the oven to 325°F (165°C). Butter and flour four mini loaf pans or a 10-inch (25-cm) tube or Bundt pan.

Measure the flour into a medium-sized bowl and whisk to break up any lumps. Cream the butter, sugar, and salt together in a medium-large bowl with a hand mixer until well emulsified and fluffy.

Break the eggs into a medium-sized bowl and add the vanilla. Slurp the eggs in, 2 at a time, to the batter. Beat until the eggs are nicely incorporated and there are no ripple breaks on the surface of the batter. Scrape down the sides between egg additions.

Add the flour in 4 increments. Scrape in a quarter of the flour, beat at low speed until creamy, scrape down the sides, and continue until all the flour has been added and the batter is thick and velvety.

Divide the batter among the small loaf pans or smooth into the tube pan and rap smartly on the counter to eliminate any air pockets. Bake the small loaves for 45 to 50 minutes or the tube pan (or Bundt) pan for 75 minutes. The cakes should be golden brown. Cool for 3 minutes in the pans. Invert the cakes onto a clean dish towel, then set on a cake rack to finish cooling. Cut and serve when completely cool.

Tadaaki began making custard when he had an excess of eggs (or milk, since I tend to order too much, a vestige of my ingredient-less childhood). He whips it up for the egg workers' ten o'clock tea break. Originally he used small fluted metal pudding cups because that was the Japanese way. And not wanting to "bother me" by asking where the vanilla was, he bought the only vanilla flavoring available locally—vanilla essence, not real extract. I stepped back and let him have at it. I had only ever made custard in the oven, so didn't really want to get involved in his stovetop method. But over the years, Tadaaki, Mr. Wing It, ended up perfecting "the recipe" and realized the benefit of sometimes following a formula. He flavors with vanilla or occasionally instant espresso powder. I thought ginger would complement the delicate flavor of this milk-based custard. And it does.

ginger custard MAKES 8
SHOGA PURIN

2 cups (500 cc) milk

¼ cup plus 2 scant tablespoons (75 g) organic granulated sugar

5 large farm-fresh eggs, at room temperature

1 teaspoon ginger juice, squeezed from finely grated fresh ginger

Pour the milk into a heavy-bottomed saucepan, stir in the sugar, and dissolve over medium-high heat. Stir occasionally. Do not let it boil!

Just before the milk reaches a boil, remove from the heat and let cool for 1 minute.

Whisk the eggs lightly until the whites and yolks are incorporated but not frothy. Pour the hot milk into the whisked eggs in a slow, steady stream, whisking continuously. At this point, the custard will naturally be at the perfect ambient temperature, about 160–175°F (70–80°C).

Preheat eight ceramic ramekins (½ cup/125 cc) in a bamboo or metal steamer set over a large pan of simmering water. Strain the milk mixture, add the ginger juice, and fill the warm ramekins about three-quarters full. Steam for 15 minutes over low to medium-low heat. The trick here is to steam the custards slowly—even taking up to 22 minutes. For the most silky results, stay on the low end of the temperature setting, and then after 15 minutes, increase the heat just a speck and check every 2 minutes. Toward the end you can gauge the doneness by giving the steamer a little jiggle and seeing how the custard reacts. It should have turned from soupy to a gentle soft consistency.

Remove the steamer from the heat. Serve warm or let cool to room temperature before serving. Also good chilled. (After cooling, cover with foil and refrigerate.)

POUNDING MOCHI

"Gacha-gacha-gacha," our monstrously heavy and equally ancient front door rattles on its metal track, quickly followed by the whoosh of the wood and glass shoji inner front door. From the energy burst of the opening and the splash of hand washing, I know it's Tadaaki, coming in for breakfast after collecting the early morning eggs. As he bangs brass against iron, I hear him hefting the antique stockpot onto our stove. He sparks the flame and the soft hum of the hood fan revs up. Christmas has come and gone, and now *shogatsu* (Japanese New Year) has arrived. *Shogatsu* is traditionally a family time, though that has been waning in recent years as family members disperse to far cities. But our family still follows most of the traditional practices.

On December 29, Tadaaki washes the organic glutinous rice (*mochi gome*) that we will pound the next day. This year Tadaaki plans to pound eight batches of *mochi*, so he has eight pails of rice to wash and soak. Each pail holds three kilos of rice that he has bought from our grower friend, Suka-san. A couple of years ago, Tadaaki discovered an antique rice washer upstairs in my collection of flea market finds and was excited to put it to use. The guy I bought it from said it was an ice-cream maker. I doubted that but was attracted by the fine craftsmanship of the old wooden bucket and the low price. Tadaaki soaks the rice overnight, and the next morning we kick off *shogatsu* with a half-day of *mochi* making (*mochi tsuki*).

Every year we do *mochi tsuki* outside in the garden, and by some stroke of luck, that day almost always dawns sunny. Tadaaki wraps a pail of soaked *mochi gome* in a muslin cloth, puts the muslin bundle into a lidded wooden steamer, and places it on top of an iron pot full of boiling water set over a wood-burning fire. The glutinous

rice steams for about an hour, then is plucked out of the steamer and dumped into a one-meter-diameter mortar (*usu*), a hollowed-out tree stump that Tadaaki has soaked overnight. Tadaaki's mother prepares a bucket of cold water next to the *usu* for dipping in the mallet or hands before touching the hot sticky rice. First Tadaaki circles the *usu*, smashing the rice grains with an oversized wooden mallet. Then he wields the mallet high above his head and pounds the mass with a series of distinctively satisfying *thumps*. The inexperienced tend toward squelchy, weak glurps when their mallet hits the rice. (They probably don't reach far enough over their heads to really get the necessary leverage.) One person pounds and another person dips a hand in the cold water, then folds the rice "dough" over itself in one quick movement while the mallet is still in the air (almost like kneading bread). We invite a few dozen friends and everyone gets a turn at pounding the *mochi*. In the past, Tadaaki and his brothers worked up a sweat. But now that the kids are getting bigger and friends have gotten more skillful, the mallet gets passed around, and *mochi tsuki* is truly a community event.

As soon as each batch of *mochi* is pounded, we must work quickly before it cools to an unpliable mass. We smooth the hot *mochi* into moon-shaped dumplings called *kagami mochi*, which will be stacked in two tiers and offered to the house gods. Tadaaki continues to pinch off misshapen globs of *mochi* as we flatten them into rough circles and stretch them around a ball of *anko* (simmered organic azuki beans smashed with organic sugar and a little sea salt). As more batches of *mochi* are pounded, I take my turn at rolling the *mochi* into a rectangular slab. *Mochi* is much less temperamental than piecrust and just needs a firm, even hand. Tadaaki's mother used to roll the *mochi* out on the hall floor, which opens up to the garden, but in recent years Tadaaki drags out Christopher's

Ping-Pong table for the operation. Once the *mochi* is rolled and well powdered with potato starch, Tadaaki flips the several-centimeter-thick slabs onto a wooden board to dry for a couple of days before cutting. The air-drying process is essential to create a wicked surface against which the *mochi* will push off and puff up when broiled.

Some of my oldest friends have come and we fall easily back on familiar topics. I uncork the stopper of Harigaya-san's homemade lager and pour a glass. Life couldn't get any better, and this day is one of my favorite days of the year: (almost) no responsibility, the warm winter sun, and talking leisurely with friends. Sometimes it's nice not to be in charge.

But the real truth is that Tadaaki and I share an intertwined responsibility, and this is why we are able to preserve age-old farm customs or create our own. Our partnership, along with our family and community (those people in our life who share those same ideals), and the fact that that community is a world community, gives us an immeasurable amount of collective energy to keep on growing and creating. And, when I think about it, that is a powerful feeling that brings me to my knees.

My mother-in-law has a severely bent back caused by the postwar calcium-poor diet and years of working in the rice fields. But at eighty-three, she still makes *ohagi* on every traditional farming holiday. These sweets go very well with tea and make a tasty and healthy afternoon snack.

The first time I made *ohagi* with my preschool students, they had a grand old time and begged to make them again the following week. Sadly, sweet bean paste *(anko)* is not wildly popular with Japanese children today, and chocolate has replaced this traditional azuki bean paste as the flavor of choice. Perhaps it is because so few people make it by hand and because it is often overly sweet. There is a myth that making *anko* is difficult. Not true. Use organic azuki beans and organic sugar, and what can go wrong?

pounded sticky
rice sweets MAKES ABOUT 24
OHAGI

2 cups (500 cc) glutinous rice
 (*mochi gome*)

2 cups (500 cc) minus 3 tablespoons
 filtered or spring water

TOPPINGS

4 tablespoons sesame seeds

1 tablespoon organic sugar

¼ teaspoon fine sea salt

4 tablespoons soybean powder
 (*kinako*, page 9)

1 tablespoon organic sugar

¼ teaspoon fine sea salt

1 cup (250 cc) azuki beans

¼ cup (50 g) organic sugar

¼ teaspoon fine sea salt

Wash the glutinous rice until the water runs clear. Place the rice in a rice cooker. Add the filtered water and let stand overnight. Cook in the rice cooker on the *okawa* (おかわ) setting or in a heavy saucepan according to the cooking method for Plain Rice (page 143).

Transfer the cooked glutinous rice to a large mixing bowl and mash with a large wooden pestle (*surikogi*) until the rice grains adhere into a sticky mass. There should still be visible grains. Let cool 20 minutes for easier handling.

Set a small bowl of cold water by your side. Dip your fingers in the water to keep the rice from sticking to your hands. Shape the rice into 4 by 2-inch (10 by 5-cm) oblongs. Finish by using one of the three toppings.

Sesame: Toast the sesame seeds in a dry pan over medium heat just until they start to pop. Grind roughly in a *suribachi* (page 14) or mortar, add the sugar and salt, and mix. Pour the sesame mixture onto a small plate and roll the rice oblongs in it to coat.

Soybean powder (*kinako*): Mix the soybean powder, sugar, and salt. Follow the above procedure for rolling the rice pieces.

continued on next page

pounded sticky rice sweets

Azuki bean paste (*anko*): Measure the azuki beans into a medium-sized, heavy pot and fill the pot three-quarters full with cold water. Bring to a boil over high heat, remove from the heat and let sit 1 hour. Drain, return the beans to the pot, and fill with cold water to about 2 inches (4 cm) above the beans. Bring to a simmer and cook for about 15 minutes, then throw in a ½ cup (125 cc) of cold water. This is known as "surprise water" (*bikkuri mizu*): it shocks the beans and softens them. Bring back to a simmer and cook until the beans just get soft (about 10 or 15 minutes). Stir in the sugar and salt and continue cooking uncovered, stirring occasionally, until the beans start to fall apart and most of the water has evaporated. If there is still too much liquid left in the pan, boil over high heat to reduce (but take care not to burn the bottom). Mash roughly. The paste should be about the consistency of mashed potatoes but still chunky (technically this style of *anko* is called *tsubu-an*). Smooth the *anko* around the rice oblongs. This recipe makes 3 cups (750 cc), but leftover *anko* keeps well for several months or more in the freezer.

My youngest son Matthew was hot to become a *wagashiya* (traditional Japanese sweet maker) several years ago, and he set about making all sorts of Japanese sweets. But a few years ago, after being homeschooled all their life, Matthew and brother Andrew entered Japanese junior high. No more dreams of being a *wagashiya*, no more going up to the pottery studio to throw plates or bowls—it was basketball and school all the way (though Matthew did pick up the guitar a year or so ago and Skypes with brother Christopher about music and chords). Matthew and Andrew ducked out whenever Miura-san was photographing for the book, so other than a couple photos, are absent from these pages. The boys have some contrived idea that taking their picture takes a part of their souls. Okaaay . . . I wonder where they picked that up?

Kuzu mochi may not be traditional to Tadaaki's farm family, but I include it because, unlike some of the other sweets, it is uncomplicated and quick to make. *Kuzu mochi* also combines a couple of my favorite elements in Japanese sweets: *kinako* and *kuromitsu* (soybean flour and black sugar syrup). Originally from *warabi* (bracken) roots, nowadays this is made from *kuzu* starch. At the height of Matthew's *wagashiya* days, he made these often, so this recipe is for Matthew.

kuzu sweets with black sugar syrup MAKES 16 PIECES
KUZU MOCHI

⅔ cup (3.5 oz/100 g) *kuzu* starch (*hon kuzu*, page 11)

¼ cup (50 g) organic sugar

FOR SPRINKLING

6 tablespoons soybean powder (*kinako*, page 9)

1½ tablespoons organic sugar

¼ teaspoon fine sea salt

Black Sugar Syrup (page 319) or blackstrap molasses (optional)

Sprinkle 1 tablespoon of the sweetened *kinako* powder on each bottom surface of two 8 by 4-inch (20 by 10-cm) metal loaf pans.

Fill a wide pan about halfway with water, set a steamer basket over the water, and bring to a simmer over high heat.

Measure the *kuzu* and sugar into a medium-sized pan and whisk in 1 cup (250 cc) water until no *kuzu* lumps remain. Add 1½ cups (375 cc) more water, whisk briskly, and cook over medium heat, stirring constantly with a flat wooden spoon. After a while, you will be able to see a few rice-shaped clear gobules here and there. At this point, turn the heat down to low and continue cooking (and stirring) until the liquid thickens into a smooth, milky-white paste, then finally changes to become almost clear. Remove the saucepan from the heat and smooth the hot paste into the two prepared loaf pans. Most likely both pans will not fit in the steamer, so steam one by one over medium heat for 20 minutes (before steaming the second pan of *kuzu mochi*, be sure to add more hot water to the pan under the steamer since it will have evaporated).

When the *kuzu mochi* is cool, cut each pan into 8 pieces. To serve: sprinkle a little sweetened *kinako* on a small plate, lay a piece or two of *kuzu mochi* on top, sprinkle with some more *kinako*, and drizzle to taste with some black sugar syrup or molasses, if using.

Kuzu mochi only keeps for a day or two, so serve and eat quickly. Do not refrigerate because the sweets will harden and fade in both color and flavor.

I never really loved the texture of steamed buns, and by the time I came on the scene, my mother-in-law was using store-bought flour and locally made azuki bean paste (*anko*). Like many farmer women of her generation, decades of postwar privation while raising kids and helping on the farm paved the way for embracing ready-made or store-bought when more prosperous times came. Tadaaki's father had also stopped growing wheat for flour, so there was that as well. After college, Tadaaki returned home to work on the farm and not only revived old growing customs but also added new. He began to grow wheat again for the udon noodles they ate every night for dinner, and after we were married he experimented with growing hard red wheat for bread flour. There was a bit of trial and error involved in finding the right variety and drying method (the heating hopper overheated the grain, often rendering it gummy). In the meantime, Baachan lost the energy to make *manju*. Tadaaki occasionally would pair up with Matthew for a *manju*-making session, but by this time I had given up on sampling them (especially since I don't take tea breaks). Baachan often asks me, *"Ocha arate kun nai?"* ("Won't you drink some tea?") when I'm dashing out the door. She always asks with a giggle, because she knows I can't stop. (And don't.)

Flour from homegrown wheat and *anko* made at home are sublime. Such homemade *manju* are nothing like the factory-made *manju* that abound in Japan, a favorite *omiyage* (presents from trips to other areas of Japan). But that's another story.

steamed buns stuffed with azuki paste MAKES 12
SAKAMANJU

1 cup (250 g) *anko* (page 354)

1 ⅓ cup (200 g) or more good-tasting unbleached cake or pastry flour (page 10)

2 tablespoons organic sugar

2 teaspoons baking powder

¾ cup (8.8-oz/250-g package) organic *amazake* (page 11)

Make the *anko* earlier in the day or the day before because it needs to cool before handling.

Measure the flour, sugar, and baking powder into a medium-sized mixing bowl and whisk to break up any lumps. Stir the *amazake* in slowly with a wooden spoon. Turn the dough out onto a clean, flat surface dusted with flour. Rub off any lingering wet dough scraps left on the sides of the bowl with some flour and drop them on top of the dough. Knead the whole mass gently, adding flour as necessary, until the dough has developed the soft consistency of your earlobe. Return the dough to the bowl, cover with a damp cloth, and let rest for an hour.

While the dough is resting, make 12 *anko* balls, drape with plastic wrap, and set aside on a medium-sized plate.

Cut parchment paper into twelve (3-inch/7.5-cm) square pieces and place in a bamboo steamer.

After an hour, the dough should have risen a bit but will not be as active as a typical bread dough leavened with yeast. Dust very lightly with flour (this is a slightly sticky dough) and knead a couple of turns. Separate the dough into 4 equal sized balls, roll those into short, fat sausage-like shapes, and pinch each of those into 3 balls for a total of 12.

Working with 4 balls at a time, reroll each dough ball so it is evenly rounded. Flatten the dough on the palm of your hand a bit, then roll/ stretch into a ⅓-inch (8-mm) thick, 2½-inch (6-cm) wide circle. Pinch around the perimeter of the circle to thin the edge and to increase the size of the circle to about 3½ inches (9 cm). Place 1 *anko* ball in the middle of the circle and pinch up the outside edges of circle to form a dome-shaped bun. Arrange, seam side down, on top of the parchment paper pieces in the bamboo steamer. Let rest 30 minutes before cooking.

Fill a wide pan halfway with water and bring to a boil over high heat. Set the steamer vessel on top of but not in the boiling water and steam for 20 minutes. Remove from the heat and serve at room temperature. Do not open the steamer while cooking or cooling, except for one peek after 20 minutes to make sure they are done! The buns are best the same day but will keep wrapped in plastic then stored in a resealable plastic bag for a day or two. Do not refrigerate.

Not all tea snacks need to be sweet, and since farm work can be quite physical, salty flavors are also welcome. These *dango* were traditionally made unsweetened, brushed with soy sauce and slow grilled over a charcoal fire. If you have never smelled that indescribable aroma of gently caramelizing soy sauce intermingled with the tantalizing smoke from artisanal Japanese charcoal, well . . . you haven't lived. For me that is the smell of Japan.

You will need six (6-inch/15-cm) bamboo skewers to make this recipe.

soy sauce–broiled
dango balls MAKES 6 STICKS OF 4 DANGO
DANGO

1 cup (175 g) rice flour for *dango* (*joshinko*, page 10)

3 tablespoons organic soy sauce

Sweet Soy-Flavored Sauce (optional, page 319)

Bring a large, wide pot of water to a boil.

Set a large bowl in the kitchen sink and fill with cold water. Drop the bamboo skewers into the bowl.

Measure the *joshinko* into a medium-sized bowl. Whisk to break up any lumps and slowly add ¾ cup (175 cc) hot water to form a firm but pliable dough. Grasp the side of the bowl with one hand and knead the dough briefly with your other hand.

Divide the dough into 24 equal-sized balls and drop into the boiling water. After about 8 or 10 minutes, the balls will rise to the surface. Cook for another 4 minutes and remove from the boiling water by scooping up with a wire mesh strainer and dumping into the bowl of cold water in your sink. Run more cold water into the bowl to keep the overall temperature cool, but be careful the *dango* don't flow out of the bowl and escape into the sink.

Prepare a small charcoal "hibachi"-style brazier (*shichirin*). The charcoal takes some time to burn down and the low embers are best for cooking. Alternatively, set the broiler rack on the third position from the top and heat the broiler.

Remove the skewers from the bowl before draining the cooled *dango*.
Let air dry for a few minutes on a non–terry cloth kitchen towel. Pat dry
if you are pressed for time.

Thread 4 *dango* balls onto each skewer so that they are gently nestled up
next to each other but not smashed together. They should be centered
on the skewer. Brush with soy sauce and broil or grill about 2 minutes on
each of their 4 "sides," brushing with more soy sauce each time you turn
the skewer.

Serve hot from the grill with a cup of Japanese green tea for a
midmorning or afternoon snack. If you prefer a sweeter flavor, dip in the
sauce before serving.

The Tohoku Earthquake

At 2:46 p.m. on March 11, 2011, an earthquake of magnitude 9.0 struck the Tohoku region of eastern Japan. Our area was rocked at about magnitude 5.0—strong enough for my husband to see out into the garden where the earthen walls of our house separated from the posts in the rolling motion of the quake. When the earthquake shook Tokyo at about magnitude 6.0 or stronger for six long minutes, the city came to a halt. All public transportation was suspended, and people poured up from the underground malls and rail stations; office workers emptied out from buildings into the already swollen streets; and that vast city of speeding trains and bustling streets slowed to a crawl.

By a stroke of very bad luck, I was standing on the train platform in central Tokyo's Otemachi subway labyrinth at the moment the Great East Japan Earthquake hit. When the ground of the massive station structure stopped rippling and the initial terror had passed, the other commuters and I waited quietly, backs leaning against the station walls. All eyes were fixed on our cell phones in hand, trying unsuccessfully to get a signal. No one said a word.

At that point I still thought the trains would be running again because announcements were telling us there had been a "big earthquake" and to wait while the train lines were being checked. I dutifully waited forty-five minutes before realizing it was pointless. And so I made my way through underground walkways to Tokyo Station, unaware of just how long that distance is, and began to realize the enormity of what had just happened.

Student groups trapped on their way through Tokyo for their annual school trips were seated on the floor as teachers gave instructions. The bullet train would not be running that day or the next. Businessmen stood crowded around television screens, listening to news updates. But I knew time was an issue and kept moving, so did not hear of the horrific devastation wrought by the postquake tsunami.

I looked for a hotel right away but wasn't quick enough. Everything took an inordinately long time—so many people were flooding onto the walkways and streets after the trains stopped. That night in Tokyo was kind of like an out-of-body experience. Just moments before the great earthquake began, I had been thinking about food. My iPhone battery was dying, I was getting cold, and I knew I needed to get to a safe haven to recoup my energy before the night ahead of me. I needed food, and I needed good food.

When I finally got my bearings, it was getting on toward 5 p.m., already two hours after the quake. All hotels were full, so I lined up for a public pay phone to call home and make a restaurant reservation. I waited forty-five minutes.

I also waited forty-five minutes (in vain) for a taxi. I tried to gauge how long it would take by talking to others around me in line—I'm not sure what we were thinking. We somehow believed that if we stood there long enough, a taxi would take us where we wanted to go. But what exactly was "long enough"? One hour . . . five?

The alternative was unthinkable. Walk. But I now had a restaurant destination and nothing would deter me from having a good meal. Nothing. So I walked—power walked, that is.

Thanks to a fellow map-toting "traveler" met early on in my trek, I got to the restaurant in about an hour and a half. We stopped one time on a pedestrian bridge over a main thoroughfare. Beneath us a massive river of automobile headlights barely inched forward. No taxis were getting through that night. Walking had been a good decision.

A flute of champagne in hand, my iPhone charging, I heaved a huge sigh of relief. I was "home."

For the next two hours, a surreal dinner like I had never had before unfolded. It almost seems obscene in retrospect: tree bark, tree sap . . . bread baked before my eyes in a small stone capsule. Unusual and whimsical morsels from land and sea played together on the equally fanciful "plates." I was the only customer that night. Perhaps I was the only one crazy enough to take refuge in such a place. Shut off from the outside world, none of us in that hushed room of Les Créations de Narisawa really knew or understood the gravity of the earthquake and the monstrous destruction it had brought. Nor had any of us imagined the unthinkable happening—the meltdown of the Fukushima Nuclear Power Plant.

At ten o'clock, I stepped back out into the brisk night and started my return voyage. Long (useless) waits for trains, a night spent shivering on the marble floor of Tokyo Station, and more endless lines later, I finally got home late the following day. And for now we are safe, though 215 kilometers does not seem far enough from the Fukushima debacle. At the time of this writing, hundreds of thousands of Japanese are still in shelters, and many will not be able to go home for many years to come.

And in the aftermath, we try to pick up our lives. I am planting seeds for the summer and looking toward the future. We cannot control the amount of radiation that may or may not be in the environment around us, but we can control what we choose to put in our bodies. Now, more than ever, is the time to make careful and conscious decisions about the food we eat and to strive to find the cleanest, most chemical-free food we can. That is a choice we can make every day for ourselves and for our families.

ACKNOWLEDGMENTS

There are many people who contributed to making this book a reality, and to them, I am eternally grateful. But without the "you-can-do-anything" attitude instilled in me as a child by my unconventional parents, I don't think I could have seen this project through to the end. Also, growing up in a Japanese-inspired house on a woodsy back lot in Atherton, California, prepared me in a strange way for this farm life I lead today. And because of that, I feel deeply at home in this very foreign country.

As a lifelong cook, writing a cookbook was always on the far horizon—a goal I worked toward slowly—first teaching local cooking classes, then entering the global food world through Slow Food, and eventually publishing small articles and a blog. How I got to this place right now is thanks to the relationships built up over the years, but also to a chain of events that resulted in this book.

I want to thank the people involved in that chain: Toshiya Yoshikai, for opening the door to freelance writing jobs; Joanne Godley and Sylee Gore, for encouraging me to write a blog and pointing me in the right direction; the Undam(n)ed Women Writers group, for friendship and moral support; Malena Watrous (Stanford Continuing Studies), for invaluable editorial advice and mentoring; my old (and new) friends who read my blog and keep me on the straight and narrow; Mora Chartrand-Grant, for her most thorough feedback on recipes;

Sylvan Mishima Brackett and Sharon Jones, for propping me up and being my sounding boards; Patricia Wells and Alice Waters, for their inspiration and generosity; Amy Katoh, for opening up the world of Japanese country things in her books and for introducing me to my dear friend and editor in Japan, Kim Schuefftan (who was with me every step of the way from inception to completion); Kenji Miura, my talented and indefatigable photographer; David Lebovitz, for galvanizing me to put this particular book on the front burner and move the others back; writing coach Dianne Jacob, for pushing me through the onerous book proposal process; my agent, Jenni Ferrari-Adler, for her acerbic humor and straight-shooting editorial advice; designers Julie Barnes and Diane Marsh for completely "getting" me and my vision for this book; and Jean Lucas, my editor at Andrews McMeel, for not only choosing to publish *Japanese Farm Food*, but also for allowing me so much input and creative control—an anomaly in the publishing world (or so I am told).

But most of all, I thank my farmer husband, Tadaaki, without whom there would be no book; sons Christopher, Andrew, and Matthew, for their patient good humor throughout the more hectic phases; the Sunny-Side Up! staff, Alyssia, Yumiko, and Chizuru, for their unwavering support; and all the little crazies at SSU! for the unadulterated love and joy they give me each and every day. Life should be so simple!

Glossary of Japanese Produce

ROOTS, VEGETABLES, GREENS, MUSHROOMS, AND AROMATICS

ROOTS

DAIKON: A large white radish. If possible, buy with the leaves intact and still springy. The surface skin of the daikon should be crisp and not withered. Remove the leaves and store both leaves and root separately in the fridge.

GOBO (BURDOCK): A long (usually) thin, fibrous root used in stir-fries, simmered dishes, and soups. Store in a cool, dark place. Scrub the surface but do not peel before slicing.

KONNYAKU: Refers to both the root (inedible corm) and the gelatinous processed food (blocks, blobs, and noodles) made from the corm, which is used in soups, simmered dishes, and stir-fries. Store in water in the refrigerator. Keeps well.

SATO IMO (TARO ROOT): Small round, pleasantly slimy potato-like roots with a fibrous skin that is normally peeled. Lovely in soups and simmered dishes, and particularly tasty steamed whole (unpeeled), popped out of the skin while blisteringly hot, and eaten dipped in salt. If you find these, the skin should look fresh and not excessively dried out. Store in a cool, dark place.

SATSUMA IMO (SWEET POTATO): Pretty much the same as the sweet potatoes familiar in North America. Used in simmered dishes, Japanese sweets, and tempura. Most popular as a snack roasted in hot stones, sold by venders with small pickup trucks who cry (amplified: *"Yaki-imooooh, ishi yaki imooooh."*) to call people to come buy as their trucks cruise through neighborhoods. Store in a cool, dark place.

YAMA IMO (MOUNTAIN YAM): A tan, thin-skinned tuber speckled with small brown eyes. The bright white flesh is grated into a wonderfully slimy mass and eaten raw with soy sauce or as an accompaniment to noodles. Also sometimes used as a binder when making soba noodles or *ganmodoki* (page 110). Look for ones that appear fresh and not shriveled. Store in sawdust or rice husks in a cool, dark place.

VEGETABLES

EDAMAME (YOUNG SOYBEANS): Sold on the branch or in small net bags in Japan. Best fresh picked. Store in the fridge if not using right away, but better to use soon.

KABOCHA (WINTER SQUASH): Usually round, with dark green skin, heirloom varieties of kabocha may have light green or peach-colored skin or be oval in shape. Store in a cool, dark place if whole. If cut, wrap in plastic and refrigerate.

KYURI (CUCUMBER): Should be thin, usually about 7 inches (17.5 cm) long, with dark green shiny skin. They are not peeled or seeded. Store in a plastic bag in the refrigerator.

NASU (EGGPLANT): About 4 inches (10 cm) long. Look for ones with glossy purple skins. Store in a cool, dark place overnight, otherwise in the fridge.

NEGI (JAPANESE "LEEKS"): ½- to 2-inch (1.25- to 5-cm) thick Japanese green onions. Substitute fat scallions or spring onions. Store in a cool, dark place or the fridge.

RENKON (LOTUS ROOT): Comes in sausage-like links and is harvested from deep mud. Good sliced into thin half-rounds and sautéed with soy sauce and red pepper (*kinpira*, page 199). Look for pieces that are not discolored.

GREENS*

HAKUSAI (NAPA CABBAGE, CHINESE CABBAGE): *Hakusai* ("white vegetable") is widely used in one-pot and simmered dishes and to make pickles. Large heads are tied up while still in the field and kept out in the winter cold for about a month; this sweetens them and makes the leaves ideal for pickling.

KARASHINA (MUSTARD GREENS): Spicy greens available much of the year, though perhaps best in the winter.

KOMATSUNA: (BITTER GREENS): A brassica, relative of bok choy, but with thinner stems and leaves. An extremely versatile green grown all year-round in Japan. Good in *nabe* (one-pot dishes), sautéed, or blanched, squeezed and dressed (page 171).

MIBUNA (BITTER GREENS): A bitter green with long ⅓ inch (1-cm) wide leaves good in salads, stir-fries, and *nabe* (one-pot dishes).

MIZUNA (BITTER SALAD GREENS): A peppery salad green with zigzaggy leaves. Also good in *nabe* (one-pot dishes) or blanched, squeezed, and dressed with *shira-ae* (page 299) and slivered dried persimmons (*hoshigaki*, page 10). Often found in salad mix seed packs.

NANOHANA (FLOWERING TOPS): There are many varieties of flowering brassica (crucifers), including *komatsuna*, mustard, or turnip greens. Late winter and spring. Substitute rapini or any flowering tops sold at Asian farmers' markets.

SHUNGIKU (CULINARY CHRYSANTHEMUM GREENS): Good blanched, squeezed, and dressed with *shira-ae* (page 299) and exceptional in Sukiyaki (page 278).

*All greens should be perky and not wilted when you buy them. See Washing Vegetables sidebar for storage, page 170.

MUSHROOMS

ENOKI: Mild white or orange-colored mushrooms that go well in miso soup or *nabe* (page 90). Slightly slippery. Store in the fridge.

SHIMEJI: Spongy, gray-capped mushrooms that are good in *nabe* (one-pot dishes) or *chawan mushi* (page 119). Look for small caps and white stems. Slice off the bottom connecting portion. Store in the fridge.

SHIITAKE: Dark-capped meaty mushrooms grown on logs in the forest. Stems are thick, so cut them off the caps but do not discard. After removing the raggy bottom ends, the stems can be used like the caps in *nabe* or soup or to make a shiitake stock. Look for dusky gray-brown caps with cracks; avoid wet or discolored shiitake. Wipe if necessary; do not wash. Store in a cool, dark place, cap side down.

AROMATICS

MYOGA: A relative of ginger that shoots pinky-brown, candle flame–shaped buds up from the root area. If you find it, it should be fresh-looking and not tired. Spring to summer.

MITSUBA: An aromatic herb with a light, astringent flavor. Substitute a peppery cress. Spring and early summer.

NIRA (GARLIC CHIVES): Used in *gyoza* filling (page 128) and *kimchee*. Available most of the year.

SHISO (PERILLA): The most common Japanese herb, used in many, many dishes. Very easy to grow, a perennial that will happily reseed itself each year in the late spring and last into the early fall. Green and red varieties. The red can be used to make a refreshing drink.

SANSHO (PRICKLY ASH): Tiny tannic, strong-flavored leaves that are good in dressings (page 30) or *chawan mushi* (page 119) in small doses. Spring to summer. The dried seeds are also known as Japanese, Chinese, or Sichuan pepper.

CITRUS AND OTHER FRUITS

CITRUS*

OTACHIBANA: A native Japanese grapefruit-like citrus that yields hauntingly aromatic zest. They do not have much juice because the white pith inside is unusually thick.

DAIDAI: A native bitter orange used to make ponzu (page 309)

KABOSU: A small green citrus with a wild limelike flavor.

MIKAN: Technically a mandarin, but I use the more colloquially understood term, tangerine, in this book.

*Citrus season is winter, but the fruit should be harvested before the first frost. Wrap individually with a small piece of newspaper, pack in a box, and store in a cool, dark place.

NATSUMIKAN: A pale orange-skinned, mildly sour citrus. Good eaten as is, juiced in a salad dressing (page 306), or as a *chawan mushi* cup (page 120).

SUDACHI: A very small aromatic orangey-yellow citrus with bright-tasting juice and fragrant zest.

YUZU: A small yellow citrus with a sweet, mild (indescribable) taste. Juice and zest are both used. Recently available in the U.S.

OTHER FRUIT

KAKI (PERSIMMON): Round *kaki* (U.S.: *fuyu*) are eaten raw (peeled, seeds removed, and cut into sixths). Oval *kaki* (U.S.: *hachiya*) are eaten raw (only if not bitter), or peeled and dried for *hoshigaki. Kaki* season is late fall.

NASHI (APPLE PEAR): Round crispy fruit that has a mild pearlike flavor but resembles an apple more in texture. *Nashi* are harvested in the summer and are prized for their refreshing juicy crispness more than their flavor. Served peeled, cored, and cut into eighths.

UME (SOUR "PLUM"): A member of the apricot family ready to harvest in June. *Ume* are soaked, packed in salt, then sun-dried for *umeboshi* pickles (page 64) or added to a generic white liquor with sugar to make *umeshu* (page 59).

VEGETABLES BY METHOD

	Raw	Pickled	Ohitashi	Goma-ae	Shira-ae	Salad	Salt-Massaged	Tempura	Stir-Fried	Grilled	Simmered	Nabe
Asparagus	✳	✳	✳	✳	✳	✳		✳	✳			
Bitter Melon		✳						✳	✳			✳
Bok Choy			✳						✳		✳	✳
Broccoli		✳	✳	✳	✳	✳		✳	✳			
Cauliflower		✳	✳	✳	✳	✳		✳	✳			
Cabbage		✳				✳	✳		✳			✳
Carrots	✳	✳				✳		✳	✳		✳	
Celery	✳	✳	✳			✳		✳	✳		✳	
Chayote		✳							✳			
Corn		✳				✳		✳	✳	✳		
Cucumbers	✳	✳				✳	✳					
Daikon		✳				✳			✳		✳	
Edamame			✳			✳			✳			
Eggplants		✳					✳	✳	✳	✳		
Fava Beans	✳		✳					✳				
Garlic	✳	✳						✳				
Green Beans	✳	✳	✳	✳	✳	✳		✳	✳			
Green Peppers	✳	✳				✳		✳	✳			
Greens (Bitter)			✳				✳		✳			✳
Gobo								✳	✳		✳	
Kabocha								✳	✳	✳	✳	
Lettuce	✳					✳						
Lotus Root				✳	✳			✳	✳		✳	
Mizuna	✳		✳	✳	✳	✳	✳	✳	✳			✳

	Raw	Pickled	Ohitashi	Goma-ae	Shira-ae	Salad	Salt-Massaged	Tempura	Stir-Fried	Grilled	Simmered	Nabe
Mushrooms								*	*	*	*	*
Negi			*	*	*	*	*	*	*	*	*	*
Okra	*	*	*	*				*	*	*	*	
Onions	*	*				*		*	*	*	*	
Peas	*			*	*			*				*
Potatoes								*	*	*	*	
Radishes	*	*				*	*					
Snap Peas			*	*	*			*	*			
Snow Peas	*		*	*	*			*	*			
Spinach			*	*	*				*			*
Sweet Potatoes								*	*	*		
Taro Root										*		*
Tomatoes	*					*		*				
Turnips		*						*		*	*	
Zucchini	*	*	*				*	*	*	*		

FISH AND SEAFOOD BY METHOD

	Sashimi	Raw Chopped	Kelp Wicked	Vinegared	Sake Steamed	Miso Broiled	Butter Broiled	Salt Broiled	Tempura	Patty	Nabe	Simmered
FISH												
Anchovies	✳							✳	✳	✳		✳
Bonito	✳	✳										
Cod			✳	✳	✳			✳	✳	✳		✳
Flying Fish	✳	✳	✳	✳	✳			✳	✳	✳		✳
Halibut	✳		✳	✳	✳		✳	✳	✳	✳	✳	✳
Herring								✳	✳	✳		
Mackerel	✳	✳						✳	✳			
Monkfish					✳	✳	✳	✳	✳		✳	✳
Salmon					✳	✳	✳	✳	✳	✳		
Salmon Trout								✳	✳			
Sardines	✳				✳	✳	✳	✳	✳	✳		✳
Sea Bass	✳		✳	✳	✳	✳	✳	✳	✳	✳		✳
Sole			✳	✳	✳		✳	✳	✳			✳
Snapper			✳	✳	✳		✳	✳	✳	✳		✳
Sturgeon					✳		✳	✳	✳			
Swordfish	✳				✳	✳	✳	✳	✳			✳
Trout					✳		✳	✳	✳			
Tuna	✳	✳										
Yellowtail	✳				✳	✳	✳	✳	✳			✳

	Sashimi	Raw Chopped	Kelp Wicked	Vinegared	Sake Steamed	Miso Broiled	Butter Broiled	Salt Broiled	Tempura	Patty	*Nabe*	Simmered
SHELLFISH												
Clams	✳				✳	✳	✳	✳	✳		✳	✳
Crab					✳	✳	✳	✳	✳	✳	✳	
Mussels	✳				✳		✳	✳	✳		✳	
Octopus	✳							✳	✳			
Oysters	✳							✳	✳		✳	
Shrimp	✳						✳	✳	✳	✳	✳	
Scallops	✳				✳	✳	✳	✳	✳	✳	✳	
Squid	✳					✳		✳	✳	✳	✳	

Resources

Mail-order sources are probably your best bet for high-quality Japanese staples. Once you have acquired a minimal number of essential seasonings (namely, soy sauce, miso, sesame seeds, rice vinegar, *hon mirin*, *katsuobushi*, and konbu), I recommend buying fresh vegetables, fish, and meat at your local farmers' market, fish market, or butcher.

UNITED STATES

GOLD MINE NATURAL FOOD COMPANY (WWW.GOLDMINENATURALFOODS.COM): An online macrobiotic store based in San Diego, California, that sells a wide range of Ohsawa organic products, including some from our local company (Yamaki Jozo): miso, soy sauce, tamari, brown rice vinegar, plum vinegar, pickled plums, plum paste, wakame, kelp, nori, agar, *nigari*. Very highly recommended source for most staple ingredients you may desire for your (organic) Japanese pantry.

NATURAL IMPORT COMPANY (WWW.NATURALIMPORT.COM): Distributor for Mitoku macrobiotic and organic foods and a comprehensive source for many high-quality, hard-to find Japanese ingredients such as *amazake*, *koji*, and *kuzu*. Also sells Japanese cooking equipment.

EDEN FOODS (WWW.EDENFOODS.COM): A reliable purveyor of many organic Japanese ingredients. Available in the natural food section as well as online.

MEGUMI NATTO (WWW.MEGUMINATTO.COM): High-quality organic natto made in Sebastopol, California. Available online.

FROG EYES WASABI (WWW.FROGEYESWASABI.COM): Real wasabi roots grown on the Oregon coast. Available online. Pricey, but well worth it for the occasional sashimi or sushi feast.

MASSA ORGANICS (WWW.MASSAORGANICS.COM): Small producer brown rice in California, available online. Top-quality rice grown by a conscientious community-oriented farmer.

SOY MILK MAKER (WWW.SOYMILKMAKER.COM): Tofu-making supplies, including American-made cypress tofu forms, which are roughly 30% larger than Japanese-made forms.

KING ARTHUR FLOUR (WWW.KINGARTHURFLOUR.COM): The oldest flour company in America (founded in 1790!), which also happens to be a 100 percent employee-owned company committed to producing beautiful flour that tastes good. (And coincidently, is located in Norwich, Vermont, one town over from where my mother was an English professor for ten years.)

GIUSTO'S (WWW.GIUSTOS.COM): A three-generation-old family-owned company in the San Francisco Bay Area dedicated to providing top-quality flours to home bakers and professionals.

ARROWHEAD MILLS (WWW.ARROWHEADMILLS.COM): A fifty-year-old organic grain company that sells "adzuki" beans, soybeans, unhulled sesame seeds, and a wide range of flours online or in natural food stores.

PLEASANT HILL GRAIN (WWW.PLEASANTHILLGRAIN.COM): A mind-boggling array of old-fashioned cooking tools and grains, including organic soybeans. Located in Nebraska, but the business is conducted online or over the phone (800-321-1073—allow twelve rings!).

KITAZAWA SEED CO. (WWW.KITAZAWASEED.COM): The oldest Japanese seed company in the U.S. An essential source for home gardeners interested in trying their hand at growing Japanese vegetables. Kitazawa Seed Co.'s distinctive yellow ochre seed packets with forest green lettering can be found in Japanese supermarkets or through the company's web site. Inventory includes heirloom varieties of about any Asian vegetable you could ever imagine and many common Western ones as well.

KORIN (WWW.KORIN.COM): A large Japanese kitchenware store located in Manhattan but also accessible online. A good source for Japanese barbecuing supplies, knives, and a wide range of Japanese kitchen equipment or tableware.

TOIRO KITCHEN (WWW.TOIROKITCHEN.COM): Perhaps the only U.S. purveyor of *Iga-yaki donabe* (Iga ware refractory clay pots that can be used on direct flame for cooking rice or *nabe*). I have (and recommend) the black *donabe* rice cooker they call "Kamado-san." It comes in different sizes, and is not cheap. Although designed for cooking rice, it also pinch-hits as an excellent vessel for cooking *nabe* (one-pot dishes).

HIDA TOOL & HARDWARE CO., INC. (WWW.HIDATOOL.COM): A compact but comprehensive traditional Japanese hardware shop at 1333 San Pablo Avenue in Berkeley, California, or by phone 510-524-3700 (excellent customer service). A smaller selection of the wares are available for purchase online through their Web site. Highly recommended for Japanese knives and sharpeners.

AUSTRALIA/NEW ZEALAND

CHEF'S ARMOURY (WWW.CHEFSARMOURY.COM): A Japanese knife, cookware, and grocery store located in Sydney. An extensive array of products are also available online, including the most essential Japanese ingredients (many of which are organic). A very useful one-stop source for most of your Japanese grocery or cookware needs (including tofu-making supplies). They also sell the only Japanese-made vegetable scrubbing brush (Kamenoko brand) as a cast-iron cleaning brush (it does double duty in Japan). Nowadays most of the brushes are made in China and quickly lose their bristles.

UNITED KINGDOM

CLEARSPRING (WWW.CLEARSPRING.CO.UK): An extremely high-quality Web site dedicated to selling and promoting organic and traditional foods.

FRANCE

SUSHI BOUTIQUE (WWW.SUSHIBOUTIQUE.FR): Good knife selection as well as a wide range of Japanese kitchen or cooking supplies.

JAPAN

GOOD FOOD JAPAN (WWW.GOODFOODJAPAN.ORG):
An organization created to promote and provide the
latest information regarding top-quality Japanese foods.
The food items endorsed by Good Food Japan have
been carefully selected by food journalists and editors,
and the products are all locally produced and sourced.
Products include a special variety of rice (*tsuyahime*),
Wajima sea salt, soy sauce, miso, rice vinegar, spices,
fermented fruit and garlic, and yuzu juice products.
Good Food Japan introduces producers but does not sell
directly. I am a consultant with this group.

JAPANESE FOOD-RELATED BLOGS AND OTHER

WWW.INDIGODAYS.COM: My blog about life in Japan
on the farm—sometimes about life more than food.

WWW.LAFUJIMAMA.COM: Although not strictly about
Japanese food, Rachael Hutchings is a mad Japanophile
and has some excellent archive posts about making tofu,
gyoza, sushi, and more.

WWW.NORECIPES.COM: Marc Matsumoto's passionate,
well-written blog also includes a fair amount of
Japanese recipes put together with some poetic license.

WWW.HIROKOSHIMBO.COM: Author of *The Japanese
Kitchen* and *Sushi Experience*, Hiroko has solid, well-
researched posts and books. Hiroko is based in New
York City and also teaches cooking there. Highly
recommended.

WWW.JAPANESEFOODREPORT.COM: Harris Salat's
informative blog about cooking Japanese food in the
U.S. or eating it in Japan. A lively and interesting site.

WWW.JUSTHUNGRY.COM: Maki Itoh, author of *Just
Bento,* blogs from the south of France about all things
Japanese, though mainly food. The most comprehensive
(and long-running?) Japanese food blog around.

WWW.SAKE-WORLD.COM: John Gauntner's Web site on
everything you need to know about sake. A long-time
resident of Japan, John is indisputably *the* expert in sake
in the English-speaking world.

WWW.TASTEOFCULTURE.COM: Elizabeth Andoh's Web
page. Author of many Japanese cookbooks, notably
Washoku and *Kansha*, Elizabeth is an expert in the
landscape of Japanese food.

BIBLIOGRAPHY

Homma, Gaku. *The Folk Art of Japanese Country Cooking*. Berkeley: North Atlantic Books, 1991.

Lebovitz, David. *The Perfect Scoop*. Berkeley: Ten Speed Press, 2007.

Ruhlman, Michael. *Ratio*. New York: Scribner, 2009.

Shere, Lindsey Remolif. *Chez Panisse Desserts*. New York: Random House, 1985.

Shimbo, Hiroko. *The Japanese Kitchen*. Boston: The Harvard Common Press, 2000.

Shurtleff, William, and Akiko Aoyagi. *The Book of Miso*. New York: Ballantine Books, 1976.

Shurtleff, William, and Akiko Aoyagi. *The Book of Tofu*. Berkeley: Ten Speed Press, 1975.

Tsuji, Shizuo. *Japanese Cooking: A Simple Art*. Tokyo: Kodansha International Ltd., 1980.

Waters, Alice. *The Art of Simple Food*. New York: Clarkson Potter/ Publishers, 2007.

Wells, Patricia. *Patricia Wells at Home in Provence*. New York: Scribner, 1996.

Wise, Victoria. *The Vegetarian Table*. San Francisco: Chronicle Books, 1998.

Yoneda, Soei. *The Heart of Zen Cuisine*. New York: Kodansha International Ltd., 1982.

Metric Equivalents and Conversions

APPROXIMATE METRIC EQUIVALENTS

VOLUME

¼ teaspoon	.1 milliliter
½ teaspoon	.2.5 milliliters
¾ teaspoon	.4 milliliters
1 teaspoon	.5 milliliters
1¼ teaspoons	.6 milliliters
1½ teaspoons	.7.5 milliliters
1¾ teaspoons	.8.5 milliliters
2 teaspoons	.10 milliliters
1 tablespoon (½ fluid ounce)	.15 milliliters
2 tablespoons (1 fluid ounce)	.30 milliliters
¼ cup	.60 milliliters
⅓ cup	.80 milliliters
½ cup (4 fluid ounces)	.120 milliliters
⅔ cup	.160 milliliters
¾ cup	.180 milliliters
1 cup (8 fluid ounces)	.240 milliliters
1¼ cups	.300 milliliters
1½ cups (12 fluid ounces)	.360 milliliters
1⅔ cups	.400 milliliters
2 cups (1 pint)	.460 milliliters
3 cups	.700 milliliters
4 cups (1 quart)	.0.95 liter
1 quart plus ¼ cup	.1 liter
4 quarts (1 gallon)	.3.8 liters

WEIGHT

¼ ounce	.7 grams
½ ounce	.14 grams
¾ ounce	.21 grams
1 ounce	.28 grams
1¼ ounces	.35 grams
1½ ounces	.42.5 grams
1⅔ ounces	.45 grams
2 ounces	.57 grams
3 ounces	.85 grams
4 ounces (¼ pound)	.113 grams
5 ounces	.142 grams
6 ounces	.170 grams
7 ounces	.198 grams
8 ounces (½ pound)	.227 grams
16 ounces (1 pound)	.454 grams
35.25 ounces (2.2 pounds)	.1 kilogram

LENGTH

⅛ inch	.3 millimeters
¼ inch	.6 millimeters
½ inch	.1.25 centimeters
1 inch	.2.5 centimeters
2 inches	.5 centimeters
2½ inches	.6 centimeters
4 inches	.10 centimeters
5 inches	.13 centimeters
6 inches	.15.25 centimeters
12 inches (1 foot)	.30 centimeters

METRIC CONVERSION FORMULAS

TO CONVERT	MULTIPLY	TO CONVERT	MULTIPLY
Ounces to grams	Ounces by 28.35	Cups to liters	Cups by 0.236
Pounds to kilograms	Pounds by 0.454	Pints to liters	Pints by 0.473
Teaspoons to milliliters	Teaspoons by 4.93	Quarts to liters	Quarts by 0.946
Tablespoons to milliliters	Tablespoons by 14.79	Gallons to liters	Gallons by 3.785
Fluid ounces to milliliters	Fluid ounces by 29.57	Inches to centimeters	Inches by 2.54
Cups to milliliters	Cups by 236.59		

COMMON INGREDIENTS AND THEIR APPROXIMATE EQUIVALENTS

1 cup uncooked rice = 195 grams

1 cup all-purpose flour = 140 grams

1 stick butter (4 ounces • ½ cup • 8 tablespoons) = 110 grams

1 cup butter (8 ounces • 2 sticks • 16 tablespoons) = 220 grams

1 cup brown sugar, firmly packed = 225 grams

1 cup granulated sugar = 200 grams

OVEN TEMPERATURES

To convert Fahrenheit to Celsius, subtract 32 from Fahrenheit, multiply the result by 5, then divide by 9.

DESCRIPTION	FAHRENHEIT	CELSIUS	BRITISH GAS MARK
Very cool	200°	95°	0
Very cool	225°	110°	¼
Very cool	250°	120°	½
Cool	275°	135°	1
Cool	300°	150°	2
Warm	325°	165°	3
Moderate	350°	175°	4
Moderately hot	375°	190°	5
Fairly hot	400°	200°	6
Hot	425°	220°	7
Very hot	450°	230°	8
Very hot	475°	245°	9

Information compiled from a variety of sources, including *Recipes into Type* by Joan Whitman and Dolores Simon (Newton, MA: Biscuit Books, 2000); *The New Food Lover's Companion* by Sharon Tyler Herbst (Hauppauge, NY: Barron's, 1995); and *Rosemary Brown's Big Kitchen Instruction Book* (Kansas City, MO: Andrews McMeel, 1998).

Index